Destination North Pole

5,000 km by bicycle

Gary W. Wietgrefe

Cora 6

Destination North Pole

5,000 km by bicycle

Gary W. Wietgrefe

Adventures forty days through the Dakota Plains,
Prairie Provinces, northern British Columbia, the
vast Yukon and Alaska

GWW Books
Sioux Falls, SD

GWW Books *GWW*
801 E. 8th St., Suite 214-730, Sioux Falls, SD 57103-7011
Website: www.RelatingtoAncients.com   Email: gwwbooks@outlook.com

Ordering Information
Quantity sales. Special discounts are available on quantity purchases by organizations, businesses, associations, and others. Submit a request through the website www.RelatingtoAncients.com, or gwwbooks@outlook.com.

Individual sales. GWW Books publications are available through most bookstores and on-line retailers. See www.RelatingtoAncients.com, or gwwbooks@outlook.com.

Orders for textbook/course adoption use. Please make contact through the website www.RelatingtoAncients.com, or gwwbooks@outlook.com.

Orders by U.S. trade bookstores and wholesalers. Please contact BCH Fulfillment & Distribution, 33 Oakland Avenue, Harrison, New York 10528; Orders: 1 (800) 431-1579, Email: orders@bookch.com; Tel: 1- (914) 835-0015; Fax 1-(914) 835-0398; Website: http://bookch.com.

Print management and credits:
Cover photo design and permissions: Chad Phillips Photography, Sioux Falls, SD with bison insert from Adobe Stock #184603593 used with permission.
Book production: Western Commercial Printing, Sioux Falls, SD.
Bicycle graphic: Cora Wietgrefe, North Pole, AK.
Photos: Gary and Patricia Wietgrefe

Name: Wietgrefe, Gary W., 1953— author.
Title: Destination North Pole—5,000 km by bicycle/Gary W. Wietgrefe,
Sioux Falls, South Dakota: GWW Books, 2020.

Identifiers: Library of Congress Control Number: 2020903977 / ISBN 9780999224960 – hardcover, ISBN 9780999224977 – paperback, ISBN 9780999224984 - e-book.

Subjects: Non-fiction: Adventure Travel, Sport & Recreation, Cycling, Natural Therapy

Classification: BISAC Codes: 1. TRV 001000 Travel/Special Interest/Adventure; 2. SPO 011000 Sports & Recreation/Cycling; 3. OCC 043000 Body, Mind & Spirit/Natural Therapy.

First Edition   Printed in the United States of America

This is dedicated to my travel companion and lovely wife, Patricia, and to our children Michelle, Charmion, and Wyatt._

Cover

I departed Fort Nelson, BC June 16 at 4:45 a.m. At 6:10 dawning midnight sun casted larger-than-life shadows as I stopped with trepidation and took the cover shot and a series of photos.

This crisp morning, I had already biked about an hour and a half. Both sides of the ALCAN were many signs of caution—including permafrost humps. Onward were Yukon's whitecapped mountains.

After twenty-five days and 3,000 kilometers of biking with wonderment, out front lay a riddle of conflict.

Could I make it?

Services this far north were rare. A sign immediately after "Steamboat 75…" read "Next Services 188 km."

Really?

Twice past Steamboat, then 38 km I would find the next services?

On a bicycle, more than petrol was needed!

The Milepost noted reality including: "*Watch for bison alongside and the middle of the Alaska Highway….*"

For another 2,000 kilometers, what was ahead?

Soon, herds of frightened bison crossed as bulls turned to block me while mothers and calves rushed on. Porcupines and other critters entered the road, or lay dead as roadkill—or were they playing possum?

Meanwhile, baffling drivers stopped to feed bears.

I biked on.

Table of Contents

Preface   *viii*
The Route   *ix*
Introduction   *x*

1.   Summary Questions   1
2.   Bike Idea   7
3.   Muster   11
4.   Packing   13
5.   Considerations   15
6.   The Blog   20
7.   Day 1: 90 km/56 miles   22
8.   Day 2: 76 km/47 miles   30
9.   Day 3: 92 km/57 miles   36
10.   Day 4: 103 km/64 miles   42
11.   Day 5: 177 km/110 miles   48
12.   Day 6: 114 km/71 miles   53
13.   Day 7: 85 km/53 miles   64
14.   Day 8: 90 km/56 miles   70
15.   Day 9: 267 km/166 miles   75
16.   Day 10: 90 km/56 miles   94
17.   Day 11: 156 km/97 miles   98
18.   Day 12: 130 km/81 miles   103
19.   First day off   108
20.   Day 13: 140 km/87 miles   111
21.   Day 14: 132 km/82 miles   114
22.   Day 15: 129 km/80 miles   117
23.   Day 16: 95 km/59 miles   121
24.   Day 17: 43 km/27 miles   124
25.   Day 18: 172 km/107 miles   126
26.   Day 19: 126 km/78 miles   129
27.   Second day off   132
28.   Day 20: 143 km/89 miles   135

29.   Day 21: 74 km/46 miles   141
30.   Day 22: 89 km/55 miles   147
31.   Day 23: 119 km/74 miles   152
32.   Day 24: 87 km/54 miles   157
33.   Day 25: 92 km/57 miles   162
34.   Day 26: 109 km/68 miles   165
35.   Day 27: 77 km/48 miles   171
36.   Day 28: 117 km/73 miles   174
37.   Day 29: 209 km/130 miles   180
38.   Day 30: 24 km/15 miles   184
39.   Day 31: 114 km/71 miles   188
40.   Day 32: 126 km/78 miles   194
41.   Day 33: 117 km/73 miles   202
42.   Day 34: 68 km/42 miles   208
43.   Day 35: 156 km/97 miles   214
44.   Day 36: 156 km/97 miles   218
45.   Day 37: 140 km/87 miles   223
46.   Day 38: 185 km/115 miles   233
47.   Day 39: 172 km/107 miles   241
48.   Day 40: 140 km/87 miles   245
49.   Chapter 49: Biker Summary   252
50.   Chapter 50: Why Bike?   256

Epilogue: A Tragic Recovery   261
Appendix 1: Bicycle Specifications   272
Appendix 2: Supplies   275
Bibliography   279
Acknowledgements   281
About the author   284

Preface

A deep bark from roadside woods meant a savage dog or worse—half wolf/half dog. Spiking adrenaline was unavoidable from piercing eyes of a roadside grizzly. Of the hundreds of bears and wood bison, which would attack?

Solo he owned peacefulness of the Prairies into northern wilderness. Glaciated runoff from enchanted mountains backgrounded rainbowlike flowers in the midnight sun.

Legs kept pedaling with mind at peace yet conflict was constant. Why else would a grey wolf drag his prey further from the road as his bicycle approached?

Is this trip for others? Maybe. The path has been laid. Risks? Many!

How would you react to attack dogs at isolated cabins, spring-foraging bears, moose guarding young, and wild bison blocking your path? Think fast...or you're dead!

No radio. No headphones. No earbuds. No music. No static. Nowhere but ahead for an old guy on an old bike towards the Arctic Circle. Excitement. Danger. Humor. Scenery. Satisfaction. Serenity...at every turn. A solo, unexplored bicycle journey awaits.

Despite age, distance, dangers, and protracted recovery, a retired 65-year-old corporate manager, researcher, and author peddled nearly 5,000 kilometers for 40 days.

Logging only seven kilometers on his ten-year-old hybrid bike before departure, the senior pensioner decided...why wait? Age was not in his favor. What was ahead? Errant vehicles with drowsy drivers, road debris, construction, mushers, permafrost, biting flies, mosquitos, moose, wolves, half-wolf dogs, and bears! The adventure... legendary...and sometimes quirky.

Where was the water? Food? Lodging? Could exhaustion, cramps, falls, foul weather, or a gun stop him cold? Yes.

Many would not attempt the trip in a vehicle. He did it on an old bicycle.

Join readers on this thrilling, fast-paced North American travelogue through the Dakota Plains, Canadian Prairie Provinces, northern mountains of British Columbia, vast unpopulated Yukon and Alaska toward the Arctic wilderness.

The 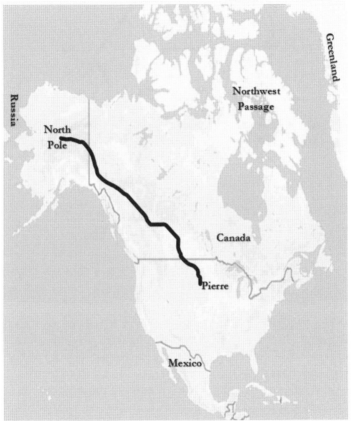 Route

(Map developed from computer screenshot using MAPQUEST®)[1]

---

[1] MAPQUEST® is a trademark of Verizon Trademark Services LLC.

Introduction

Explore forty days solo on two wheels.
Look ahead. Look around. It's more dangerous to look back from a bicycle.

With the journey complete, my goal is to encourage others to bike, drive, or simply be carried through an adventure into the northern wilds. Often health can be reclaimed through exercise, travel, and imaginative adventure.

Everyone, young, old, cycle enthusiast, or those open to a premonition trip of a lifetime are in for an exciting adventure. Go somewhere, perhaps towards the Arctic Circle. Clear your mind and find serenity.

This travelogue may be enjoyed for its adventure, route, connection with nature, emotions, family support, near misses, and unexplained happenstances.

People can be allusive—so is the north pole. It moves; some sit.

Chinese used compasses 2,000 years ago and the St. Nicholas (a.k.a. Santa Claus) legend originated about three hundred years later. Finally, an Englishman, William Gilbert, in the 1600s proposed the compass needle was pointing to a huge magnet in the northern wilderness.

Magnetic north has shifted hundreds of miles in my lifetime and moved about 1,094 kilometers (680 miles) in the twentieth century. As I am writing this, a year after I arrived in North Pole, magnetic north pole moved about a hundred kilometers (62 miles). Many bicycle owners do not pedal that far in a year. Perhaps, just air the tires and go. I did.

Find North Pole or come along with me.

Long-distance bicyclists will discover a new route. Motorcyclists and RVers will find this guide alluring. Rather than speeding north, vacationers can follow unexpected descriptions and distractions not found in tourist guides. Adventurous readers will be carried on a journey they may never take.

This is practical and intellectual.

Wilderness is no-man's-land. Dakota Plains and Canadian Prairie Provinces have been settled for well over a century. Northern British Columbia served 100,000 Klondike Gold Rush prospectors in the 1890s. Yukon and northern Alaska today remain mostly wild and unsettled. The Alaskan Highway, an eight-month war effort, was built in 1942.

Bicycling is an alternative to dog mushers, airplanes and vehicles.

Peddle to North Pole. After the first revolution, approximately 1,350,720 remain.

Beware! Observe. Road-travel can be far more than endless highways.

I carried no camping gear. My travel distance was metered to find a clean bed.

Lodging in many towns was not available. Since the 1960's 15-cent-a-gallon gasoline, plainspeople drove to town, often fifty or more miles, for supplies. Dinner guests came at noon. Mimicking fur trading outposts, most grocery stores have long-since closed.

If you travel at bicycle speed, new sights, sounds, smells, and the feel of nature are endless. Planning is required. This book may entice you to make your own adventurous journey.

Conveniences? Few.

Your brain will stymie you. Your gut says go.

Unless you survive on beer, canned soft drinks, candy bars and chips found at gas stops, consider going another twenty or thirty miles to a convenience store/fuel station. There, you may detect hot-food similarities--microwave pizzas, frozen hamburgers, and machined Frappuccinos.

Convenience stores were a lucky find, before they disappeared farther north.

Then, scattered in valley outposts, fresh bakery smells enticed with mouth-watering treats. Many health experts expect you to avoid pleasures attracted by sweet smells.

Smells are healthy. They add no calories. They gratify. Smells bring memories. Who would deny you the smell of mom's apple pie?

Early morning, sweaty, yet cold, emerging from a mountain pass, I cannot describe the euphoria of Maillard Reaction[2] aroma (dough proteins and sugars chemically caramelizing sticky buns). Just imagine. Smell. Feel your saliva building. Taste. Mmmmm. Bike on.

Northern British Columbia, the Yukon Territory, and eastern Alaska are permafrost, mountains, glaciers, and sparse.

In this story, distances between nightly stops are noted and indicate lodging, food, and water locations. Do not count on extra anything to recharge your supplies, find parts, or tires. The resource is you.

Plan. Water, food, fuel, and nightly accommodations should never be taken for granted anyplace along this route. In late spring and summer the few beds fill well before dark.

Dark? There is little to none as you approach the Arctic Circle on summer solstice as I did.

The Gold Rush ended. Early stages of ghost towns became outposts. Natural expanses are all-inclusive.

The ride was invigorating with life-long satisfaction. Avoid mistakes. It took three weeks from being in the best shape of my life to being bedridden, traumatized, hospitalized, and on medications. Tenacity was rewarded with physical and mental freedom.

Advice: Actively travel, be alert, read cautions from your body, pray, and always be kind. For affirmation, travel north.

---

[2] Maillard Reaction, first described in the early twentieth century by French chemist Louis-Camille Maillard, is the chemical process of heat converting dough sugars and proteins giving bread and rolls brown crusts.

Chapter 1: Summary Questions

It has been a year since I made the bicycle journey to North Pole. Too many people were interested and too many asked too many questions not to summarize it into an adventurous travelogue. May others seek the same personal journey.

Before details, here are some of the questions.

1. Did you ever think of quitting?
A. No. Anticipation only leads to opportunity.

2. What bike did you ride?
A. My 10-year-old hybrid Trek worked fine.

3. Why didn't you follow your wife's advice and get a new bike?
A. I enjoy both older models.

4. What music did you listen to?
A. None.

5. What did you think about those forty days?
A. Nature.

6. What was your biggest challenge?
A. I never stopped on any hills or mountain passes.

7. How long did it take to go up the highest mountain passes?
A. Sometimes it took me an hour and half.

8. What were the steepest grades?
A. The toughest were eight to ten percent inclines up and down.

9.   Did you take the Alaska Highway?

A.   Yes. For anyone considering this journey, I highly recommend using *The Milepost* of Alaska highways.[3]

10.   How was the Alaska Highway?

A.   Wide shoulders made for good cycling. The road was an amazing feat by man.

Originally, the Alaska Highway stretched 2,800 kilometers (1,700 miles) and crossed eight mountain ranges separated by marsh, permafrost and rivers with over 300 bridges. Under threat of invasion, the U.S. Army built it in eight months. Yes, eight months— a timely feat unmatched in human history!

11.   How fast did you go?

A.   I averaged 16.9 kilometers-per-hour (10.5 miles-per-hour).

12.   How many hours did you bike each day?

A.   From departure to arrival time, I averaged eight hours and three minutes per day.

13.   I know you say you biked 5,000 kilometers, but what was your actual mileage?

A.   It came close to 5,000 kilometers (3,000 miles).

Distance biked was actually 4,823 kilometers (2,997 miles). I caught a ride for about three-miles (5 km) after a flat tire, and a required ride in Yukon construction for less than a kilometer.

14.   Why didn't you bike a little more to get to exactly 3000 miles or 5,000 kilometers?

A.   Numbers would have replaced my goal—getting there alive.

15.   Did you have any days off?

A.   Yes. Two. I took one rain day in western Saskatchewan and a day in western Alberta to visit friends.

---

[3] *The Milepost* 2018, Alaska Highway, (Legendary Alaska Trip Planner), 301 Arctic Slope Avenue, Suite 300, Anchorage, Alaska, 99518, phone (907) 272-6070; https://www.themilepost.com/, pp 166-127.

16. What time of the year did you bike?

A. I left May 20th from Pierre, South Dakota and arrived in North Pole, Alaska June 30.

17. What route did you take?

A. What I thought would be the easiest—the flattest.

18. How many gears did you have and did you use them all?

A. Twenty-four gears (three drive gears and eight in back) were used nearly every day.

19. How many tires did you blow out?

A. Four. All on the back. The last flat was within a mile of my destination.

20. Did you have any other mechanical breakdowns?

A. Yes. I lost a pannier support screw in North Dakota and I broke a nearly new spare drive chain in the Yukon being chased by two dogs.

21. How much weight did you carry?

A. Including me and an eight-pound daypack, the bike was loaded at 285 pounds (129 kg) when I left. See Appendix 1 for details.

22. How much weight did you lose during the trip?

A. Negligible. I weighed 83 kg. (183 lbs.) when I departed and 82.6 kg. (182 lbs.) when I arrived.

23. How many calories did you burn each day?

A. My Garmin® calculated 132,469 calories (3,312 per day) used while biking, plus the normal calories during the other 16 hours each day.

24. Did you condition on a bike, like spinning classes?

A. No. I have never taken spinning classes, cross-fit, nor pumped weights. I walk regularly.

25. How did you get in shape?

A. I did no special training. Since growing up on a South Dakota farm, I was never really out of shape. I walk and in the summers bicycled some. I never considered it training—just normal living.

26. Have you ever done a long bike ride before?

A. Yes. Seven years earlier, my wife and I biked an 800-kilometer (478 mile) Tour de Kota—a group bike ride over six continuous days.

27. How many miles (*seat time* in biker lingo) did you log before take-off?

A. Total before my May 20th takeoff was 7.1 kilometers (4.4 miles).

Over the winter and early spring, I had not been on a bike for over eight months. The day before I left, I purchased an odometer from Walmart; replaced my old one and tested it for exactly one mile. I ordered a small Garmin® Edge 20 GPS from Amazon and calibrated it to the odometer for 3.4 miles to our State's Capitol building.

28. Did you have much wind?

A. Does the sun rise each morning? One thing a biker can count on, especially in the Plains, is wind, and more wind—usually in your face, especially heading northwest—its primary source.

29. Most bicyclists do not like hills. What was your total elevation gain?

A. My bike Garmin®4 recorded total elevation gain of 59,200 feet (18,044 meters). Google®5 Maps estimated the bicycle route at 65,548 feet (19,979 meters).

30. How far did you bike each day on this trip?

---

4 Garmin® is a registered trademark of Garmin® LTD.
5 Google® is a registered trademark of Google® LLC.

A. The average was 121 kilometers (75 miles) per day. My shortest day was 24 kilometers (15 miles) and my longest day, though not the toughest, was 267 kilometers (166 miles).

31. What were your bike's specifications?
A. Obviously, you are a techy biker.

See Appendix 1 for weights and measurements of various components, gears, tires, pedal type, handlebars, odometer, and safety equipment.

32. What did you expect to be your biggest obstacle?
A. My wrists. They would always get sore on 50 plus kilometer bike trips. That was why I built (invented) a **wrist support bar**.

33. Is it like a second handlebar? Tell me about it.
A. It functions like an additional (inside) handlebar used to support both wrists and absorb vibration on rough roads. It worked well beyond expectations

34. You have several patents. Are you patenting the **wrist support bar**?
A. No. Every long-distance bicycler should have opportunity to use one.

35. What did you carry?
A. Too much! Half the clothing and supplies would have been more than adequate. See Appendix 2 for details.

36. What was the most useless item carried on your bike?
A. Three cans of Spam®6 I carried and only ate one in a town with no café.

37. Did you take energy supplements?
A. I have never consumed steroids or sports drink energy boosters. Each day I would drink at least 20 ounces of electrolyte supplemented water. Each evening, upon arrival, I would mix up 20

---

6 Spam® is a packaged luncheon meat and registered trademark of Hormel Foods Corporation.

ounces of water with a whey protein supplement. Only a couple days did I take electrolyte tablets. I weaned myself from caffeine decades ago. I do not drink coffee, tea, soft drinks, and seldom eat chocolate.

38. What medications do you take?

A. None. One evening, my wife thought I acted stiffer than normal, so she gave me a Tylenol®[7]. That is the only medication I took the whole trip. To avoid issues down the road, my goal was to be extremely sensitive to what could be going wrong--blisters, chaffing, aches, and pains.

39. What time of day did you start?

A. I liked to get going about sunrise to see wildlife and before the wind started.

40. What was your daily routine?

A. It is detailed in the book.

41. What was your most unique observation?

A. Serenity. Expect nobody to change but yourself. Biking without radio, earbuds, or music allows time to think, observe and absorb nature.

42. I heard you were hospitalized six days afterwards. Why?

A. Since mind controls the body, I was in the best shape of my life and thought I could do anything. I could not. That's the epilogue, not the story....

43. You biked from Pierre, the South Dakota capitol, to North Pole, Alaska. Can you tell us a funny story?

A. You will have to read the book, but I can tell you about our French-speaking Canadian friends who were visiting France while I was biking. They wanted to check on my progress and went to my website www.RelatingtoAncients.com and clicked on my blog *Pierre-to-the-Pole*. The wife asked, "Why is Gary calling himself Pi'erre?

---

[7] Tylenol® introduced in 1955 is a form of acetaminophen used as a pain reliever (analgesic) owned by McNeil Consumer Healthcare, a subsidiary of Johnson & Johnson.

Chapter 2: Bike Idea

An idea is like light, if turned off you cannot return what you have seen.

Like many ideas, this one started at home.

Mid-winter, huddled in our cozy 380 square foot loft in downtown Sioux Falls, South Dakota with snow on the windowsills, I thought of our nephew, Seth, and his wife and family in North Pole, Alaska. Cold here. Colder there.

Rumor was the week-long bike ride, Tour de Kota, 400-500-mile group bike trip through small towns in South Dakota was going to end. My wife, Patricia, and I had taken part in all or part of that group ride for three years. Approaching sixty-years-old was not our concern as we peddled along, behind, or ahead of inexperienced riders four decades younger and some much older.

"I guess there is no reason to make the ten or so training loops around the bike trail this spring," I said to Patricia.

Our city's twenty-mile bike loop along the Big Sioux River only had one hill—a 100-foot switchback climb around the falls (as in Sioux Falls). The gradual downhill flat paved path along the riverbank mimicked much of South Dakota highway shoulders between corn, soybeans, wheat and sunflower fields. Flat. Where a creek intersected endless flatness, we called it two hills—up and down.

The daily newspaper flopped across my lap as I recalled a ten-minute conversation with a fellow Tour de Kota rider the previous spring.

"That's a nice jersey. Do you race competitively?" I asked the guy across the table from us. Patricia was also admiring the jersey and the muscular physique wearing it. The red flashy biking jersey was plastered front and back with such names as Waste Management, Ford, and other corporate logos. Likely in his early 70s, the tanned and toned biker appeared in much better shape than 345 of the 350 riders that day.

"Oh. This is my son's jersey," he said modestly.

Somewhat surprised, I said, "Well, you must ride a lot because you are in great shape and it sure fits you." Patricia and I bought Tour de Kota jerseys each year, but my 205 pounds on a five-ten frame compared to his physique appeared more like a traveling corporate gut than a regular bicyclist.[8]

"Yes. I do like to ride. Over the years, I have been on many tours like this in several states," he said as he casually ate an omelet and toast.

"What was your most interesting ride?" I asked inquisitively.

With a casual reply, "That would be biking to Alaska with my two brothers. We had another brother living in California and he also had a place in Alaska, so we decided to bicycle up to see him one summer."

Excitedly, I asked: "Where did you start?"

"Dell Rapids".

His hometown is euphemistically referred to as the Dells for its deep quartzite chasm south of town where a rock cliff overlooks the narrowly channeled Big Sioux River as it spread, cut, and often flooded its way to the Missouri River about seventy miles south where Iowa, Nebraska, and South Dakota meet.

Adventurers make history.

About the time bicycles got pedals, notorious bank robbers, Jesse and Frank James, obviously on athletic stolen steeds, reportedly jumped a similar chasm, Devil's Gulch, at Garretson—the next town to the east. At least that is the 1876 tale on Garretson's historic marker.

Whether on horse or bicycle, there are prohibitive destinations. In my mind, sitting at the café breakfast table that morning, biking to Alaska was a mysterious trail to explore.

The idea of biking to Alaska never left me.

What can stop an idea?

With imagination in overdrive, I asked the aging bicyclist, "What did you take along?"

---

[8] Tour Makes SDSU Stop, Interesting people, good food part of Tour de Kota for SDSU folks, Feature, South Dakota State University, Brookings, South Dakota, June 5, 2011, https://state.sdstateconnect.org/tour-de-kota/ (Sourced January 16, 2019).

"We carried everything! Tent, sleeping bags, cooking gear, food, water, and bike parts. We had no idea what we would need, or where we would get it."

"You camped the whole trip?" I quizzed.

"No." He replied. "We hauled all that camping gear and only used the tent four nights."

Thinking about all that extra weight, I asked, "How long did it take you?"

Not bragging, he said, "Forty-four days."

"That is amazing," I said unable to concentrate on breakfast and the calories I would need to finish the day.

I rattled off the next question, expecting vehicle close calls, getting lost, and bear attacks. "What was the worst part of the trip?"

Without hesitation, he replied: "My oldest brother always thought he was in charge."

My thoughts were scrambled. A massive distance. Grueling pace. Group travel. Physical differences. Unprepared meals. Unknown lodging. Rain. Wind. Cold. Hot. Mountains. Wilderness. Road conditions. Pavement or gravel? Construction. Which route? Wrong turns? How far each day? The next and the next? Road shoulder width. Morning start time. When to call it quits for the day? Breakdowns. Spare parts. Attacks: Bears. Moose. Wolves. Dogs. Cars. Campers. RVers and trucks. Robbed at gunpoint?

What a wild idea—bike to Alaska.

Being the oldest of six boys, I did not want to think about my brothers allowing me, or anyone of us, to be in charge of speed, intermittent stops, daily distance, or accommodations for hungry, thirsty, bickering brothers in their 60s on what seemed like a months-long...Mission Impossible.

I picked up the newspaper and asked Patricia, "Next spring I'm biking to Alaska. Are you going along?"

The remainder of that winter, I spent planning a route to Alaska by bike and petitioned my senior corporate managers for leave-without-pay to bike there. To make me feel better, I suppose, they thought my work was more important than bicycling.

Instead of cycling to Alaska that summer, I worked. The next winter we bought an RV (recreational vehicle) and we retired the following spring.

On a beautiful day, driving away with our bicycles mounted on the hitch visible through the rear camera, we never looked back—except I kept thinking someday I would bicycle to Alaska.

That day came May 20th--eight years after sitting at a breakfast table with a fellow bicyclist.

After using our RV two summers, we traveled extensively often with only a backpack. We searched for continuous summer.

Two U.S. winters we enjoyed Australian and New Zealand—their summers. A couple years, we enjoyed house-sitting in southwest Mexico. We traveled most of the U.S. and in fifteen countries. Looking for opportunities, we took a transition cruise to Venice, hiked and biked in various states, countries and continents. In the back of my mind I yearned to bike to Alaska.

Families, friends, funerals, months and years slipped by....

Six years after retiring, at age 65, I dug out my pre-retirement biking-to-Alaska maps.

That's it. I am leaving from Pierre (SD) and biking to North Pole (AK). Patricia quizzingly smiled.

We flew back from Mexico where we had spent the winter. Supplies and equipment were organized and packed. A week later I began peddling north.

Chapter 3: Muster

Thinking is a step, but a step takes you toward your goal.

How far should I bike each day?

I better start slow—maybe 80 to 100 kilometers (about 50-60 miles) per day.

What if I bicycled six hours per day? At ten miles-per-hour average, verses eight mph, would mean 48 to 60 miles per day—a 12-mile (19 kilometers) difference. Extrapolated, a 5,000 km (3,000 mile) trip could take an extra two weeks at the slower average speed.

A hundred kilometers (62 miles) per-day seemed like a good target. A few rest days could be scattered between. With breaks, six hours cycling could make ten-hour days on and off the bike.

Sixty days—two months—May 20th to July 20th with summer solstice assured long days. That was my plan. With no schedule, days off would allow my muscles to recover.

Hotel reservations for July 20 to 26th were made before departure. If I did not make it, I would cancel, but at least a comfortable bed was envisioned two months hence.

If three athletic brothers, my age or older, only slept in their tent four nights, lodging may not be the biggest obstacle. Hmmm. Where would I stay?

Initial logistics suggested no assured lodging every 48 to 60 miles even in well-settled South Dakota, North Dakota, Saskatchewan, and Alberta. Lodging in northern British Columbia, Yukon Territory, and eastern Alaska may have required an average of 160 kilometers (100 miles) or more per day.

Be logical. I had been a corporate traveler--usually drove, sometimes flew. I desired at least a sit-down evening meal, a shower, comfortable bed, and morning breakfast. My camping days were over. RVing would be ok.

My endurance? Questionable.

Occasionally, each summer we biked sixty-miles a day—sometimes, we did several days in a row. Considering mountain travel on a bicycle, rain/snow/wind and mechanical delays, and 160 kilometer (100 mile) per-day sustained travel appeared a stretch far beyond my capabilities.

Tenting, and the extra supplies needed, added too much weight. Tenting was scratched. If motels, lodges, bed-and-breakfasts, and Airbnbs were not available, the alternative, sleeping in our vehicle, would be threatening to stiff muscles. That was my second to last resort.

Alone, with no other alternative, a lightweight, emergency weatherproof bivy bag[9] was my roadside last-resort lodging.

Biking longer distances each day carrying less weight seemed like the most viable option.

After a winter in Mexico, my wife scheduled family visits around her hometown the week I departed. She was excited to catch up with me someplace in Canada. There, long distances between lodging were inevitable. By throwing both panniers and other dead weight into our vehicle, my bike load would be trimmed.

Back to logic. Bikeable miles, meals, and lodging are required.

Where would I eat? How could I get enough calories without junk food overload?

I packed enough protein bars, two or three per day, to last a week. Cafés, grocery stores, convenience shops, and gas stations were my declining choices.

I was off May 20th—destination North Pole, Alaska.

Why North Pole?

My nephew, an army sergeant, was assigned to a base near North Pole thirteen years earlier. He, with wife and dog crammed in the front seat, hauled their life's possessions in a small pickup truck from Tennessee to North Pole, Alaska. Born of that union were three Alaskan girls that fish, hunt, and clean their prey like pros.

If all went as planned, my wife and I would see them July 20th.

---

[9] Bivy is often considered a bivouac shelter, but in my context, it is a rolled, weather protectant bag, (e.g. sleeping bag) about four inches (10 cm) in diameter which would hold in body heat and keep out varmints, mosquitos, and moisture.

Chapter 4: Packing

You cannot use what you forgot.

My Trek® bicycle was purchased at Scheels® All Sports[10] ten years earlier. As an authorized Trek dealership in Sioux Falls, South Dakota, they became our reliable sporting goods store.

Not only did Scheels® have a selection of bikes, but they had a bike service department, clothes, and accessories. The best part, Scheels® staff had actually street, road and mountain biked. Ten years earlier, I did not pick this bike, their bike specialist selected one that fit me.

The insert photo was taken the morning of May 18th, 2018 before I started packing for "Pierre-to-the-Pole".

Take special note of mirror, seat suspension, used tires and chain, no handlebar modifications, nor odometer or Garmin®.

For years, I used the mirror in the down position, because without a kickstand, the mirror needed to be readjusted every time I laid it down. My **wrist support bar** (described in chapter 1 and Appendix 1) was designed to be long enough that my mirror could be used in the normal upright position.

It had been a very reliable bike—an expectation of all American-made Trek bicycles. Trek started making durable mid-cost bikes in a Wisconsin shed in 1976. Forty-four years later, they still did.

---

[10] Trek is a registered trademark of Trek Bicycle Corporation, Waterloo, WI and Scheels® is a registered trademark of Scheels® All Sports Inc.

This Trek hybrid fit me. For ten years it had been used on dirt, gravel, pebble, and paved paths, on roads, and some (but limited) mountain-trail biking in Arizona.

Usually, I put on about a thousand miles (~1,600 km) biking spring, summer and fall.

My bike was serviced every fall at a bike store and stored inside every winter, except two years we carried our bikes on the back of our RV (covered when traveling).

Drive gears had been changed once, and the rear cassette (eight-gear set) had been changed thrice. Brake pads were changed once and chain replaced about every couple years.

Tires were replaced about every three years, and since biking cactus strewn paths in Arizona, I used a liquid sealant in tubes. It proved beneficial on this trip as you will read later.

Friday afternoon and Saturday (May 18 and 19) were used for packing. My two panniers and tote bags were packed, stuff removed, repacked, weighed, stuff removed, repacked and reweighed.

What was necessary?

What was a want instead of a need?

What could be packed into our SUV[11] for later use?

Bottom line: What could I get by without? What could wait until my wife, Patricia, caught up with me in Saskatchewan or Alberta?

If you are curious what I carried and packed on my bike (in panniers, backpack, rear tote, small bags on handlebar and under the seat), see Appendix 2. Additional supplies, like extra tires, big air pump, water jugs, packaged food, camping stove, etc. were packed in our SUV.

Taking her time driving, my wife was not expected to supplement my stash for at least two weeks and possibly up to a month.

---

[11] SUV is a vehicle designation for sports utility vehicle.

Chapter 5: Considerations

The initial mapped route was prepared in early May 2018 before I left wintering grounds in Mexico. Actually, it is very close to the route initially developed in 2011 when I planned to take a couple months off from work.

The route to North Pole was long. Miles traveled in forty days from Pierre, South Dakota could have traversed Mexico to the Caribbean, or to the Northwest Passage on route to Greenland. But, water, ice and bikes do not match.

The objective was to conserve energy. To do that, the shortest, most level route was desired. For the most part, hills through the Northern Plains could be avoided, but not the eight mountain ranges.

Likewise, strategy to minimize weather issues would make the trip more enjoyable. About half the trip was through the Plains of the Dakotas and Canadian Prairie Provinces. As an agronomist, I knew most precipitation was expected in June often from intermittent showers. Continuous drizzling days of spring generally trend toward sunny skies with thunderstorms as summer approached.

The hottest months were July and August. Frost-free months were generally June into mid-September. For me, a perfect temperature to bike was a wind-free day of 70 Fahrenheit (21 Celsius).

Wind cannot be avoided but effects can be minimized. Wind in the Dakotas is primarily out of the northwest. Westerly winds prevail in central Canada.

Weather forecasters drop wind-chill ratings by May. As I have experienced many times, one can figuratively freeze your butt off during blustery May and June showers.

For a quick reference to wind direction, check out airport runways. They run parallel to the primary wind direction because airplanes take off into the wind to gain air-speed and land into the wind to slow ground speed.

For a while, I was on the board of directors of the South Dakota Aviation Association whose primary members were aerial applicators. Whether spreading fertilizer, fungicides, or dousing fires, regulations required application between sunup and sunset based on wind speed and direction. Most of their flying occurred between sunup and 9:00 a.m. when the winds were lowest.

My plan was to maximize distance with minimum wind which meant covering as much distance as possible from dawn until sun's intensity ignited Prairie breezes.

Each day I recorded departure and arrival time. For bicyclists contemplating this trip, note my departure time, arrival time and distance.

As a rule of thumb, I began biking between sunrise and 9:00 a.m. At least thirty percent more miles were covered the first three hours than the next four hours.

Mountains:

The second half of my trip was through mountainous areas of British Columbia, the Yukon Territory, and Alaska. My bicycle was not designed to bike through snow or ice. Nor was I.

Continuous summer was our goal since retiring. As you will soon discover, weather affects apparel. (Note Appendix 2: I did not pack winter gloves.)

Although life-long South Dakota residents, we spent a few winter months in Arizona and Florida. However, we found Australia, New Zealand, Fiji, Mexico, Guatemala, Honduras, Belize, and even a trans-Atlantic transitional cruise from the Caribbean through the Canary Islands into southern Europe more compatible to our retirement wardrobe.

Highways through mountains follow rivers. Upstream or down, roads are mostly level, but occasional flooding forces builders to construct over nearby hills which bicyclists' legs do not appreciate.

When traveling in a vehicle, mountains and passes are breathtaking. Biking added dual meaning to breathtaking, and enhanced peaks and valleys.

I peddled by the largest glacial ice-field in the world outside the Arctic. A blind person could experience the feel, smells of fragrant flowers, breezes, sounds from birds, wildlife, rustling leaves and trickling water. A potent feeling awaits your presence at this geologic marvel.

Paths are made for taking. I wanted to watch, breath, smell, and absorb my surroundings, not just take a path. Anybody can do that by car six times faster.

A bicyclist must not always watch the scenery. Two inches of tire contact with road embody two elements: efficiency and death.

Sand, gravel, rocks, unmaintained weeds, wet or icy pavement, construction, cracks, and permafrost heaves are as treacherous as glass, vehicle plastic, metal fragments, equipment parts, shredded aluminum, mower debris, blown tires, cables, hitch pins, roadkill guts and everything else on road shoulders, including errant drivers.

Rumble Strips:

Rumble strips are bikers' nemesis. They warn drivers and bicyclers of impending danger. Except on a few Provincial highways, rumble strips were a constant caution avoided.

Rumble strips are dangerous and can kill a bicyclist!

Civil highway engineers know drivers are inattentive. On modern highways, rumble strips border most driving lanes. Into their design beyond the rumble strips, highway shoulders have been widened the last couple decades to provide passing space between speeding vehicles and inoperable and emergency vehicles.

I was pleasantly surprised at the width of paved shoulders on Canadian highways. Many must be three meters wide.

Unfortunately, bridges, being costlier to build, are narrower than highways. Where are bridges located? Over beautifully distracting streams and rivers, but worse than that, at the bottom of hills and mountains.

I must let you in on an unsuspecting secret. Forget for a second about grizzly bears at streams and errant drivers watching both.

One of the most dangerous parts of my trip was coasting downhill at 30 to 40 miles-per-hour (48-64 kmph) next to a guardrail where the highway rumble strip met the narrowing road shoulder at a bridge abutment on the bottom of a long steep winding hill with only a couple inches of bike tire touching pavement.

Rabbits, skunks, porcupines, foxes[12], wolves, deer, elk, bison, moose, and bears use guardrails as paths to streams below bridges. Emerging without warning, wildlife are exciting and deadly. So are drivers watching them.

Tires bounce more radically with speed. Keeping touch with pavement is key. Double braking (front and back) to keep speed under 40 mile-per hour (64 kmph), my tires would bounce over frost heaves and cracks while trying to avoid stones and other debris.

Now magnify the problem. In the north, mountain highways are sanded in winter and some of the shoulders are mechanically swept clean in the spring. That's great. Right? Except!

Now what?

As road sweepers approached bridges, they must have moved onto the highway. Result: A layer of slippery sand was swept, or with runoff, ran down hills into bridge abutments. No RED FLAG!!! No caution. Sand and camouflaging rumble strips often blended into a tapered ridge up to the bridge. At the far end, the sand again covered the rumble strips up to the guardrail until the sandy road shoulder widened for the uphill climb.

Scared shitless cyclists, like me, were granted two good things. Fortunately, with rare exception, rumble strips were not carved into bridge decks, and wildlife seldom crossed bridges. Dampen cockiness! Critters cross suddenly from hiding in untrimmed brush at the end of bridges and under and over guardrails.

Ever hit a porcupine on a bike? My advice: Don't.

Departure dates:

Mid-May to mid-September is the bicycling window to avoid the most ice. Mosquitos, moose baring young, and bears hungry from hibernation are a given. Avoid them.

Rather than flying to Fairbanks, Alaska with my bike and riding east/southeast pushed by prevailing winds, I decided to start from Pierre, South Dakota which was my home from 1978 to 1992, and my wife's hometown.

Why depart May 20?

---

[12]Fox and foxes can be used as plural, but in this cases "es" is added since red, silver and Arctic fox could be found.

Since the ride was expected to take two months, I decided to maximize day-length. I considered it mandatory to ride during daylight hours.

No commercial lodging was available in Blunt, Onida, or Agar, the first three towns north of my starting point. If it is sparse in central South Dakota, lodging would certainly become increasingly sparse heading into the thousand mile stretch of the Yukon and eastern Alaska.

Camping along roadsides is an option for others. At age 65, a hot shower and soft bed were my preferences.

Depending on weather, winds, road conditions, construction, and mountain terrain, long stretches required long biking days.

Another benefit to ending the trip near the Arctic Circle was the teasing midnight sun. It lasts from June 12 until July 1 as days lengthened moving north.

With summer solstice occurring around June 20 each year, departing May 20th gave me the year's longest sixty days with plans to arrive in North Pole July 20th.

Pre-booked lodging:

Lodging only for the first ten days was confirmed before departure. In case of delay, I would reschedule.

Adventurous salmon and Arctic grayling fishermen and tourists flock to Fairbanks, Alaska (the largest city in northern North America, population ~32,500) for the longest summer days. Rooms are limited. A week's lodging, beginning July 20th, was confirmed before departure.

Chapter 6: The 🚲 Blog

You cannot climb a mountain before visualizing it.

My daily blog was code named "Pierre-to-the-Pole". See https://www.RelatingtoAncients.com/Pierre-to-the-Pole-1. Daily blogs have been included in each day's summary.

After enjoying the last three years writing and publishing two books, Pierre-to-the-Pole challenge was to take a couple months to rebuild my body.

After seeing some friends and family physically and mentally deteriorate as they aged, losing some was frightening.

Seven years after my initial yearning for a long-distance bicycle ride, we continued retirement—sitting, traveling by RV, plane, bus, tuk tuk, boda boda,[13] taxi, train, ferry, cruise ship, walking, hiking, and bicycling. I wanted to keep my brain and blood flowing.

A decade earlier, we abandoned television. Continual travel during retirement precluded reading daily newspapers, which had already faded from those under forty and from those aging on social media.

A two-month bike ride should prove interesting. So, I decided to use my books' website, www.RelatingtoAncients.com, to publish a daily blog from Pierre-to-the-Pole.

Initially, I had no plans to report my progress. It was a personal journey. My patents, research, and other books were available. I had nothing to prove. Explaining a risky bike ride, I figured would interest many. This book is a continuing result.

---

[13] Tuk Tuks use a motorcycle engine to power a small three-wheel vehicle with a driver's seat in front and two to three passengers can sit on a back seat. Boda bodas are small motorcycles used to taxi people and supplies in Uganda from "Border-to-Border". In Ugandan English lingo that is "boda boda".

Too many people talk about doing things. Many intentions are not lived. Inflated words without action is naught. That was not my way. As Spanish/French artist Pablo Picasso (1881-1973) said, "What one does is what counts. Not what one had the intentions of doing."

As my departure day neared, more friends and family wanted to track my progress.

Being worn out from biking, hungry, or over-relaxed from stuffing myself, resulted in minimal blogs. As you read through them, please note blogs have not been changed or updated except to make necessary corrections, like spelling.

It was difficult to put exhilaration, tranquility, thoughts, solitude, the day's sights, and anticipation of the next day's ride into words. May my attempts give you hints of what I experienced.

Better yet, try it yourself. Put air in the tires of your old bicycle and go.

If you have convinced yourself you cannot bike 5,000 kilometers, pick a bed and breakfast or motel in the next town. Go there. Bike a few days in a row. Stay overnight. Bike on. You may not want to stop.

(Note: I did not carry computer, nor tablet. All blogs were from my Apple iPhone®.[14] Entering data on my website blog was very difficult. The display program only allowed viewing three short lines of text. Entering one letter at a time, with many correction delays, it took a minimum of an hour, when Wi-Fi was available, to post each day's blog. More details were written in a daily journal and data charted in my trip guide.)

---

[14] iPhone® is registered trademark of Apple Inc.

Chapter 7: 🚲 90 km/56 miles
Day 1, May 20, Pierre to Forest City, SD

Depart time: 6:30 a.m.
Arrive time: 1:25 p.m.
Highways: 34/14, 1804, 212
Day km/miles: 90/56
Day average speed: (kmph/mph): 15.4/9.6
Day elevation gain (m/ft): 220/722
Calories daily: 2,292
Daily dangers/excitement: Family, Fishing, Missouri River bluffs

Begin blog:

Departed Pierre, South Dakota (population 14,008) to Forest City (population zero)

Moved out from South Dakota Capital building in Pierre and turned north.

-----Blog end-----

No. My blogs were not all that short and boring. After I set up the blog page on my website a few days before departure, https://www.RelatingtoAncients.com/Pierre-to-the-Pole-1/, I unwittingly assumed photos, videos and text could quickly be added. After spending a couple hours the first couple nights trying to download videos and multiple photos, I realized no videos and only a single photo could be used on a single blog.

Can you sleep soundly knowing you are departing on a two-month trip—a trip of a lifetime? I did not.

A 7:00 a.m. Sunday departure was planned since my first day was to be less than the average plan of 60 miles (97 km). At 6:30 I pushed the heavily loaded bike down the second-story flight of stairs into a cool, clear, calm 47°F (8.3°C).

As the odometer flicked to the first mile mark, I deliberately passed Prairie Pages, our local bookstore, which sold my latest two hardcover books. It was closed—for a couple months. Old and new owners were redesigning layout and exchanging inventory. As many of us authors experienced in the last decade, local bookstores are becoming a rarity.

Another block I stopped for a photo at our local bike shop (Pedal and Paddle). Like all such shops, Tom not only repaired and sold bicycles for a meager living, he provided healthcare. Strange? No. Far exceeding hospitalization, bike shops provide a lifetime exercise program for young, old, and workers of all ages.

My wife and sister-in-law were following closely behind-- checking tires and flashers to insure (primarily for themselves) that the bike was road-worthy. Likely, they had more questions about my sanity than roadworthiness. For one thing, in a rush to start, they realized I had forgotten my hydrate (back) pack. It was always the last thing to put on and the first thing I needed.

With the State Capital building behind, I pedaled out of the Missouri River valley onto Highway 83/14 heading north of Pierre. Friends, Carol and Joel, who had biked with us on our first Tour de Kota trip, asked if I could swing by their place on the way out of Pierre. Preparing for church, they reminded me Sunday was to be a day of rest—not heading to North Pole.

No worries! I had all day. After well-wishes, I began to realize how many friends and family would be following my journey, if not physically, spiritually. Prayers were welcomed to avoid expected dangers and tragedy.

After a short visit and visual rundown, I left town. Within a mile, I left the main highway, and turned onto Highway 1804—the highway named and dated after Lewis and Clark's Expedition.

Biking north, I was making personal history, but real history was hidden in the valley and bluffs below. Native tribes in permanent settlements had preceded the French by hundreds, if not thousands of years.

Near our small farmstead east of Pierre, I would occasionally walk up to a huge earthen berm and explore an ancient Native settlement. With years of experience in military intelligence, I was curious how they built their fort, how they protected their gardens, and where they sourced water beyond the Missouri River in the valley below.

Fur trappers and traders had traversed the area for centuries. On a gumbo bluff overlooking what is now Fort Pierre, an inscribed lead plaque was placed by Chevalier and Louis la Verendrye claiming the area for France in 1743. In 1913 playful teenagers discovered it.

Fort Pierre, the longest permanent settlement in South Dakota, dates to 1817. However, explorers Lewis and Clark fourteen years earlier had a tense standoff with Natives seeking compensation for passage north. Sharing a peace pipe settled nerves.

During my long ride, I decided to rest at each historical marker. They would provide mental fodder for the miles ahead.

The first marker north, noted the landing of Charles Lindbergh at exactly 4:00 p.m., September 1, 1927 in a field beside Highway 1804. Only twenty-four years earlier, 1903, the Wright brothers had made human mechanical flight possible. Lindbergh was promoting punctuality of commercial use of *aero planes* on a cross-country tour less than four months after making the first solo flight from New York to Paris.

I certainly will not take the time to explain each marker where I paused, but the second is certainly noteworthy considering the numbered highway I was using. In the majestic river below, 295 steamboat wrecks were identified on the Missouri River above Saint Louis. The 1897 report indicated twenty steamboats were lost in South Dakota, the first, Kate Swinney, on August 1, 1855.

Fifty-one years after Lewis and Clark's journey, Kate Swinney, the 328 tonne steam side-wheeler, had been loaded with furs and hides heading downriver to Saint Louis.

As I would learn biking to North Pole, many towns' signs and historical markers documented history of Natives, fur trading, military action, and original settlements.

Bicycling provided an atmosphere of unparalleled autonomy. My mind wondered without restriction.

As I am writing this (and other sections) I will refer to my daily journal. The one thing summarized on today's notes was a list of wildlife and roadkill. Although it is brutally sad how many native creatures are killed by vehicles, the following list is testament to the wildlife conservation practices of area farmers and ranchers.

Wildlife included nine antelope, two deer, and many birds. Birds were mainly mourning doves, woodpeckers, and swallows around farmsteads. Open areas had larks, blackbirds, king birds, ringneck pheasants and others, including a nesting Canada goose. Ponds hosted a variety of ducks—mallards, teal, pintails, and a group (5 or 6) I could not identify.

With that much wildlife, even with limited traffic, especially Sunday morning, roadkill was prevalent, including an antelope, skunk, racoon, prairie dog, field mouse, a frog, dove, and a mangled hen pheasant with scattered feathers. On her last effort to reproduce, an intact egg lay strewn in guts behind her.

Even before vehicles, South Dakota game has been sought by licensed hunters, unfortunately, some wildlife gets recklessly killed by licensed drivers. Bikers beware!

A century ago, bicycles quietly passed horses, buggies, and pedestrians. Once vehicles hit the road, drivers claimed road passage their right-of-way and have hit all others.

Inventions change culture. Bicyclists often start young with training wheels. Many young adults get their driver's license based on age, not training.

Some say hitting pavement can be the scariest thing about biking. Are cars hitting bikes worse? No. It is drivers hitting bicyclists.

Oncoming self-driving vehicles will provide a non-mechanical dilemma—a moral one. Will vehicles be programed to hit a bicyclist rather than another vehicle? Will it avoid a deer and hit the bike?

Futuristically, will radar avoidance technology be required for road-shoulder bicyclists to alert autonomous vehicles? (For technology geek readers, you cannot patent that idea because I just made it public. Patent designs are welcome.)

Bicyclists are wildlife friendly. That is another good reason to cycle rather than drive. Cyclists can quietly observe and enjoy sights and sounds of feeding, flying, mating, and nesting wildlife without endangering them.

For many days and weeks, I pedaled into a northern wilderness I had never seen. Mellowing was easy as highways opened spaces. Traffic was generally light to non-existent in early mornings when wildlife abounded. If an animal got in my way, the goal was to enjoy it, not kill it as had inattentive drivers.

What should I think about? What was worthy of an empty journal? Having traveled to over thirty countries, I had never tried to do a daily journal. What should I write?

What brought me the biggest joy was unplanned.

After bringing my hydrate pack earlier, my wife and sister-in-law passed me late Sunday morning to see if we could check into Bob's Resort where we had a reservation for the first evening. The fishing outpost, sixteen miles from the nearest town, had a well-known steakhouse.

The last couple miles of today's ride, I turned right off Highway 1804 onto U.S. Highway 212. Foster City, population zero, had its own historical marker, but not a building remains to be called a ghost town.

About fifty miles into my ride, five miles before Highway 1804 turned onto Highway 212, I could feel early signs of leg fatigue. On rides in previous years, those signs led to leg cramps. I stopped, took a drink, walked a bit and took a few more swallows.

Leg cramps are a hindrance. As a blessing, they indicated dehydration. That first day's reminder was the only time in forty days I had cramp warnings.

A cramp never happened. Of course, I constantly sipped from my backpack water bladder, and very often wondered where I could pee discretely. Most of the roads on this route one can pee freely. Do it.

That reminded me of an eighth-grade jokester in our one-room grade school when I was the sole third-grader developing an interest in books. He told me about *Mist in the Wind* written by I. P. Freely and another (imaginary) book I thought would be more interesting, *Trails in the Sand* by Peter Dragon.

It would not take two hands to count the times I used gas station bathrooms. But, it took planning. Padded bike pants (men and women's) are made without seams to minimize rubbing the narrow seat. On your trip, seriously consider wind and bike to your back, and two hands to bare necessities.

That may be more information than you need but let this be a warning: Do not stop drinking water because you do not know where to pee. Nature always provides.

In the driving lane, a vehicle was slowing to my pace. Trying to avoid rocks, glass and other debris from the gravel shoulders I constantly glanced at the highway shoulder ahead.

After I turned on Highway 212, heading east, a mile remaining on my final leg, someone hollered from the open window, "Hey Gary! You're almost there!"

What a surprise. It was my brother Neal as passenger with brother, Mark, from Colorado. Mark had taken a few days' vacation to fish in Lake Oahe. He had invited me to Mobridge to fish with him for a few days. After I told him I was packing to bike to Alaska, he called my brother, Neal, who joined him for the weekend.

"I'll meet you at Bob's Resort," I yelled and motioned ahead.

My wife, and brothers met me at my first stop.

As I pulled into the gas station/convenience store/cabins/steakhouse, I was cheered to a halt by my wife, Patricia, her sister Sharon, and my brothers Mark and Neal.

"Ready to fish?" Mark asked.

"You might as well," said Patricia. "It's only 1:25 and we can't check in yet."

"Let me grab something to eat and pull my rod and tackle from the vehicle," I said while removing my helmet and skull cap. Like rural convenience stores, they had ample supply of chips, frozen sandwiches, and an assortment of drinks.

We grabbed some beef jerky, sandwiches and chips. The brother trio jumped into Mark's vehicle after I slipped his dirty fishing pants over my bike outfit and replaced clipped biking shoes for flat walking shoes from my pannier.

Within minutes, we were fishing at East Whitlock Bay.

Sunday, after a 90-kilometer (56 mile) bike ride, I fished.

Since the late 1950s our parents had taken us to the Missouri River to fish. My mother grew up in the 1930s and '40s riding horse and gathering cattle on the Missouri River bluffs. As it was being dammed in the 1950s, water backed into the rivers, creeks, and prairies that surrounded the treacherous muddy river, known then as the Muddy Mo. Settled and calm, it now has some of the clearest fishing water in United States.

By 1959 the earthen dam near Pierre reached its maximum height of 245 feet (74.7 m). On August 17, 1962, with my (future) wife and family in attendance, the Oahe Dam was officially dedicated by President John F. Kennedy. What then was the largest rolled earthen dam in the world backed water 372 km (231 miles) to Bismarck, North Dakota (my fourth stop).

Northern Pike were my grandfathers, fathers, and six siblings' favorite fish. The native species, *Esox lucius*, produced abundantly in the newly flooded grasslands. Sixty years later Northern still reproduce and are known as the toughest fighter from shore, boat, or through the ice.

On my two-month trip from Pierre-to-the-Pole, I had not anticipated fishing until I reached Alaska. Within eight hours of departure, I fished with my brothers, and casted for Northern Pike just as we had decades earlier as children.

Hungry, we returned to Bob's Resort, where I quickly showered and joined the rest who had gathered in the Steakhouse.

The day was one for surprises. Our grandson Willie, a farmer and avid fisherman, came in. So did Andrew, my nephew, who had recently returned from the Navy.

Family came to wish me success. (Unconsciously, they perhaps thought they may never again see me alive.)

How could the first day be any better? It was a Sunday blessing! Pierre-to-the-Pole was going to be one pleasurable surprise after another.

(My daily notes were personal. Anyone taking this ride, or any ride they plan, will likely develop a personal connection bringing relevance to their potential.)

Chapter 8: 76 km/47 miles
Day 2, May 21, Forest City to Selby, SD

Depart time: 6:45 a.m.
Arrive time: 11:10 a.m.
Highways: 212, 83
Day – total km/miles: 76/47—166/103
Day average speed: (kmph/mph): 18.3/11.4
Day – total elevation gain (m/ft): 129/423—349/1,145
Calories daily/total to date: 2,138/4,430
Daily dangers/excitement: Passing cross-country bicyclists near my first-grade one-room country school, visiting cousins.

Begin blog:

The original Forest City (population 0) in central South Dakota is now under the Missouri River's Oahe Dam. Today I paralleled the Missouri River bluffs north of Pierre 56 miles to Bob's Resort (near the Forest City landmark).
-----Blog end-----

Today I started at dawn. It was beautifully calm. It was my fifth shortest ride as my stops were dependent on lodging. It was only 76 kilometers (47 miles) to Selby, mostly on Highway 83, a road I would be on for the next 443 kilometers (275 miles).

For the next couple days, Patricia decided to rejoin me after returning her sister, Sharon, to Pierre. By 11:10 a.m. without breakfast, I arrived in Selby. I ate a protein bar 30 miles earlier.

I gave my two bananas to a couple that were bicycling through South Dakota to the Pacific Coast. Camping along the way, seldom did they get fresh bananas by 9:00 a.m. They had departed West Whitlock State Park an hour before my departure. Pulling a fully loaded single-wheel trailer, I caught up with him first and offered a banana.

"My wife is somewhere ahead," he said.

I returned to my bike and grabbed a second banana for his wife whom I passed about twenty minutes later.

In hindsight, I should have suggested dust masks, goggles, and a couple innertubes besides bananas. After leaving the paved road at Akaska, they had perhaps thirty kilometers of gravel.

That area I knew well. Beautiful. Rurally quaint. Grandfather had emigrated from South Russia (now the Ukraine) and settled in the Akaska (not Alaska) area a century earlier. Forced to flee Bolshevik extremism [15], many German-Russian farmers resettled into the Dakota Plains with similar weather, land and crops as the Russian Steppes[16].

My mother grew up riding horse, checking cattle, and avoiding rattlesnakes on those Missouri River breaks. As a first-generation American, survival was their goal in the blowing dirt, drought, and grasshopper infestations of the 1930s. Second generation Americans, like me, tend to take religious, economic, and lifestyle freedoms for granted. This bicycling adventure would not be possible without those established rights.

This part of the trip, a few miles northwest of Gettysburg, I felt at home. It was in that area my father took a job as a ranch-hand in 1959. Four miles to the east, I started first grade in a one-room country school that fall.

By then, my sister had more education. She was in the second grade. Confirming she had a head start, she also attended kindergarten for one day—actually, one half-day at Harmony Center in May 1958.

---

[15] Bolsheviks were a militant socialist political party officially founded in 1912 by the brutal Vladimir Lenin supposedly representing workers through violent economic and ethnic cleansing as a breakaway group of the Marxist Russian Social Democratic Labour Party.
[16] Russian Steppes are an inhabitable geologic ecoregion of farmable grassland and shrubs stretching from southeast Europe across southern Asia.

We grew up almost as twins since she was only eleven months older. Of course, I was jealous because she was better able to advance through her school years because she attended kindergarten—a program not offered at Fuller School, the one room where I started.

(I'm being sarcastic. My book, *Learning as it influences the 21st century*, pointed out pre-school scholastic benefits lasted only through the third grade while parents were suckered into work.[17] Learning from family and nature transitioned to a school system.)

With about a dozen kids in school, and being the sole first grader, I was outclassed.

My mother received her teacher's certificate with only ten weeks of college and taught for a year before she married a schoolmate's brother, my father. According to my parents, I could count before I started school. Halfway through the first grade, when we moved back to our family farm near Ipswich, I could still only count as I did at age five.

Older kids, like my sister, must have been smarter because mostly I remember listening to their lessons. To my knowledge, I never had a school lesson at Fuller. My schoolteacher impressed me because she dated an Air Force pilot that would occasionally fly over a nearby radar site.

Looking east while biking, I could see the grassy hills, radar site and farm ground near my first school.

Tracking pheasants, raccoons, skunk, deer, and coyotes were lessons taught by the older boys.

We would leave the playground at mid-morning recess and track animals until lunch. After lunch, our teacher would read a story. I would doze off until the afternoon recess.

Being likely hunters when we grew up, from afternoon recess until it was time to walk home after school, we tried to find the pheasants, raccoons, skunk, deer and coyotes we had tracked in the morning.

---

[17] Gary W. Wietgrefe, *Learning as it influences the 21st century*, GWW Books, pp 41-42, with references to John H. Bishop's Cornell University study "Domestic Trends to the year 2015: Forecast of the United States" (July 1, 1991).

When blizzarding, we had to stay in school. Older kids would climb up the extra stacked desks and stools in the storage closet, lift the attic hatch and watch television.

Too young and inexperienced to watch that television, I was intimidated. Television was a new invention and not all families had them. In 1956, I remember when my father brought our first television home—only black and white, of course.

Fuller School had electricity for lights, fuel oil stove, no running water or telephone, and two outhouses differentiated for the dozen boys and girls. We moved that winter back to Ipswich, South Dakota. A couple years later, I realized Fuller's attic television was bogus and I was the stool pigeon.

I have no memory of books at Fuller country school, but I remember tracking wildlife. Wildlife observation was a goal of this trip and I took a journal to record events. My memory was better when I could not read or write. Literacy replaces memory.

Many more details on memory are found in my book on *Learning as it influences the 21st century*.

"Memory was expected and a powerful learning tool before the advent of writing. Memories create thoughts. Thoughts develop into ideas. Ideas become innovations. Unfortunately, using inventions of the past generations in a structured school system, today's students are losing their ability to remember."[18]

In the past, elders passed on culture, genealogy, and traditions from memory. For those of us approaching life expectancy, age is not an excuse to forget. I cheat--memories in this book were aided by daily blogs, journal notes and chronological photos.

After arriving in Selby, Patricia and I enjoyed a relaxing lunch. Before the motel was open, we caught up on fond memories with my mother's cousin, Darlene, and her husband, Bob. Being they were only about a decade older than I, we reminisced about retirement, travels and playing on their family farm six decades earlier.

---

[18] Wietgrefe, Gary W., *Learning as it influences the 21st century, Relating to Ancients* series, 2018, pgs. 285, 296.

Before I get too far into my trip, it may be beneficial for followers to detail my daily routine.

After long hours on the seat, to enjoy a large relaxing meal and maximize rest time upon arrival, I established a routine.

Upon arrival, after checking into lodging, I would immediately head to the shower where I washed my clothes. Every day my jersey, padded pants, skull cap, handkerchief, socks were drenched as I entered the shower then stripped to soak as I showered. Undershirt, arm-slipovers, and long stretch pants were washed daily if used. My gloves, containing leather and pads, were washed about every week.

It was not unusual for me to go years without taking a bath. Daily showers were always preferred since I entered the military as a teenager. They were fast and efficient.

After my wife rejoined me in Saskatchewan, she suggested that I soak in warm Epsom salt-water after each day's ride.

Serene, I weakened while washing my daily uniform. Bathing was amazing. Relaxing. Thereafter, whenever lodging had a bathtub, I used it immediately upon arrival.

Lights out was planned for 8:00 p.m.

Departure was anticipated at dawn. It was dark outside during morning preparation. To start, I shaved each morning to minimize face irritation and to effectively apply sunscreen. Being fair-skinned, before I dressed each morning, I always liberally applied sunblock to face, ears, neck, and feet (before I put on my socks). If not wearing the long-sleeved bike underwear and long bike pants, I would apply a uniform layer of 50 SPF sunblock to my arms, legs and feet.

Sunblock lotion was foot lotion applied after showering. Foot power and other lotions were not taken along. Dual-purposing was key to minimizing weight.

Chamois Butt'R®[19] was liberally applied wherever seat chaffing would be expected. "Butt butter" is its colloquial name for obvious reasons.

Time in the mornings from wakeup through cleanup, applying lotions, dressing, packing a light snack, taking daily vitamins,

---

[19] Chamois Butt'R® is a registered trademark of Paceline Products, Inc.

repacking bags on bike, putting on helmet and gloves, turning on helmet, arm, and bike flashing lights, resetting odometer and Garmin® GPS, checking tire pressure, and kissing my wife goodbye until the first pedal revolution took 45 to 50 minutes.

My phone alarm was generally set for 4:15 a.m. but I always woke beforehand. When planned daily rides were shorter, I departed an hour or so later.

Most mornings, other than drinking water with vitamins, I ate little before biking. When we stayed at a place offering breakfast, usually their offering would not open until 6:00 a.m. about an hour after I departed.

Some places offered juices, milk, fruit, bread, peanut butter, and jelly on the counter from which to make a couple sandwiches to be eaten later. When available, I consumed a couple glasses (cartons) of milk or juice to start my day. A banana, orange, or apple, when available, was happily taken along for a mid-morning break.

My bike was kept in our room. Very rarely, a secure storage room was available next to the check-in counter where my chained and locked bike was held until morning.

That was my general routine. Daily summaries include other details.

Chapter 9: 🚲 92 km/57 miles

Day 3, May 22, Selby, SD to Linton, ND

Depart time: 7:01 a.m.
Arrive time: 12:01 p.m.
Highways: 83
Day – total km/miles: 92/57—257/160
Day average speed: (kmph/mph): 16.9/10.5
Day – total elevation gain (m/ft): 166/545—515/1,690
Calories daily/total to date: 2,883/7,313
Daily dangers/excitement: Curious sheep and cattle, Mound City Park, small businesspeople.

Begin blog:

Another peaceful day with 7-8 mph southeast tailwind. Can't get better as my wife, Patricia, met up occasionally as my "sag wagon." I entered North Dakota today.
-----Blog end-----

Today was similar to the first day, only 92 kilometers (57 miles). I simply headed north. Elevation gain of 166 meters (545 ft.) was also similar to day one as Highway 83 skirted east of the Missouri River bluffs. Traffic was light and the highway shoulder adequate as the countryside passed.

Two days of bicycling in South Dakota accounted for five percent of my ride, but only two percent of elevation climb. Average speed was exactly the same as the whole trip average but I only biked 83 kilometers per day (51.5 miles)—a third less than the trip average.

My trip started with less distance per day to build stamina and confidence.

Luckily, small rural towns in the Dakotas provide services to farm and ranch families laboring to produce enough to support their families and a bit extra to recover from drought, hail, blizzards, prairie fires or other calamities.

As I quietly pedaled past cattle, they would look to inspect the passing sight. While continuing to graze as cars and trucks passed, they were far more alert as I passed. Was it sound, sight, or potential predator that caused an alert glance?

If predator, sheep should be more concerned. As I passed a small flock of sheep grazing a shelterbelt of trees, they were not overly concerned. Grass and flocks were reminiscent of Ireland on a spring day. Still bushy with winter wool, some came to the fenceline for a closer look.

Earlier I mentioned drinking a lot of water each day. Not all perspires. Traveling through the Prairies, drivers realize bathrooms are seldom convenient. Road approaches and tree-belts provide discretion for bicyclists. Urinating drivers are conspicuous.

When speed limits were lower and roads rougher, highway departments or local communities built and maintained roadside parks. They are rare today. Small towns, and vast distances between them on main routes more likely had rest stops.

One small town, Mound City, South Dakota, (population 72) not only has a city park next to the only highway running through town, it is fully functional. Toilets, paper and paper towels, and sheltered picnic tables on well-kept grounds provided an excellent place to relax. Halfway between Selby and my destination, Linton, I enjoyed a peanut butter breakfast sandwich in their roadside park.

Over the years, I had been through this area many times. Occasionally, I would stop in the Mound City café for the main course—the only course, some type of German-Russian meal. It always consisted of meat, potatoes and wheat (in many different forms)—sometimes including sauerkraut or cabbage. Servings were more than generous.

If anything less, customers (local farmers) or their retired parents would complain before boycotting. Their boycott would not last but a day or so since there was no other place to eat, except at home. A small pleasure for wives was having their husbands gone for hours.

Back home, when I was not traveling for work, at 7:00-8:00 a.m. I would stop at our local coffeehouse to join the guys and often one lady to catch up on local sports, business activity, and in some way political discussions. Religion and politics were off-topic, but some could not resist.

One morning, idiosyncrasies of small-town coffee groups were the topic of the day. True stories were always welcome. Mound City was a particular day's favorite.

Traveling from Bismarck, North Dakota back into South Dakota one of the older guys stopped in the Mound City café for breakfast. As he walked in, everyone looked to see who entered. He sat at an empty table, and a guy at the next table said, "That's Rudolph's table." My friend got up and sat at another table. "That's Joe's table," another fella impolitely, but succinctly, explained the rules. German Russians are not known to beat around the bush.

Before he could sit at the only other unoccupied table, someone said, "That's John's table." Hungry and disgusted, he looked at the waitress, an older maiden who obviously knew the routine, pointed to a half-table between a wall and unpacked supplies.

Coffee was apparently pour-your-own, but he waited to get it until he had ordered breakfast. It did not take long for him to consume eggs, sausage and toast before departing.

Like many ethnic communities around the world, the small pocket of German-Russians in northcentral South Dakota and southcentral North Dakota are friendly people. Just consider, as a stranger, you are not their friend.

Mound City, like many small towns, had its system. It was no different than visiting a church. Everyone had their place. Outsiders are welcome—just do not sit where someone else had unknowingly reserved it.

Please do not avoid small town cafés, their churches, or visiting with locals. Feel very free to buy from small-town businesses. Likely, you will be the only stranger they see that day, and you will be their topic of conversation for the next week or two or longer. Besides, that stop may give you a story to tell the rest of your life.

If you are tired of urban life, move to a small town. Freedom abounds! Never assume you will fit in. It may take two decades or more to be considered a resident. You will never be considered a local.

It matters not what area of the world, small town and village businesses survive off locals—not you.

As a visitor, when entering a local business, always assume you are an outsider. Be pleasant. Ask. Never demand. Thank them for their service. Tip heftily at cafés and coffee shops. Depart with a smile, even if you did not get what you wanted. Likely, a substitute will be offered. Be thankful, because it may be many miles to the next outpost that may have less.

Bicycling is freedom. It is joy. Biking disgusted is like searching for your own peril.

The route I planned avoided cities. Their traffic is dangerous. I like small towns. They are all unique. When you take this trip, look for them. Eat in them. Stay in them. Enjoy them.

It is my hope followers on bicycles, motorcycles, cars, campers, and RVers will take this uncommon vacation route. Settlements offer only recent history.

Some say the Plains have little to look at, probably because highway speeds are fast, and metered only when a cop is seen or anticipated. Bicycling in the quiet surroundings slows to a pace allowing details to be appreciated and contemplated.

Drivers speed down the road racing the mind to look distant thereby failing to realize what was passed. Zooming by, the past is not readily evident and the present not enjoyed.

Can the future be enjoyed without admiring the past?

The future will never be reality—only unrealized intentions.

When you get my age, it is better to enjoy the present.

As the train era began in the nineteenth century, readily bypassing horse and cart, a rumor spread that any person traveling faster than 25 miles-per-hour (40 kph) would lose their mind. Are we?

I rode without listening to radio or music. On our city's bike trail it was not unusual to see bicyclists wearing headsets. Some music was so load I could hear it.

Those over-stimulated, some addicted to electronic impulses, cannot appreciate nature's subtleties. It remains elusive.

As a military intelligence interceptor, for four years I wore headsets trying to separate reality from static. This trip, I wanted to identify nature's reality.

Growing up with electronic stimulation, rationalization seemed to divorce those born in the 21st century from reality. Instantaneous digital snippets are mind-boggling. Ever-present smartphone impulses beg attention. Young ears and eyes have become shock absorbers.

What is learned?

Sadly, yesterday's reality, history, culture, tradition, and nature lays hidden—anticipating another incongruous snippet.

Gadgets occupy time. Being at work does not get work done, nor does access to knowledge make one wise. That is as foolish as saying the bicycle in the garage kept me in shape.

Communication and transportation technology have quickened the mind. Cycling slows it while muscles reactivate. Reality reappears.

Another stop was at the South Dakota/North Dakota state line. Scant evidence indicated it offered a bit more than a photo stop. (Do not count on finding trees for discretion in the Prairies.)

Coasting into Linton, at 1:10 p.m., I remembered a café I had frequented before and stopped there to have lunch with my wife who had arrived an hour earlier. A local motel was gracious, if not surprised to have a guest, especially one arriving so early in the afternoon. They were grateful, accommodating and curious.

"They have a local bakery," my wife reported.

Lunch, bakery goods, and a large dinner sounded good to me.

When in small towns chat with business owners. They are usually the ones in the public, if not serving you.

The bakery owner, 64, and her husband had recently bought a small house for $35,000 and were converting it into a "Bridal Suite" for wedding couples and anniversary get-a-ways. She had seen small houses used as such in France, but was not aware of any in the U.S.

You may find it confounding, but Prairie Dakotans and Canadians are generally well traveled.

Using a quaint European idea, buying and renovating an old house too small as a starter home was risky. Besides ambition, small townspeople must be progressive or their town dies.

Linton, North Dakota and many towns I passed through had business after business and farm after farm that indicated a positive attitude and conviction to make a living where few others remained. Give them business.

(As you will notice, my daily blogs lengthen as daily ramblings shorten. This could be a personal journey for you as it was for me. Pedal, ride, think, hear, see, smell, feel, and absorb surroundings.)

Chapter 10: 🚲 103 km/64 miles
Day 4, May 23, Linton to Bismarck, ND

Depart time: 6:20 a.m.
Arrive time: 1:10 p.m.
Highways: 83, 1804
Day – total km/miles: 103/64—360/224
Day average speed: (kmph/mph): 12.7/7.9
Day – total elevation gain (m/ft): 315/1033—1,830/2,723
Calories daily/total to date: 2,974/10,287
Daily dangers/excitement: No wife support, German/Russians, bakery, and abandoned school.

Begin blog:

Sixty percent chance of showers as I departed Linton was aided by a slight east breeze which supported peddling on this 6 hr. 50-minute ride.

For a bit of background, Dakota Territory was split into North and South Dakota in 1889–86 years after President Thomas Jefferson bought the Mississippi River drainage area from French military leader, Napoleon Bonaparte in 1803.

Napoleon, running short of cash, supposedly worried he would lose the major shipping port at New Orleans. Trying to protect his expanded French territory in Eastern and Western Europe, he quickly made a cash offer to the young country—the United States. Napoleon's enemy, England, likely would have made a quick move to control New Orleans. For three cents per acre, Jefferson bought

42

828 million square miles for $15 million which basically doubled the U.S. in size. Jefferson, a U.S. Founding Father and drafter of the Declaration of Independence, had served in France as Minister (ambassador) of the young country. He had likely heard about Pierre Gaultier De La Verendrye's March 30, 1743 claim of the Mississippi and Missouri River drainage for France.

Interestingly, the Verendrye expedition placed an inscribed lead plate on a bluff overlooking what is now Ft. Pierre, SD two weeks before Jefferson was born.

Anyway, three school children found Verendrye's lead plate February 26, 1913, 109 years after President Jefferson sent Meriwether Lewis and William Clark on the 1804 to 1806 journey to find a water route to the Pacific Ocean. The highway I took north on my departure from Pierre was Highway 1804. It is the same uncompleted road I took into Bismarck today.

Up to the mid-1800s, water was the main mode of travel. It took Lewis and Clark from September 29 to October 24, 1804 to travel upstream on the Missouri River from Pierre, SD to what is now Bismarck, ND. I made the fairly easy trip (224 miles) in four days by bicycle. It is no wonder pedals and chain driven rear wheel in the 1880s created the Bicycle Craze of the 1890s. It was the first efficient, mechanical mode of personal transportation.

Today I took a break on the front steps of another symbol of days gone by—an abandoned one-room country school south of Hazelton, ND. It was bigger than the two country schools I attended, but today's Internet-based learning requires no school structure. It made me wonder…how long will schools named after President Jefferson last?

----Blog end-----

As I mentioned yesterday, before I left Linton, my wife and I stopped at the local bakery. Small towns are so fortunate when bakeries survive. Fresh bread, donuts, rolls, and cookies grace the sidewalk with appetizing smells. Desire to enter cannot be replicated.

When biking you smell the bakery invite. Meanwhile, vehicles drive by.

My uncle was a baker. His older brother was a baker. His younger brother was a baker. Each had their own special recipes, called formulas, that were seldom shared.

During high school, a classmate of mine worked for my uncle. When he graduated, he moved to a small town in Minnesota. I lost track of him. About 35 years later, I stopped into a small-town bakery run by my former classmate. His donuts and rolls were exactly like my uncle's. When my uncle and aunt left our town, Ipswich, SD, they ran a commercial bakery in Pierre. Fortunately, their hometown recipes were still enjoyed many decades later.

One day, my mother, my wife and I stopped into a bakery owned by my uncle's older brother. That brother had passed away a couple years earlier. His widow and daughter were still maintaining the bakery. As I was selecting the noticeably different rolls and donuts, I asked the widow about her younger brother-in-law.

"I bought his filled donut holes whenever I was back in Pierre," I said.

As I was making my selection, I asked the widow if she had filled donut holes like her brother-in-law. She did not. Before I could make a different selection, she asked if I could get the recipe for the custard filling used in the donut holes.

If she had not received the donut hole filling recipe (called a formula) in the last forty years, I was not about to ask him.

Local bakery formulas were family secrets.

During and after World War II larger "commercial" (rather industrial) bakeries developed to minimize labor and supply bread to working men and women employed in the war effort. Those large bakeries sought, bought, and even recruited local bakers for their formulas. Baking formulas were needed to make products taste better and last longer as they were placed on grocery shelves instead of bakery shelves.

I could have biked 5,000 kilometers and eaten bread and rolls every day from convenience stores without eating anything less than a week old. In the "old days", when I was young, day-old bread and rolls were discounted. Expiration was dated in hours, not months.

Espionage was not the only way to gain secrets during the war. Industrial secrets were sought from humble bakers.

Likely, bakery formulas are like beer recipes. They die with the owner/inventor or their widow. Why?

In the twenty-first century, children are extremely unlikely to take over bakeries or breweries from their parents. Why?

Small-town bakeries were like dairy farms. They died a slow death by industrialized baking as twentieth century milking machines eliminated hand milking.

Cows had to be milked morning and night. Dairymen, their wives and children were up before dawn and finished the evening milking about dark. Feeding and preparing feed filled the rest of their life, 24-7-365.

We milked cows on our farm. Hitting the road at 6:20 this spring morning was much more pleasant than washing, milking and feeding cows mornings and evenings. Today, all I had to do was get on a bike and pedal.

A century ago, every farm had dairy cows if only for their own use. On this route, I did not see one dairy cow in five thousand kilometers.

Like dairymen, bakers rose earlier, about 2:00 a.m. With ovens warmed by 3:00, the first batches were mixed and in pans. That process continued until customers arrived around 6:30 or 7:00 a.m. Small-town bakeries usually closed by late afternoon. They still do. Industrial bakeries deliver 24-7.

Sundays off may be the only difference between a baker's and dairyman's life. It is no wonder few towns have bakeries or dairies, or fresh bread or fresh milk.

For refreshments, rather than a carbonated soda, I drank a fresh glass of milk. It was fresher than canned chemical formulas or highly processed dairy milk alternatives.

If you do find a bakery while traveling, buy more than you can eat. An hour later, all the goodies will be gone and you will be wondering why you did not buy more.

One of the wonderful, certainly surprising, experiences on this bicycle odyssey was that bakeries were prevalent. Based on my experience, if an outpost had an oven in North Dakota, northern British Columbia, or the Yukon, they promoted gigantic sticky buns (Americans call them caramel rolls).

Stop. Enjoy. Eat another.

Bicyclists survive on carbs. Bakeries fill the need.

As we departed Linton, Patricia headed south to Pierre for Memorial Day with many of her eight remaining siblings.

Depending on my speed and her family commitments, we had not planned to see each other for two to three weeks. By then, I would likely be in western Saskatchewan or Alberta.

I biked north on Highway 83 through German-Russian settlements and farmsteads until I turned west on Highway 1804 all the way to North Dakota's capital, Bismarck.

The area had been settled for hundreds of years by Hidatsa and later Arikara Natives before Lewis and Clark arrived in 1804. They crossed the Missouri River to visit the unique buildings of permanent Natives and named the area "Missouri Crossing".

When the Northern Pacific Railroad arrived only decades later, in 1873, the growing town was renamed Bismarck after German chancellor, Otto Von Bismarck, to attract German settlers. It worked. Germans still dominate the area today.

Although English is universally spoken, the German-Russian brogue (distinct accent) is very recognizable along Highway 83 from Akaska (my mother's hometown) through Lowry, Selby, Java, Mound City, Herreid, Hague, Strasburg, Linton and up to Bismarck.

In less than four hours one can drive from South Dakota's capital, Pierre, to North Dakota's capital, Bismarck, without perceiving the regional peculiarity—the German-Russian brogue.

This is just another example of how bicycling with regular stops enables appreciation of parochial idiosyncrasies.

These are twentieth century communities--unique as any on this 5,000 kilometer (3,000 mile) journey. They are young communities.

Even Native Americans did not settle the plains but had encampments along rivers, like the Missouri.

For example, the first baby born in the small hamlet of Akaska, now a sports fishing village, was Caroline Kalmbach born October 21, 1907 which was only four years before my grandfather emigrated from South Russia.

When traveling through this area, or for that matter any area of the world, notice the different accents. Even if you do not know their foreign language, you can still notice differentiating accents, inflections, and phraseology.

It is one of the joys of biking through an area at a slow pace.

Traveling by car, train or plane, uniqueness of communities is missed. Sounds, like smells, cannot be missed when not encountered. How sad.

Bicycling allows encounters. Satisfaction guaranteed.

Chapter 11: 🚲 177 km/110 miles
Day 5, May 24, Bismarck to Minot, ND

Depart time: 6:13 a.m.
Arrive time: 6:02 p.m.
Highways: 83
Day – total km/miles: 177/110—538/334
Day average speed: (kmph/mph): 14.8/9.2
Day – total elevation gain (m/ft): 396/1300—1,358/4,454
Calories daily/total to date: 4,737/15,024
Daily dangers/excitement: Wind behind and against! Under-estimated calories burned, wind turbines, and trucks hauled oil equipment.

Begin blog:

I had planned two days to get from Bismarck to Minot, ND with the first stop 54 miles at Underwood. I was there by 11:15 and the lodge was closed (probably after the last guest left and before the afternoon guests arrived). It indicates small town folks do not wait around for someone to show up. They have more productive things to do during slack parts of their day.

With a ~7 mph (11 kmph) tailwind from the southeast and forecast of southeast winds up to 25 mph (40 kmph), I decided to push through the next leg to Minot. I should have checked Minot winds rather than Bismarck.

As I moved north, winds shifted to the southwest, then west, then northwest with rain clouds building as I moved north. I fought 25-30 mph winds the last 20 or so miles but arrived after consuming about two gallons (~8 liters) of water.

I also learned my new Garmin® Edge 20/25 only had battery life for about 7 hours of biking. Luckily, my $12 Walmart bike odometer kept me updated on speed and distance. When I compared the two after about six hours, they were within a couple tenths of a mile.

Today's trip was into one of the most prolific energy producing areas in the world. Trucks were passing me loaded with oil pipes and tanks for the Bakken oil fields ahead of me. Then I passed active surface coal mines and coal fired power plants—one co-generating ethanol from the area's farmers. I did pass a solar panel supplier. Some may cuss constant wind, but I passed hundreds of 200 foot electricity-generating wind turbines strategically scattered in fields and pastures. Northwest North Dakota is likely unsurpassed in potential renewable and non-renewable energy.

-----End blog-----

For European readers, distances in Canada and the United States are sometimes difficult to imagine. Therefore, my distance from Pierre, South Dakota to Minot, North Dakota would be like biking 478 kilometers (287 miles) from Paris, France through the Chunnel to London in five days and still not have been far enough.

Over two hundred bicycles were used during construction of the fifty kilometer underwater tunnel between France and England completed in 1994. Luckily, I was biking outside in nature.

Clouds predict weather. Likewise, investors have predicted wind farms would make money and be beneficial.

June has been Dakotas' rainiest month. Usually, beginning in May, thundershowers begin popping up in late afternoon. As spring progresses into summer, storms appear more quickly and become more violent. Lightning can precede the storm.

It may seem illogical for lightning to strike with few clouds above. It does! I learned from personal experience. Luckily, not today. That lesson happened about 50 years earlier. Sitting atop a bicycle on raised pavement sometimes miles from habitation, I did not want to be an unwitting lighting rod today or the next two months.

One day, as a teenager, in early August I was sitting in the dust-free tractor cab pulling a baler. My brother was on the trailing bale skid stacking straw bales. After applying the sixth to the top, our custom was to use a four-foot iron crowbar to stab the ground between the skid boards. As the tractor and bailer moved forward, the stacked bales would slide off. The crowbar was quickly replaced in its pipe holder before the next bale dropped onto the skid.

Farmers always try to gather hay and straw quickly to keep it fresh. Continuous moisture will rot it within days. That day I noticed a rainstorm developing in the west—the most common direction. Since there were no clouds above, I decided to make one more mile roundtrip.

About halfway down the field…BAM! Not BOOM.

Without notice, I was thrown back in the tractor and my brother, Wesley, was thrown off the skid. Without thinking, I instantaneously hit the clutch and brake. Never should I have stopped that suddenly, because forward motion would have thrown my brother into the back of the crunching metal baler.

Instead, I looked back and my brother was thrown behind the skid. The impact blew him backward.

What exploded? I quickly looked forward and a few yards in front of the tractor a column of dust or smoke rose straight into the air. There was no wind.

I repeat. With no clouds above, lightning struck the ground in front of us. Apparently, we were so close that the customary thunder was not heard.

While the storm seemed to be miles away, we stopped immediately and headed home.

On a bicycle, though rubber tread prevents grounding, seek shelter from lightning storms. Lay flat in a ditch away from your metal bike. Avoid trees. They are likely the tallest thing around, are grounded, attract lightning and can fry you.

WATER:

About forty kilometers (25 miles) north of Bismarck I stopped at a gas/convenience store and picked up two ham and cheese breakfast sandwiches. My backpack water bladder was also refilled.

Knowing I never want to run out of water, I refilled three times today.

One Friday, a year before I retired, our daughter had an overnight meeting in Mitchell, SD (113 km/70 miles) west of Sioux Falls where we were living at the time. My wife had gone back to Pierre to visit family. Rather than spend the weekend by myself, I decided to ride with my daughter from Mitchell to Pierre. I phoned our daughter the night before and told her my plan to bicycle to Mitchell by noon (when her meeting ended) and put my bicycle in her vehicle for the ride to Pierre.

I departed Sioux Falls in the dark about 5:00 a.m. carrying an extra change of clothes, my backpack bladder full and a spare bottle of water. Fifty miles into the ride I was running short of water and no place to fill.

Ten miles remaining, I stopped to suck out the last drops of water. Every couple of miles I stopped regularly to avoid leg cramping. My water bladder was removed hoping for another drop or two. Thirsty. Extremely thirsty, I needed water.

Luckily, our daughter's hotel was on the edge of town. When I entered the lobby, I found water and quickly changed into street clothes before my daughter finished her meeting. Then refilled my water bottle again.

That morning I made a personal commitment to never run out of water while bicycling or hiking. I have not.

The whole trip to North Pole I carried an unopened 25-ounce bottle of water. It was "emergency water" I never used. It was a pound-and-a-half extra weight considered mandatory.

Some runners and road bikers minimize weight by carrying little or no water. In my opinion, that is foolish.

When you take a cycling trip to North Pole or wherever, carry plenty of water.

Based on my travel journal for day five, I noted: "This evening I feel a bit stiffer—like every other night but not worse. I brought a small bottle of Ibuprofen along but did not take any to date."

I never used it.

Arriving in Minot later than expected, my wife was upset I had not messaged her of my change in plans. Besides an extra bicycle chain, we discussed what other things I might need in Canada.

Patricia was as excited to begin her journey north as I was to have her join me.

Chapter 12: 114 km/71 miles
Day 6, May 25, Minot to Bowbells, ND

Depart time: 6:20 a.m.
Arrive time: 5:55 p.m.
Highways: 2, 52
Day – total km/miles: 114/71—652/405
Day average speed: (kmph/mph): 9.7/6
Day – total elevation gain (m/ft): 131/431—1,433/4,701
Calories daily/total to date: 2,580/17,604
Daily dangers/excitement: Strong wind in my face! Hot! 87 °F. Calories severely underestimated, Wind 9-20+mph dropped to 16 mph by 8:00 pm. Spaghetti dinner $9.98 perfect.

Begin blog:

Besides nearly a 12-hour ride with wind in my face for 70 miles, the greatest experience was mechanical. Why do I say "great"? Northwest North Dakota is sparse with few towns—actually only three in 70 miles that have any surviving retailers. A new Cenex truck stop/convenience store in Carpio was where I stopped for a breakfast sandwich after fighting wind for 25 miles.

I was less than a 100-yards on the highway again and I noticed my gears grinding. A quick check found the right pannier support resting on the gears. Without that single screw holding it, I could not go on. Searching the highway and parking lot proved futile.

Reluctantly, I went back into the store and asked if they sold nuts and bolts. I was escorted to a full hardware section. They had the exact Allen wench headed metric screw I needed! The 26-cent screw didn't blow my maintenance budget, so I bought two more in case it happened again.

I could have been anyplace on today's 70-mile leg, or in any U.S. city, and not found a retailer to help me in the two minutes it took to resolve my problem.

One guy asked about my problem. After telling of my breakdown, he said, "I guess you were lucky." It is more like Divine intervention!

-----End blog-----

Mechanical things force reliance on others. Let me give you a geographic perspective. A history you do not see surrounds you.

Two hundred years ago, although this area (Louisiana Purchase) was bought from France to become part of the United States, French fur traders were the established business entities as they had been for the previous century or more. Roadkill, easy to spot and smell on a bike, gives some evidence of the historic past.

Those of the past could not rely on a convenience store to fix broken equipment or resupply wants or needs. This day I was lucky to have access to a needed part.

Who were previous explorers? How did they continue? What did they learn?

Solo bicycling frees the mind. Fighting wind and more wind, constant wind, then gusts can be frustrating. Physically fighting it at 30.6 Celsius (87°F) can turn the day into a mental battle.

That was someplace I wanted to avoid on this trip. It was much more relaxing to imagine an indigenous aura, a sweat lodge for example, or running after game animals on a hot summer day. Imagining the past removed mental obstacles.

For example, all bicyclists have experienced wind. Behind: Good. To the side: Oh, well. Facing it: A clash with reality.

Today I biked eleven hours and thirty-five minutes. Most of it into the wind. With my mind on the past, I actually cannot remember much about fighting the wind. Twice I called to notify my bed and breakfast host that I would be later than expected. They were providing dinner. There was no place else to eat. I was late.

About ten hours into the ride, I looked ahead into a valley. I peddled going down to the bridge. No momentum was gained to propel me into the steep rise out of it. A glimpse of frustration hit me.

"Relax Gary. You're only a week into this trip," I thought. "Wind hasn't been too bad. Guess I've been lucky. If I struggle now, the rest would be worse."

Relaxing concentration all day on something other than wind and bicycling was the trick.

Rather than thinking how hard it would be to peddle out of that valley, I realized it was easier than it should have been. With wind in my face, I looked down. One problem solved: It's not in my face.

Did explorers of the past have wind? Of course. Did they move on? Of course. They faced starvation as an alternative. My worst case? Dinner would be late.

After I returned home from this trip someone asked me if I ever thought of quitting during the trip.

My reply was quick. No thought needed. My answer: "No! Why would I want to do that? Every day was a new adventure."

In reference to today's breakdown, can you imagine a fur trader, or mountain man, traipsing through the prairie plains giving up because he had a screw loose? Some think I did…someplace above the bike.

Using the eighteenth-century vernacular "screw loose" dates to the origin of cotton milling equipment in the beginning of the mechanical revolution. Bicycles reached their revolutionary period a century later. Most fail to realize European exploration of this stretch of the North American Prairies dated back hundreds of years—pre-Columbus.

Many may traverse this area and see only a wind-swept barren prairie dissected occasionally by rivers and roads. They miss what really happened. It was mythical. Without indigenous writing systems, and scant written records, its retained mysteries have gradually exposed a prehistoric past.

Biking allows unrestricted imagination. Today I could be the modern-day Erik the Red while smelling the same roadkill scent trappers and traders experienced when days warmed their dressed furbearers.

Sufficient historic evidence exists proving I am not the first unusual flaming-red-headed novelty, traveling by unusual means, through this area.

A thousand years earlier, Nordic explorer Erik "The Red" Thorvaldsson's (c. 950-1003 A.D.) family was banished from Norway, lived in Iceland, and based on Nordic sagas, Erik the Red established settlements on another island he called Greenland to attract settlers from Iceland. Moving to a place 'green' from 'ice' must have sounded enticing. Having your children visit, and likely settle, Vineland (wine land) would have been better.

Eric the Red not only explored, his clan created major settlements. Eric the Red's son, Leif (surnamed Erik's son) Eriksson has been credited to be the first European to see North America. It is extremely likely he was not. Fellow Viking, Bjarni Herjolfsson, or other sailors or fisherman should likely be credited. Some moved inland. The timing of the move has not been established before the 1300s.

Claims have been made that Eric the Red's descendants, maybe his sons Thorvald and Thorstein, explored and settled in North America around 1000 A.D. (See the Saga of Greenlanders.) It is not speculation that red-haired, blue-eyed natives settled the area I am biking (central North Dakota along the Missouri River).

Let's jump ahead. About 250 years after Christopher Columbus landed in America, a French-Canadian fur trader, Pierre Gaultier de Varennes Sieur de la Verendrye (1685-1749), in 1738 explored the Missouri River and described a tribe thought to be of European origins. He supposedly was shown a Nordic Runestone on the North Dakota Missouri River near a Mandan village and had it shipped to France. Its whereabouts remains unknown, but one tribe he met, the Mandan, appeared European—white skin with different customs and hair color.

With authority to explore and establish new lands in North America on behalf of France, two of Pierre Verendrye's four sons, Louis and Francois de la Verendrye, inscribed a lead plate in 1743 and placed it on a Missouri River bluff overlooking Fort Pierre, South Dakota. That plate, about 250 miles south of where I'm bicycling, was not rediscovered until 1913 and remains in the Cultural Heritage Center in Pierre, South Dakota.

The first successful daily newspaper in the United States, the Pennsylvania Packet and Daily Advocate, on August 24, 1784 had a story about a plain's tribe that included white people.[20] The Corp of Discovery team, Lewis and Clark, in 1804 into 1805 wintered (in what is now central North Dakota) with the Mandan considered a most hospitable tribe. Mitutanka village, the closest Mandan tribe to the Expedition wintering grounds was the Mitutanka village who's chief, Sheheke, was called "Big White" by Lewis and Clark.

Does every distance bicyclist write about their journeys? Of course not! Neither did explorers and sailors a thousand years ago. Many of them likely could not write.

Today, people look to written records and assume if some European group settled in North America, they would have maintained a written record, had extended communications with their home country, and returned there.

I will politely call it an assumption of ignorance. Some present-day historians who would never survive by hunting, making shelter or their own clothes, and would likely have starved gathering their own food have rejected early European, pre-Columbian presence in middle America. When written records were left, like Runestones, many historians question their originality or history.

It may have been just the opposite. Why would they return? For hundreds of years, many people and affiliated groups left overbearing landlords in Europe because of persecution, famine, poor living conditions, limited tillable land, warlords, bland diets, pests, threats, accusations, or they sought religious freedom and economic opportunity elsewhere.

Evidence proves Vikings settled Iceland and Greenland by 1000 A.D. Proof keeps mounting. The Kingittorsuaq Runestone found in

---

[20] Brent Swancer, The Mysterious Tribe of Blue-Eyed Native Americans, Mysterious Universe, October 13, 2017, https://mysteriousuniverse.org/2017/10/the-mysterious-tribe-of-blue-eyed-native-americans/ (Sourced March 29, 2019).

1824 on a North American island northwest of Greenland is considered authentic, though uses old characters not totally cipherable. Placement dates vary from the early 1100s A.D. to early 1300s--hundreds of years before Columbus. However, scholars question the authenticity of three Spirit Pond Runestones found near Phippsburg, Maine though they contain similar characters.

Of course, once scholars object to some evidence, they must reject other finds like the ancient Norwegian coin, circa 1067-1093, referred to as the Goddard coin found at Naskeag Point Brooklin, Maine. How did it get there? Likely, it moved through trading channels with Natives.

Iceland, about 1,200 kilometers (~750 miles) of open ocean from Norway, was a trading route. Island hopping was possible with about 400 kilometers to the Shetland Islands, another 350 kilometers to Faroe Islands, and 500 additional kilometers to touch the nearest spot of eastern Iceland. From western Iceland to uninhabited rock on eastern Greenland would have been at least 530 kilometers.

Just as I biked nearly 5,000 kilometers in forty days, it is therefore very reasonable to assume sea-faring Vikings of Greenland had far more skill and endurance than I had. They certainly had the talent to sail west an additional 380 kilometers or so to the North American continent and explored much of it.

After crossing the last short stretch of the North Atlantic to North America, sailors would have found abundant furbearers, plenteous fish, and wood (a rarity in Greenland) for cooking and heating. All those resources were scarce in northern Europe and its islands. Once such resources were found on the North American continent, it would be illogical for the Vikings to ignore them.

The adventurers would have found the large continent's inland bays, lakes, and long flat rivers easy sailing as they made way into Hudson Bay up the Nelson River and lakes to Lake Winnipeg fed by the flat, slow-moving Red River all the way to northern South Dakota.

Travel slowly by bike as I have, or by vehicle. Stop often and observe. This is an area mostly ignored by educators and historians.

Documented facts like an ancient Runestone with peculiar Nordic script, holestones, a Viking axe head, a sextant, a firesteel and a chisel are reported as speculative or forged when found in Minnesota or the Dakotas. Will additional iron tools, knives, whetstones, kitchen utensils, and drinking horns sent with Viking explorers also have to be found to finally prove arrival of Norse in central North America hundreds of years before Columbus? Its curious archaeology has been more ignored than explored.

We live in a generation where proof must be in writing. Readers have become leery. Need evidence? "Facts" are often sought by querying multiple sources on the Internet. A fact is no longer a fact. If evidence was written—ancient script with uncommon characters like Runestones, they have been considered a hoax. If characters are not understood, it must be a hoax. If not documented by other evidence, it must be a hoax. If exploits were not written, they must be a hoax. Why? Well…because explorers would have written of their travels? Ludicrous!

Scholars write. Those that did not, or used unknown figures and letters, must be fake. Professional historians often live in an illusion created by their fellow illusionists.

Did I really bike nearly 5,000 kilometers in forty days?

Where is the evidence?

Six months after I arrived in North Pole, we were vacationing in southwest Mexico. An acquaintance questioned Patricia about our summer and my long bicycle ride.

Later that evening over dinner, Patricia confessed, "It is sometimes hard to believe you actually biked that far in forty days. It doesn't seem real."

It had only been six months before mind questioned memory. What seems unbelievable makes it harder to imagine facts. Memories fail. Generations pass. I wrote this to document reality.

The Viking travelers, much younger than I, left clues--genes. What did their North American ancestors look like a few hundred years later?

A detailed book published in 2012, *The Last Kings of Norse America*, by Robert G. Johnson and Janey Westin, claim King Haakon IV of

Norway was the first king of Norse America when, in 1261, he sent tax collectors to Iceland, Greenland, and Graenaveld (meaning grassland without trees).

"To summarize the picture of the Greenlander's widespread trading activities in North America, we conclude that an important part of the fur trade in the twelfth, thirteenth, and early fourteenth centuries involved a Norse colony on the Prairie veldt of South Dakota and Western Minnesota. To survive, the Norse merged with a friendly tribe of white Indians, the Mandans, when Pierre Verendrye found them living in five villages of the upper Missouri River in 1738."[21]

George Caitlin, a writer and sketch artist, lived among the Mandan Tribe (of what is now North Dakota) for several months. He wrote in 1832:

"The diversity in the *colour* of hair is also equally as great as that in the complexion; for in a numerous group of these peoples...there may be seen every shade and *colour* of hair.... There are very many, of both sexes, and of every age, from infancy to manhood and old age, with hair of a bright silvery grey; and in some instances almost perfectly white."

Caitlin provided more details.

"This singular and eccentric appearance is much oftener seen among the women...differing materially from the hair of other *colours*...the Mandans is generally as fine and as soft as silk. ...There is enough upon the faces and heads of these people to stamp them peculiar...diversities of *colour* in the complexion *slid* hair...that all other primitive tribes know in America, are dark copper-*coloured*, with jet black hair. From these few facts alone, the reader will see that I am amongst a strange and interesting people...a maze of novelty and mysteries to the knowledge of a strange, yet kind and hospitable people...."

Caitlin goes on to draw sketches of European-looking tribespeople. He differentiates the Mandan Tribe from other tribes

---

[21] Robert G. Johnson and Janey Westin, The Last Kings of Norse America, Runestone Keys to a Lost Empire, 2012, Beaver's Pond Press, Inc, Edina, MN 2014, pg. 151-152.

on the upper Missouri he studied, sketched, and wrote about in the early 1830s.

"The stature of the Mandans is rather below the ordinary size of man. In addition to the modes of bathing…the Mandans have another, which is a much greater luxury…I allude to their *vapour* baths, or *sudatories*, of which each village has several…. In every Mandan lodge is to be seen a crib or basket, much in the shape of a bathing-tub, curiously woven with willow boughs, and sufficiently large to receive any person of the family in a reclining or recumbent posture…."

Most think Plains Tribes lived in teepees wrapped in buffalo robes. Some did. Itinerants.

It is not beyond imagination that the Vikings brought their modified style of permanent homes into the Plains. The Mandan had earthen mounds over a wooden framework to protect from cold in winter and heat in summer.

While I was writing this book, my brother mentioned a new museum had opened in the small town of Mount Vernon, South Dakota with a Viking axe head on display. It was found by a farmer in a nearby slough, sent off for scholarly verification, and returned confirming authenticity.

Does it matter if scholars accept the authenticity of the Spirit Pond Runestone found on the Morse River in Maine?

Will the Kensington Runestone found in 1898 now on display in the small town of Alexandria, Minnesota ever be authenticated by scholars?

How many samples of iron residue will archeologists have to pull from holestones near Corona, South Dakota to prove placement hundreds of years before Columbian history records arrival of Spanish?

There is much to observe and absorb while riding peacefully on oil roads near oil wells, between deer and ditches, grass and gates, cars, cows and canola, wheat and water.

When it is windy and hot, thoughts of weather cannot be avoided.

I kept peddling into the wind on my ten-year-old bike and smiled as others whizzed by ignorant of their surroundings and too busy talking and texting to understand the past, contemplate history, and enjoy the future.

I found bicycling mentally liberating—free of scholarly opinion. Yet, I stopped at historical markers to gain insight of how an area developed.

Is university taught history the same as would have been reported by a slave or tribal leader? No. Therefore, history books are opinions of the writer as are my observations on this trip.

Do you think Vikings trying to survive in what is now Canada, the Dakotas, or Minnesota documented their travels when starvation and pestilence were their alternatives?

Thankfully, some did, like the Kensington (Minnesota) Runestone inscribed between 1360 and 1362. Others left or lost a chisel, knife, firesteel, sextant, iron tools, and kitchen utensils.[22]

Do you think my ride would have occurred if I had not written about it? Many would doubt it was possible for a 65-year-old. Hopefully, all ages will find solace on a similar ride.

This venture was a blend of natural observance, nineteenth century mechanization (the bicycle), and twenty-first century food, lodging, and transportation conveniences.

I used no radio--no music device.

Anticipating a storm, I tried ear plugs from a portable radio in central North Dakota. The first time the battery was dead. The next day I tried it again, but it did nothing for me. It was annoying.

How could I enjoy a bike ride with annoying announcers, most annoying commercial after commercial, and manufactured sounds?

---

[22] Johnson, Robert G., Janey Westin, *The Last Kings of Norse America*, 2012, Beaver's Pond Press, Inc., Edina, MN.; Dates: p. 62; King Haakon: p. 67; Sextant: p. 72; firesteel: pp. 84–85; Chisel: p. 126; South Dakota mooring stones: pp. 130–131; iron rod: p. 132; knife: p. 139; iron tools, knives and kitchen utensils: p. 140; Mandan Indians: pp. 169–170.

To me, nature provided the beat. Rotating pedals proved rhythmic. All the way to North Pole, I never turned the radio on again.

Today was one of those days to let music drift in and out of consciousness. A line from a 1980s Bob Seger's song, *Against the Wind*, was appropriate. The line: "I'm older now but still runnin' against the wind," seemed most fitting.

Music lines in the right setting have a way of continually repeating and repeating even when you stop thinking about them.

At age 65, I did not feel that old. I lost my father and both grandmothers from cancer and heart problems before my current age. Although "I'm older now, but still running against the wind."

I'm old enough now to stop worrying about the things not controllable. Bob Seger was right when he wrote: "I'm older now, but still running agaaainst the wind." It was freedom!

I arrived for the evening at the nine-room Main Street Hotel built in 1913. Remodeling was done room by room by ever-optimistic entrepreneurs, Theresa and Shawn. Bowbells, population 336, is quaint. A clean comfortable room awaited. So did a delayed spaghetti dinner for $9.98 made by Theresa's mother.

If you make this journey, stay there. Of course, unless you pitch a tent, there is no place else to stay for 50 miles in any direction. Relax with a glass of wine. The next morning, enjoy a coffee in their bistro all in the same room at # 3 Main Street.

Really, 336 residents? The 2010 census was obviously taken before Theresa and Shawn's son moved to Alaska and others moved out. With a post office and grain terminal, what else would you expect in Bowbells?

Don't get your hopes up. It is all at # 3 Main Street.

Chapter 13: 85 km/53 miles
Day 7, May 26, Bowbells, ND to Estevan, SK Canada

Depart time: 6:13 a.m.
Arrive time: 11:29 a.m.
Highways: 52, 39
Day – total km/miles: 85/53—737/458
Day average speed: (kmph/mph): 17.1/10.6
Day – total elevation gain (m/ft): 75/247—1,433/4,701
Calories daily/total to date: 2,222/19,826
Daily dangers/excitement: Gained an hour—to Mountain Time, hot 90°F, people inside, crossed international border, library, courteous sixteen-year-old waitress.

Begin blog:

A short, sunny, nearly windless 53-mile ride through the Canadian border crossing at Portal, ND into an even smaller hamlet, North Portal was uneventful. The border agent advised me to be careful at the bottom of the only valley/hill in the 25-mile ride to Estevan. It was a hill I could have cruised down at 35 mph, but there was no way to see an oncoming train or stop in time if I had carelessly approached.

Today I relaxed, walked most of downtown Estevan, and enjoyed a pizza served by a pleasant 16-year-old (grade 10) waitress. Skipping college, she was planning a career with the Royal Canadian Mounted Police (always referred to here as RCMP since horse mounts are only for show now).

Like weather does not respect international borders, nor does geology. However, there seemed to be far more oil wells on the north side of the border along with kilometer after kilometer after kilometer of open-pit coal mine(s).

Taking over the family business is no longer a tradition. Evidence: Estevan seems to have transitioned from a farm/ranch center to an economic cycle—rising and falling based on oil prices.

It shows, as businesses close downtown and new ones pop up on the outskirts during good times.

Meanwhile to entertain the idle, the city built facilities for year-round inside activities.

When I asked directions to the library, I was directed to a modern complex merging a library and arts center in the middle separating an aquatic center and hockey rink where perhaps 8-to-10-year-olds were being trained in Lacrosse while parents watched from the bleachers. Some moms held a fundraiser bake sale in the lobby. The Curling Centre was a separate building sharing the parking lot.

I walked the ten or so blocks from my motel but did not see one child (or parent) outside enjoying a beautiful spring day. The sunlight vitamin D is free and wasted just like south of the border. Over the past week I biked 458 miles (737 kilometers) and I had to go inside to see people.

-----End blog-----

I spent four days in North Dakota, rode 486 kilometers (302 miles) at the slowest average speed (13.5 kmph/8.4 mph), and had a total elevation gain of only 252 meters (827 ft.). Every minute was enjoyed—even the wind. Why not enjoy what you cannot control? (Note: distance in each state or province was based on nightly stops.)

The shifting winds, crops, Missouri River breaks, water crossing, and smells of fresh cut grass and bakeries were as memorable as the hospitality. That's satisfaction.

I was ready for Canada—more to see, hear and smell.

Bicycling allowed time for reflection.

People lose freedom. They give freedoms away thinking they will be socially secure. Usually, the opposite happens.

I like getting up early and taking off on my bike. The mornings are always fresher than the day. Biking gave me freedom to depart at any time without government or business hour restrictions.

By 8:45 I was at the Canadian border. It was 7:46 when I crossed into Canada. Without realizing it, I had changed time zones.

Apparently, the border guard did not often get international guests arriving by vehicle or bicycle at 7:45 a.m. A simple comparison of my face to passport photo was adequate. No electronic facial or retina recognition system was used.

China, for example, has two hundred million high-tech cameras to monitor streets and classrooms where everyone has a 'social scorecards' that can deny any person a train or plane ticket. Personal movement is recorded and limited.

Not in Canada.

Safe bicycling was freedom—at least in the U.S., Canada, New Zealand and other places we biked.

Vehicles take road precedence in Australia. Two summers we returned to the same town and even speedbumps on crosswalks were removed. Reason: "Too many cars had accidents on them." Australians are very polite except when driving.

I did find biking rural roads in northern Japan an energizing escape. City cycling was not for me.

Mountain biking in southern Mexico was exhilarating, but more than a bit frightful on two-lane cobbled street traffic with cars parked on each side. If we were lucky, our handlebars did not rub cars…too often. We biked into the remote mountains with a German guide who had married a local Mayan. It was an interesting trip. Since the Spanish invasion centuries ago, Mayans coalesced in the rugged mountains of southern Mexico and Guatemala. Their villages were unique, clean, and the people very friendly.

I like open spaces. If you do, this trip is for you—flat Plains led to majestic mountains.

At the Portal, North Dakota/North Portal, Saskatchewan border crossing, exchange of passport and stamp was quick. Obviously, I was not smuggling tons of liquor, weapons, or contraband. However, I was politely cautioned to be safe and don't speed (down the hill before the railroad tracks). It was as true for a bicyclist as it would have been a vehicle driver.

What a wonderful, courteous, unexpected welcome into the country!

The rail line at the bottom of the first (and only) hill was dangerous as the trains could approach from either direction fast and unseen.

A five-to-seven mile-per-hour southwest breeze behind me was surprisingly relaxing after yesterday's headwinds. With only 28 miles from Bowbells to the Canadian border, and the 25 miles from the border to Estevan, I arrived early at the Uptown Motel. It was not uptown.

I was ahead of schedule—arriving mid-morning. My reservation was for Sunday night, not Saturday. Fortunately, being a day early, I was more than pleased to be given a clean room before noon by a receptionist that seemed surprised to get a customer that early. He graciously obliged.

Service is more appreciated when you do not expect it. A simple gesture was great testament to Canadian hospitality.

Before I left, I stocked up on Canadian cash. Both countries use dollars and similar coins.

Sometimes the Canadian dollar is worth more than U.S. greenbacks; usually the U.S. dollar is worth more. Paper is cheap to manufacture with the color, texture, and designs differentiating the country of origin. Both countries' pennies, nickels, dimes, and quarters were of similar size, color, and weight.

It is still common to get Canadian pennies and nickels as change in South Dakota and North Dakota. Not in Canada. They dropped their pennies years earlier. Nickels are seldom used.

Minerals increased in value faster than Canadian currency. In 2012 it cost about a penny and a half to produce a penny. The Canadian penny was dropped. It made no sense.

Governments manipulate their currency. They enact laws to prohibit coins from being melted into usable metal. Value of a country's currency is usually measured against precious metals—historically, gold.

Can you imagine the government confiscating your bicycle or coins without asking? Preposterous? Not really.

It can happen. Yes, it did happen!

U.S. Presidential Executive Order 6102 by Franklin D. Roosevelt on April 5, 1933 (a month after taking office) made it illegal for Americans to own gold or use it for purchases. Not preposterous. It was a fact.

"All persons are hereby required to deliver on or before May 1, 1933, to…the Federal Reserve System all gold coin, gold bullion and gold certificates now owned by them or coming into their ownership on or before April 28, 1933…."

Hence, many consider F.D.R. America's first socialist president.

One would expect free and open governments would want people to have freedoms—like bicycling with whatever money they had. Just check your bills and coins and go.

Buying a bicycle is freedom. Personal freedom was not always possible in the United States (1933-1974), Great Britain (1966-1979) and by extension Canada (not independent of Great Britain until 1982), Australia (1959-1976), the Soviet Union, and Russia after personal ownership of gold or gold coin use were banned there and in other countries.

From 1933 to 1974 Americans could not buy a bicycle with their own gold coins. Why? Personal ownership of gold was illegal. It took decades to regain ownership.

August 14, 1974, five days after taking office with a conservative philosophy, President Gerald Ford signed Public Law 93-374 restoring the American personal freedom of owning gold. That act restored the personal freedom of buying a bicycle with your own gold money.

Public law 93-373 "…permit(s) United States citizens to purchase, hold, sell, or otherwise deal with gold in the United States or abroad…."

People want freedom to make choices.

The young waitress that served me pizza today had the choice to freely enter a profession without a college degree. She did not need a penny or nickel to do it.

Youth emulate adults and are conditioned to give up freedoms.

Many teenagers get government-issued driver's license, a government approved insurance policy, drive government roads following government laws and wear government required seatbelts just like adults. Do they want to bicycle to school?

Humans often prefer convenience and drive rather than walk or bicycle. Mental freedom, like bicycling, is hard to restore. It is easier to sleep longer and drive to work or school than walk or bicycle.

Physical motivation can be challenging. Driving is often a substitute. Hopefully, this trip encourages change—using physical activity, walking or biking, for mental satisfaction.

Spending money for the opportunity is not required. In fact, those that buy expensive exercise equipment and gym memberships usually underutilize their investment.

I used a ten-year-old hybrid Trek bicycle on this trip. A road bike would have been lighter and faster. A mountain bike would carry more weight. I needed neither.

My old bike was moderately priced when I bought it new from Scheels®, a regional sporting goods store a decade earlier.

Before I took off, my wife and others tried to convince me to get a new, expensive bicycle. I had ridden my old hybrid for ten years. To me it was free. Why would I pay again for freedom?

Today, I had entered another country. Would I see differences? Yes. In currency, certainly. Other differences may be too subtle to distinguish, but I certainly was impressed with my first motel clerk and Canadian sixteen-year-old waitress.

Both had taken jobs, accepted guidelines, were trusted with finances, and given responsibilities with the prospect of helping others. That was personal freedom they created which cannot be taken away.

I smiled at the simplicity of their freedom. They might also love bicycling.

Welcome to Canada!

Chapter 14: 🚲 90 km/56 miles
Day 8, May 26, Estevan to Weyburn, SK

Depart time: 5:12 a.m.
Arrive time: 11:10 a.m.
Highways: 39
Day – total km/miles: 90/56—827/514
Day average speed: (kmph/mph): 16.1/10
Day – total elevation gain (m/ft): 18/59—1,451/4,760
Calories daily/total to date: 2,315/22,141
Daily dangers/excitement: Started an hour early, grain terminal, 00 vs. 000 soybeans, bike time trials—fastest 5-mile laps, passed Curling Museum.

Begin blog:

I woke at the normal time of 4:50 which gave me an hour to prepare for the day's ride. When I looked at my phone for messages, it showed 3:52 a.m. without realizing it, I had biked into another time zone (Mountain) yesterday and did not change my watch.

To give an indication of how flat southern Saskatchewan is, my total ascent today in 56 miles was 59 feet (and most of that was going through a creek drainage on the north side of Estevan).

The tallest structures dotting the vast Plains are the oil well pump heads and there are many. I counted 17 in one square mile. They sit amongst spring wheat and durum emerging in last year's canola stubble with beef cattle grazing non-cropped ground.

A friend grew up near Weyburn, and her father invested in a grain terminal that is likely the largest in Saskatchewan and likely one of the tallest structures in the Province (excluding towers).

As a courtesy to my friend, and personal curiosity, I biked an additional two miles into the terminal. Like all good agri-businesses during spring planting, they were open to receive grain and deliver fertilizer on Sunday. That was service!

One segment of my career, I was as a marketing manager of a new grain terminal. January 1, 1983, I started there with not even the first grain storage tank operational. Within six months we were the largest grain terminal in South Dakota. As an economist, I was hired to do trend analysis and project a twenty-year feasibility to determine if we could gather enough sunflowers to use the storage for an oilseed crushing plant. It took 15 months buying grain and sunflowers from up to 200 miles to realize we could purchase all the sunflowers from that area, and it would only meet half the projected processing capacity.

Working with 52 commercial truckers and shipping hundreds of carloads of grain created a functional grain terminal still operating 35 years later using the initial storage facility. Fortunately, I projected correctly. The oilseed crushing plans were halted to many farmers' disappointment. That decision saved investors tens of millions of dollars, but because it was located in the right place, it benefited area farmers much more. My two-year contract ended early, but it provided a lifetime of business experience.

Opportunities are always available to spend money. Fortunately, my friend's father saw an opportunity years ago to benefit his farm and the following two (or more) generations of farmers in southern Saskatchewan.

Take a few moments as you are driving by any business and appreciate the guts and determination it took to dream, invest, and do while others benefit from the service. My friend should feel very proud of her father (and others like him) who stepped up years ago for the sake of others.

The blog photo showed my bicycle as a speck next to an efficient grain terminal benefiting Saskatchewan farmers and world consumers who enjoy eating without a hint of what it takes year-in and year-out to feed them. As Aesop might have said: "Never complain with your mouth full."

Long term efficiency, opportunity costs, and return on investment are not easy to analyze or justify. Just like my 3000-mile trip "Pierre-to-the-Pole" is hard to justify economically, but satisfaction is very seldom only economic.

-----End blog-----

So far I biked 827 kilometers (514 miles) in eight days. For comparisons, that is as if I had biked from Chicago 824 kilometers (512 miles) to Kansas City, Missouri, or New Orleans 814 kilometers (506 miles) to Dallas, Texas.

Only after I was prepared to leave did I realize I had biked into the Mountain Time zone the day before. I woke at what I thought was the normal time—4:50 a.m. I went to the bathroom where my phone was charging. It showed 3:50 a.m. After responding to Patricia's message from the night before, I casually prepared for the day's 56-mile ride. Today was short--like the first two days.

To continue my blog story, a couple we met in Mexico, Kat and Wayne, grew up on farms in southcentral Saskatchewan. By coincidence, two weeks before I departed Mexico to pack my bike for this trip, Kat's parents came for a visit. Over Sunday brunch, we enjoyed their company and I sought hints on suspected weather, terrain and interesting sites.

Our friend's father, decades earlier, was not satisfied selling all his crops to the Canada Wheat Pool. Many farmers also felt trapped by government marketing controls.

To feed the world with limited labor, farmers and suppliers must seek efficiencies and better yielding crops. Soybeans, for example, could not be grown in this area until breeders developed earlier maturing 00 and 000 varieties since the year 2000. Due to its short growing season, corn could not be grown in this area until natives gradually brought corn north from southern Mexico by genetically modifying and adapting maturities over hundreds if not thousands of years. Early maturing, multi-colored flint corn is still referred to as Indian corn.

Canola and wheat, the largest crops through the terminal are not native to the area. For thousands of years, farmers have used climate knowledge and ingenuity to meet food demands.

This terminal was an example of their ingenuity. As a result, Weyburn is the largest inland grain sourcing town in Canada.

After stopping at the grain terminal, I biked the mile back to the highway and on to Weyburn where my insignificance was blended with cars and trucks flying by at full highway speeds, or faster.

Speeding makes reality less noticeable. That is why I like bicycling.

Although the farmers' grain and fertilizer terminal was open for business, the Soo Line Railroad Museum and the other Weyburn claim to fame, the Turner Curling Museum, were closed on Sundays. Apparently, tourism was not a Sunday activity in Weyburn, or they lacked volunteers or funding for paid staff.

For a summer college job, I worked on a railroad construction crew in 1976. I was curious to see if the Weyburn Railroad Museum had a handcar. Various models were all called *handcars*, because they moved manually by pumping a gear-driven handle or pedaling. The small pedal model was basically a bicycle riding on one rail with a gauge bar extended to run on the opposing rail. In 1976 we used a handcar to move spikes, anchors, hammers and other repair equipment.

A curling fanatic, I am not. With a free afternoon, I would have enjoyed seeing curling stones dating into the 1800s and assortment of 18,000 curling pins. To the surprise of many, curling has been an Olympic sport since 1998. Some of my Canadian friends, in their seventies still play it. Most watch it on television. If you love watching bowling, try curling, or something more mentally ticklish.

Weyburn seemed like a nice, medium-sized town. If you are a bicyclist or a weekend Weyburn tourist, plan activities there between 1:00 p.m. to 5:00 p.m. Saturday afternoon. Stay awhile. If you just stop for gas and go to the bathroom, grab a fast-food sandwich or stay longer—take time for a full restaurant meal. With a full stomach and tank of gas (thanks to area farmers and oil producers) hit the highway between wheat, canola and oil fields.

Obviously, an early arrival in Weyburn and an afternoon of rest energized me for the next day—the farthest and longest ride of this trip.

As referenced in *Daily Dangers/Excitement*, today I recorded five-mile (8.3 km) time trials. It turned out to be the second flattest ride (only 18 meters/59 feet total accent). Laps included stops.

1. 27:15 minutes = 11.0 mph/17.7 kmph
2. 23:19 minutes = 13.2 mph/21.2 kmph
3. 22:23 minutes = 13.4 mph/21.6 kmph
4. 24:09 minutes = 12.4 mph/20 kmph
5. 22:23 minutes = 13.4 mph/21.6 kmph
6. 30:37 minutes = 9.8 mph/15.8 kmph
7. 36:38 minutes = 8.2 mph/13.2 kmph
8. 35:31 minutes = 8.4 mph/13.5 kmph
9. 35:17 minutes = 8.5 mph/13.7 kmph
10. 37:42 minutes = 8.0 mph/12.9 kmph
11. 57:29 minutes = 5.2 mph/8.4 kmph

The first twenty-five miles (40 km) today were quite fast averaging 12.2 miles-per-hour (19.6 kmph), but not pushed—just normal pedaling.

Curious how wind, terrain, and breaks consumed time? Wind influenced speed. Compare lap five verses six compared to laps seven through ten. Lap eleven, I obviously took about a twenty minute break.

Chapter 15: 🚲 267 km/166 miles
Day 9, May 28, Weyburn to Davidson, SK

Depart time: 4:50 a.m.
Arrive time: 8:05 p.m.
Highways: 35, 48, 1, Ring Road, 11
Day – total km/miles: 267/166—1,094/680
Day average speed: (kmph/mph): 20.8/12.9
Day – total elevation gain (m/ft): 136/447—1,587/5,207
Calories daily/total to date: 6,823/28,964
Daily dangers/excitement: Wind pushing, total miles, water shortage, low blood sugar or sodium level, nobody knows distance.

Begin blog:

Very likely this will be my longest day with bike loaded—166 miles total. My wife, Patricia, may catch up with me by tomorrow night and be my "sag wagon" allowing me to reduce pannier weight. I started this trip with the bike and supplies weighing 79 pounds. As nutritional supplies dwindled and were replaced, weight remained at least into the 70s.

Mountain Time sun came up about 5:00 as I was headed to Regina. No wind for the first 30 miles followed by a favorable 7-10 mph made today's ride easy, but long.

Arriving into Regina at 10:30 a.m. would have made a 4-5 hour wait for my hotel room. Instead, I canceled it and pushed to the next stop which was an additional 92 miles. It was 70 miles to Regina, and I was concerned the 92 miles into Davidson would have been too far with unfavorable winds.

North of Regina, towns are few and far between with at least half without services. Twice I was down to my last remaining "emergency" bottle of water. Short rides into towns added about four miles to today's run, but water is a necessity when exercising. I consumed over three gallons today and supplemented it with electrolytes.

One of the towns without services was Findlater. As I was passing it, hoping to find water, I realized I would (find some later). Actually, it appears few found the town in the first place. In the U.S., a gas symbol inevitably means an adjoining convenience store. Not here! It is quite common to see eight or more symbols on a town's highway sign—the more the better, especially when food, water, or lodging are required.

Today's ride was peaceful through what was aptly called a "Prairie Province." I hope the rest of my trip is as peaceful.

-----Blog end-----

Today, I used nature (flat ground), no wind the first thirty miles, and then 5-10 mph wind (mostly behind me). Nutrition bars, cheese crackers, two 20-ounce water bottles with Solstic® Revive,[23] two electrolyte tablets, two SportLegs® capsules[24], water, and more water in all about 50 glasses (over 11 liters) to propel 48-pound panniers, 31-pound bike, my 183 pounds, and loaded small packs for a total of 285 pounds pedaling for a grand total of 166 miles (267 kilometers).

That was a long sentence, but it was a longer ride!

This was by far my greatest distance in a day—more than the first three days combined. It was not my toughest. Though today I moved at an average 12.9 mph, it was not my fastest day. A couple days in Saskatchewan and Alberta I averaged 12 mph, but my fastest day

---

[23] Solstic® Revive and Solstic® Energy are water-soluble electrolyte and glucosamine powder supplied by Nature's Sunshine Products, Inc. Spanish Fork, UT, https://www.naturessunshine.com/us/general/search/?q=solstic+revive.

[24] SportLegs® is a company name marketing the same named vegetable based capsule product containing a patented mix of lactate compounds of calcium, magnesium and Vitamin D, http://www.sportlegs.com/.

(excluding stops) was an 87-mile day in the Yukon Territory…more on that later.

For the first ten days, advanced lodging reservations put me at the Regina Holiday Inn. After a week without a day off, advanced anticipation projected a spacious room (though expensive compared to most places). Hot extended shower, perhaps a long soaking bath, an extra-large meal, maybe a steak, a glass of wine after a beer or two and a soft bed sounded rewarding.

Seventy miles from Weyburn, Regina (population 215,000) was the biggest city I had planned to go through. As capital of Saskatchewan, it was its second largest, behind Saskatoon with about a quarter million people.

At 4:50 a.m. with panniers packed and lights flashing, I began pedaling. The first 70 miles (113 km) or so went quickly. Rolling over small undulating hills amongst emerging crops, mostly wheat and canola with a sunrise mirage, was relaxing, yet stimulating.

Bicycling is very peaceful and calming with no wind nor traffic. Mirages help visualize what you cannot see. They are personal.

What does mirage mean?[25]

Mirari in Latin has the same root word as mirror or to admire, meaning to look at and to wonder. We know a mirror (*mirare*) reflects objects.

A mirage made me wonder.

Is there a better thing to think about when biking solo on a beautiful sunny morning?

On our farm in northern South Dakota, mirages in three directions were a regular occurrence—seldom to the west. Our relatively small farm was in flat glaciated terrain. How flat?

At night from our front porch step we could see the series of Faulkton airport runway lights 30 miles south as well as the Aberdeen airport lights 30 miles to the east. That airport was at 1302 feet above sea level. The Faulkton airport (elevation 1571 ft.) was

---

[25] Mirage: (noun) an optical illusion in which the image of a distant object as a ship or an oasis is made to appear nearby, floating in air, inverted, etc.; it is caused by the refraction of light rays from the object through layers of air having different densities as the result of unequal temperature distributions; *Webster's*, p 907.

slightly lower than our farmyard with Leola (1591 ft.) 30 miles north of our farm slightly higher elevation. From Bowdle (1957 ft.) 30 miles west to Aberdeen 30 miles east elevation dropped about 12 foot per mile whereas north and south elevation changed only one-third foot per mile.

Based on watching mirages for years on our farm, the optical phenomenon refracts distant images above the ground more readily in flat terrain or sloping away. Often two or three distinct replications of grain bins, silos, farmsteads and trees in the sky can be seen some mornings above actuality at least thirty miles distance—at night, perhaps farther.

Centuries of laws of the sea assumes the earth's curvature does not allow line-of-sight beyond twelve miles. Even at night, atmospheric conditions on nearly flat glaciated plains allow distinct images to appear perhaps up to three times that distance.

For thousands of years, it was known ocean-going ships on a clear day could see shore or other vessels at about 12 nautical miles (22 kilometers).[26] "International and Territorial" waters were based on line-of-sight.

When biking long distances without music, news, radio or other twentieth century distractions, thoughts wandered as above.

Back to mirages. I have always been fascinated by them.

On Monday, May 28, day nine, as I was biking north of Weyburn, Saskatchewan my mind was wandering from a peaceful view of mirages to peaceful cemeteries with flags posted at veterans' graves and flowers on others. Today was a national holiday, Memorial Day, back in the United States.

My wife had lost family in the past year. Patricia wanted to be with me from Pierre-to-the-Pole, but rightfully so, it was far more important for her to attend Memorial Day services with her family and providing them moral support than be my sag wagon.

---

[26]When I look out into the ocean, how far away is the horizon? How much of the ocean can I actually see? Shawn Kleinart, Quora, https://www.quora.com/When-I-look-out-into-the-ocean-how-far-away-is-the-horizon-How-much-of-the-ocean-can-I-actually-see (Sourced February 2, 2019).

What better way to peacefully reflect the spirituality of the day, as I was greeted by a morning mirage of things that are, but are figuratively out of site?

As I turned northwest, 40 miles from Regina, a soft breeze five to seven miles-per-hour out of the southeast rose to push me along on a cloudless 70**°F** degree (21°C) morning. Not effortless, but close.

Our friend, Dawn put me in contact with her son, Kelly, a distance bicyclist from Regina. He had planned to ride with me today, but a business trip unexpectedly took him away.

As I peddled on, about two miles ahead I could see a recreational bicyclist heading my way on the opposing highway shoulder. It was a welcome sight. No bicyclist had been seen for the first 560 miles of my trip (except day two when I gave away my bananas).

He approached, slowed, and turned around to follow me. With plenty of energy, a gentle breeze behind me on a beautiful morning, I was clipping along.

I did not slow. His bike was stripped.

Finally, after about two miles, he caught up with me and we slowed to a stop.

"You were moving at thirty kilometers per hour (18.6 mph) so it took me a bit to catch you," he said.

The day was perfect. Two consecutive days arriving before noon, apparently gave me unexpected energy.

My new companion was a small-town newspaperman and avid cyclist. After a brief introduction, we jumped on our bikes and chatted until we reached his turnoff. He and his brother had biked many places, including my home-state's Mickelson Trail the year before.

An old mining and timber railroad branch line, abandoned in 1986, was converted to a 109-mile bicycle trail under the leadership of South Dakota Governor George Speaker Mickelson, who was tragically killed in a plane crash in 1993.

The Mickelson (bicycle) Trail leads from the ranching town of Edgemont (edge of mountains), winds mostly through the Black Hills National Forest around mountains, including four tunnels, through scenic woodlands, and over a hundred bridges to the gambling and mining town of Deadwood.

The wild-west town of Deadwood was near the longest-running gold mine in the world (Homestake). Gold made it valuable and recognizable. Science made it sustainable detecting neutrinos--the smallest particles emitted from the sun (as known to date).

With shafts and tunnels reaching 8,000 feet (2,400 meters) below the earth's surface, Raymond Davis Jr., a South Dakota scientist working at Homestake Mine, first discovered solar neutrinos in the 1960s and was awarded a Nobel Prize for his efforts.

Since 2009, Lead's Homestake has been operating the National Science Foundation project known as the Deep Underground Science Engineering Laboratory researching advanced geothermal systems, neutrinos, and other dark matter.

A bicyclist, physicist, engineer, mineralogist, geologist, hydrologist, researcher, technician, businessperson, author, mountain carver, sightseer, outdoor enthusiast, or tourist would enjoy the Mickelson Trail.

As Samuel Langhorne Clemens (1835-1910) under pen name, Mark Twain, wrote, "The secret of getting ahead is getting started."

Want a relatively short adventurous ride? Head to the Black Hills of South Dakota and ride the Mickelson Trail.

In fact, based on my freedom to think and experience offered on this trip, any expert would enhance their profession on any extended bicycle ride, no matter the scenery.

There is so much to see wherever you go. There is even more to think about when not distracted from nature.

It is impossible to clear your mind or mountain without touching something new.

Today was a pre-Yukon training day.

How far could I go? Where would I stop? Should I test my endurance?

After my few-mile companion took a selfie (photo) of us with their local grain elevator in the background, I continued toward Regina.

Just outside the city, I had to decide:

1.) Should I rest after a 70-mile (113 km) ride?

2.) What would I do if I finished at 10:30 a.m.?

3.) Will I have to wait four or five hours before I could check into the Holiday Inn?

4.) Can I make it to Davidson—another 93 miles (150 km)? or

5.) If I cannot, where will I stay?

Regina, Saskatchewan's capital, has the oldest museum in the Prairie Provinces, the Royal Saskatchewan Museum. Over the years, what I have found traveling was that Mondays were not good days for tourists. Businesses and sites open on weekends, gave owners or staff Mondays off.

Should I waste time checking hours of operation for the Museum? Promoted as having historic and ethnological interesting items, tweaked my interest. Since it was closed and displays removed during World War II, it must house some extremely valuable, or ethnically disturbing artifacts.

Should I take the quickest way, the shortest way, or the safest way? Bicycles competing with traffic in large cities is never safe.

I noticed a bike path in the city's southeast. If I got off the highway onto the bike path, what would be the quickest route all the way through? Highway 33 inbound to Highway 11 leading northwest out of the city was all four-lane limited access highway, including a short segment of Trans-Canada Highway 1. That's it!

I ate a protein bar and drank enough water to last me the next half hour. At 10:30 a.m., Monday traffic should have been manageable.

Excited. Adrenaline flowing. I quickly clipped into my pedals. Go! Exiting the bike path, after a couple stop lights, I hit the loop and made a dash through Regina.

Up an on-ramp, I stayed far right on the wide shoulder. I was clipping along about 17 mph (27 kmph). The next exit ramp came quickly. Dangerous shit!

I had to cross the off-ramp between vehicles. Thread the needle.

What's the old British proverb? A stitch in time saves nine? (Determine a solution early saves much time later.)

In this case, I'll take it to mean, I should not get hit by a car or truck; it could be painful…if I recover.

I looked in my left mirror—my only mirror. Go! Go now!

One down!

There seemed like six lanes. Intersection of Trans-Canada 1? No time to think. The on-ramp came quickly.

A friend had told me that Ring Road was the quickest way through Regina. Based on the traffic flying by, I was obviously on it. *Road* was an onerous understatement.

The next ramp was even more dangerous. SHIT was too mild.

While glancing in mirror to judge traffic spacing, I constantly peeked down the on-ramp to see what was coming. How fast are they coming?

Not the right question.

How fast are they accelerating?

Next question: Can I cross to the on-ramp shoulder before the ramp ends, or stick to the solid line until traffic clears on my right?

At a critical juncture, about where the on-ramp ends before the merge lane began, was where my neck could no longer turn enough to see on-ramp traffic. Nearing that point, glancing left into my mirror was fruitless. Ramp traffic was the concern, at least for the next few seconds, until I crossed it.

I popped horizontally crossed as the merge lane began. I picked up more speed. Took a breath.

Was I breathing? I was flying! No time to look at the speedometer. Loaded with over seventy pounds of panniers and water—I did not notice.

The next ramp came quicker than I expected.

It made me wonder: Does Trans-Canada traffic pick up speed in cities? It does on U.S. Interstates going through cities. In fact, there is likely a better chance of getting picked up by Highway Patrol going the speed limit holding up traffic than speeding with the flow of traffic.

Those behind were going too fast to exit. Instantaneously, I cleared another exit ramp.

What the heck is ahead?

A bicyclist coming up the on-ramp?

What's the idiot doing?

Better get his ass in gear!

After peddling several hundred miles, I should have welcomed a fellow rider. A half-hour earlier I even stopped and chatted with one. With traffic flying by, this was no place to gab.

Luckily, there was no traffic coming up the on-ramp with him.

I pulled within a car-length of the guy ahead. Nice bike. No bags. Is he ever going to speed up?

I have to get by this idiot before another off-ramp.

I looked in my mirror. Thank you, Canadians! You are either extremely courteous, or like some people I know, always drive in the left passing lane.

There was a gap. All traffic was in the left lane—except the bicyclist hogging the shoulder.

The 4-lane leveled off. What would you expect? It's Saskatchewan.

With a slight breeze behind, seventy some miles under my belt already today, I increased cadence.

With the shoulder hogger ahead, I snuck up behind his rear tire and switched up a gear.

Momentarily, I held my left arm straight out (to indicate I was moving left).

With unrealized strength, I flew by the guy. I had to be going 30-40 kilometers-per-hour (20-25 mph).

A couple more off/on ramps and I was in the northeast industrial side of Regina—likely outside the city limits. That was a quick seven miles!

An overpass was ahead. I slowed. Pulled into the shade. Dismounted.

Took a deep breath. Relaxed—or tried to. That was exhilarating!

It had not been a half-hour since deciding to stay or go through Regina. Now I was past and looking at fields in the distance.

I checked my water. Not good. I should have been drinking more.

The year before, I biked from Pierre, South Dakota to Onida a few times. It was about a 67-mile roundtrip. The first couple times, about the sixty-mile mark, my legs started cramping. I knew I was getting dehydrated. When I was almost done, I drank. Walked a bit. Drank more, off-and-on until I could ride the rest of the way back to Pierre.

Today, if cramps emerge in the next ninety miles, I'm toast. (It was sunny.)

I never found one place to stay before Davidson. I paged back-and-forth through my detailed travel guide.

Little towns lay either side of the highway. Well, unpopulated former hamlets may be a better description.

I was clipping along—consuming extra water to rehydrate.

The day was hot. I still had a southeast breeze behind me, but I had to refill my 100-ounce (3-liter) water bladder. It was empty, as was a 24-ounce (710 ml) water bottle.

About noon I coasted down into a valley. A sign read eight kilometers to Craven. That's not bad.

I figured I would get off my route and restock. As I started up the hill, I thought. What if Craven has no services? I turned around and coasted down to the Lumsden exit.

Snack Shack, a little fast food joint—the old-fashion kind was just off the highway. A couple cars were parked out front. A girl took orders at one window while a teenage boy was grilling burgers.

I asked for a bag of chips and a water. I was not hungry. Make that two bottles.

(Now was not time to be stingy, but at a couple dollars a bottle, I thought I would find water soon and much cheaper).

With bike parked in the shade, I sat at a picnic table looking through my travel guide.

Two girls, twenty, college-age, drove in, walked up and ordered a couple ice-cream cones. They sat at the next table. As I was about to leave, I asked, "How far to Chamberlain?"

Chamberlain appeared to be the next town with services.

"Oh, about 30 minutes," each chimed in.

Saskatchewan Highway 11's speed limit was 90 to 110 kilometers per hour (depending if it was a divided highway). I decided if they were averaging 100 kilometers-per-hour, thirty minutes would be about 50 km (or 30 miles). With a good breeze it would take me over an hour.

With two full bottles of water and an emergency bottle stashed in my pannier, I would have enough to get to Chamberlain as I started the long climb on Highway 11 out of Lumsden's Snack Shack.

I had pedaled for over an hour. No Chamberlain in sight. No signs.

My calculations were off.

I had not refilled my 100-ounce hydrate pack yet today. (Thankfully, my wife brought it to me the morning I left.) My bike-frame water bottle was empty as were the two bottles I had picked up at Lumsden. A little Solstic® Energy electrolyte mix remained in my other 24-ounce bottle. Every few minutes, I would slip the remaining bottle out of the bike frame below my legs, sip, and savor it in my parched mouth.

I needed to refill water soon.

With a slight breeze to my rear left, I was clipping along about 25 kmph (~15 mph).

Was it time to break out my emergency water?

Another fifteen minutes, I was out of water except my emergency bottle. This was not an emergency, but close.

A Bethune sign appeared.

There were no gas stations or stores along the highway, but it appeared to be a town big enough to have a business that sold water. I peddled around town. No businesses. Back and forth. I spotted the city office. Surely, they would know where I could buy water.

It was obvious the city manager did not often get a customer in full bicycle gear walking into her office. Small towns only needed small offices. It was about the size of a small dining room in a building that appeared to have been a one-bedroom single-story house at one time.

After removing my helmet, I asked, "Any place that sells water?"

"Sure," she replied. "At the Co-op grocery store."

Since I thought I had biked every street, bewildered, I asked, "Where's that?"

Smiling, she said, "Next to the lumberyard, a couple blocks away."

"OK. I just biked by there but I didn't see the grocery store," I said as I turned to walk out. "How far to Chamberlain?"

"Oh, about a half hour," was her casual reply.

Considering I had biked over thirty kilometers (18 miles) I figured Chamberlain must be much closer.

"That's interesting. I was told the same thing an hour ago by a couple of girls at the Lumsden Snack Shack turnoff." I said, a bit let down.

She said, "It depends on how fast you drive."

I replied smiling, "You have a point, but I'm on a bicycle."

A common mistake people make is not answering a simple question. Alternatively, common in politics, they answer a question that was not asked.

Was the Bethune city manager elected? She had the skills: smiling, polite, helpful, and interested with a pleasant demeaner.

But, I did not ask how long it takes to get to Chamberlain. I asked how far is Chamberlain?

Canadian highway distances are measured in kilometers, not minutes. I never asked how many minutes it would take me to bicycle to Chamberlain.

That would have been foolish, since it appeared nobody bicycled in this area. Consequently, I must estimate driving speed of a particular driver. The college-age girls likely would drive faster than a city manager.

Speeding apparently was expected in wide-open rural Saskatchewan. Perhaps Royal Canadian Mounted Police (RCMP) have a policy similar to the one Montana had back in the 1980s with a speed limit of "safe but prudent."

If you could see ten miles ahead on a clear day with no traffic, Montana patrols considered it safe to drive a hundred miles-per-hour. My question of that policy was the "prudent" part. If drivers were prudent, why were seatbelts required?

Now, besides seatbelts, airbags are installed assuming drivers are not prudent. Speed sensing and collision prevention devices are becoming a vehicle standard. On self-driving cars, they are mandatory.

Before I left, the biggest concern of family and friends was that I could be hit by a vehicle. Had I thought about it, most would be considered speeders, not prudish.

As I biked over to Co-op Foods, through the lumberyard parking lot, I realized Canadians I met were shrewd in measuring distance.

There could be several reasons. Mainly, highway signage was not always accurate. A kilometer could be one to two miles, not point six. More likely, the confusion happened decades ago when Canada switched from miles to kilometers. Signs were likely erected where highway maintenance crews thought was an appropriate spot—like where a mileage sign had been. If it was within a few kilometers of exact, who cared?

Thirsty, I rolled through the gravel lot, stopped, and leaned my bike against the entrance deck of Co-op Foods, a small concrete block building annexed to a one-pump gas station.

The checkout counter was by the door. I asked, "Do you have bottles of water?"

"Actually, we have a water purifier. You can fill your bottles," said the delightful clerk. "It's in the back."

"Great!" I said, "I'll get my bottles."

There were new twenty-liter and four-liter jugs near the purifier, but I did not want to waste a container that I would only empty into my cycling containers. I filled my backpack and bottles with 4.4 liters (4.6 U.S. quarts)—well over a gallon of water and walked to the front counter to pay. "How much do I owe you?"

"Nothing. That's ok," the clerk said.

"No. Seriously," I said. "I really needed water and I am so thankful you allowed me to fill. I want to pay."

I could tell she was a truly kind, community-minded person, like the city manager.

She did not want to take my money after I asked again how much to pay. So, I laid two loonies (dollar coins) on the counter as I thanked her on my way out.

Full of water, with a soft wind somewhat behind, I headed toward Davidson intending to bypass Chamberlain. I did—twenty miles (32 km) from Bethune's Co-op Grocery store.

Later, on another break, checking my maps, it appeared to be another 35-40 miles (56-64 km) to Davidson from Chamberlain, or up to ninety kilometers (56 miles) from Bethune.

For fresh riders on a normal day, those ninety kilometers would have been a full day's ride. That was my planned average day.

After having biked well over a hundred miles (162 km) already today, I was attempting a 3-day ride in one.

I biked on.

In less than an hour from Bethune, I coasted to today's blog photo—Findlater.

The "town" sign indicated gas was available in a kilometer. In the twentieth century, where there was retail gas, there was drinking water. That is not the case in 2018. Unmanned, twenty-four-hour credit-card controlled fueling stations were taking over.

Rural America was founded on a shortage of labor. Rural Canada was no different. It was no longer possible to have an attendant wait for a car to show up, wash the windows, check the oil, test tire pressure, and pay by check at the pump.

Those days were gone.

Would I find water in towns like Bethune? Findlater? What was the chance the next town had retail facilities?

I later learned '*Find later*', was pronounced colloquially completely different with '*f*', '*l*', '*t*' and '*r*' the only recognizable letters in an unrecognizable dialect.

After asking numerous people from Saskatchewan, apparently an ethnic group settled the Findlater area. Most apparently vanished…and not found later.

Constantly, during this trip, I interacted locally and contemplated what I would have never learned had I, like many drivers, sped through the area without stopping. Findlater was another example.

Pronunciation of Findlater in the local dialect survived as the town gradually disappeared. Perhaps locals were trying to pronounce it in French.

Interestingly, it is the only Latin-based parlance I know where '*a*' is pronounced as a soft '*i*' with '*n*' and '*d*' silent and "*u*" as an "*e*". If I tried to write the vernacular as pronounced, it may be *fi' li' tur* (soft '*i*', soft '*i*').

Hopefully, as you read this book you begin to realize someone moving, weeks on end, averaging ten miles-per-hour (16 kmph) must be thinking. Conscience. Thinking something.

It is relaxing and easy to concentrate on obscure topics seemingly floating suspended, soft air massaging face, arms and legs, as spring greenery sneaks from undercover, and nature watches with curiosity.

Heedful again.

After a quick physical check, are legs peddling? Any pains? No. Legs—ok. Wrists—ok. Back—ok. Butt—ok.

Why would I stop and rest? There was no convenient place.

No trees. No shade. No farmstead. No town. Even the small bike seat was more comfortable than shoulder gravel playing grab-ass as pavement tapered onto fall-mowed stubble.

I peddled on…seeing nothing to find, now or later. Typical— *Find later.*

What I failed to realize began to emerge.

Sometime after passing Chamberlain, distant objects seemed to be blurry.

Ever since riding a tilt-a-whirl at Disneyland with our daughters in 1983 I would get nauseous when television commercials or phone videos changed scenes too quickly. The same thing happened when I was filming an Iowa field-day from five hundred feet above in the back seat of a Piper Cub[27] as it circled the patchwork of corn plots, machinery and tents.

---

[27] Piper J-3 Cub, manufactured by Piper Aircraft, was a small, light, slow-flying American aircraft manufactured between 1937 and 1947. They were durable with simple construction making maintenance and upkeep the reason there are many Cubs still flying in the twenty-first century. Piper Cubs are most commonly used for beginner pilot training.

1940s Cubs only had two seats--one behind the other. I shot several rolls of 35-millimeter film with several lenses out the open door-window as the pilot banked twenty to forty degrees as wind jerked us around. It took me an hour after landing to get my sea-sickened stomach settled.

I slowed.

I slowed some more.

I peddled for a mile or so without looking to the distance or ditches. It got worse.

Something was wrong. I stopped before I tipped over…perhaps moments before I passed out.

To this point I had never taken even an aspirin—no medication. No blisters. No chaffing.

Evening aches? Sure. Morning stiffness? Of course. All would pass. I wanted to be super-conscious if my body gave cues.

Was I getting dehydrated? An hour ago? Maybe? It seemed I had replaced what I was losing. Electrolytes.

Was water flushing through my system too fast? I put Solstic® Energy in a full bottle of water and drank half swallowing an electrolyte capsule while straddling my bike on the highway shoulder as I did not want to tip over.

I heard about endurance athletes hitting a wall—when athletes *run out of steam.*

In my lifetime of activities, cross-country running, softball endurance (74:05 hours), marathon hikes (26-37 miles), throwing bales (thousands per day), spiking rails (in 110°F/43°C heat), swinging hundreds of bags per hour, moving thousands of salt blocks from stuffy railroad boxcars, or bicycling, I never hit the proverbial wall. Perhaps it was because I never considered myself an athlete.

Some people asked me how I got in shape for the planned two-month Pierre-to-the-Pole ride. My short answer was that I never got out of shape.

At age eighteen, during six weeks of Air Force basic training I gained twenty pounds (9 kg).

Never had I spent so much time learning to fold tee-shirts and shorts, sitting through lectures interspersed with a little exercise day-after-day standing in line to eat before smoke break. Those not smoking were given the opportunity (volunteered) to pick up cigarette butts. I figured it was the military way of getting recruits to relax--smoke.

When I started this bike ride, I weighed two pounds less than when I graduated military basic training.

I was just a regular guy that enjoyed keeping my muscles and mind active. If someone expected a 65-year-old could not do it, I would try.

Dizziness disappeared. After a short road-side standing break, I clipped into the peddles and took off.

All was fine…for a couple miles. The same faintness reappeared. I stopped. Drank more water. Recovered. Peddled on, more slowly. This happened numerous times over the next half hour.

In the past, when dehydrated, I would get leg cramps. Today, I did not.

While stopped and rehydrating, I had a couple protein bars, a couple packs of peanut butter crackers, and sucked a pack of Sport Bean® (similar to Jelly Beans®)[28].

Four or five times I had to stop and regain my senses for fear of passing out while peddling. Although my pace slowed, I was still moving along at 10-11 mph (17-18 kmph).

By the time I came within ten miles of Davidson, I was no longer getting dizzy. Rehydrated? Electrolytes? Protein? Whatever was the source of my recuperation, I did not care.

I was tired.

It had been a full 166-mile (267 km) day—4:50 a.m. to 8:05 p.m. My gadgets indicated I had averaged 12.9 mph (20.8 kmph).

Although the day became long, I was still in great spirits fifteen hours later as I coasted across the parking lot into Davidson's Jubilee Motor Inn at 8:05 p.m. It was the motel I had listed in my daily guide, just above the map of Regina to Davidson. Fortunately, my typed

---

[28] Sports Beans® and Jelly Bean® are a trademark of Jelly Belly Candy Company and Herman Goelitz Candy Co. Inc.

directions took me directly there. Construction vehicles were parked in the small lot in the old-style, split-foyer motel.

Luckily, the innkeeper had a room. My second question: "Is there a place I can still get a meal?"

"If you hurry, the café (she pointed out the door) just over there should be open for a while yet, and the Subway®[29] should be open," she explained.

"Fantastic!" I said, as I grabbed the room key pushing my bike through the entry up the five steps to the second floor. The room was typical--worn as expected from constant traipsing in-and-out of construction workers.

It was clean. I was hungry.

Without showering, my typical arrival routine, I bounded down the steps in clipped bicycle shoes, out the door, across a couple parking lots to the café.

Fortunately, it was not only open, but I loaded up on a full dinner as I looked out the double-pane window to the Subway®—tonight's second choice. Either were much better than third choice—cold Spam®[30] and crackers packed in my twenty-kilo panniers.

Once this trip I experienced an unusual mental condition. Today! I never did figure out the cause, but I did manage my water and nutrient intake better from there on.

Looking back, it is sometimes hard to believe with a loaded bike I traveled 166 miles (267 km) in a day.

With wooziness past, no side effects, and a full stomach, I washed my biking clothes while showering, rung them in a towel, hung them to dry, and looked forward to tomorrow.

My longest mileage day was a success!

Note: A few months after I had written this, on a warm August day I returned from a 48-mile (77 km) bike ride to our grandson's farm. While oiling the chain (a daily ritual), I seemed a bit dizzy. Not near as bad as I experienced from Weyburn to Davidson, but it remined me of it.

---

[29] Subway® is registered trademark of Subway® IP LLC.
[30] Spam® is a registered trademark of Hormel Foods LLC.

About fifteen minutes later, I decided to check my blood pressure. It was 71 (systolic) over 41 (diastolic) with a 112 pulse. My blood pressure was way too low!

I checked in with our son, an emergency room doctor. I have noticed it before, but he indicated that my casual exercise and high pulse likely kept lowering my blood pressure to the point of concern. He asked if I had eaten any salty items. I had not. He recommended that salt intake would help retain moisture. Likely, I had depleted internal sodium levels as evaporated sweat left residue on skin and clothes.

In hindsight, my day's ride (267 km/166 miles) had not only reduced body sodium, but also my blood pressure to a critical level. No wonder I felt dizzy and about to pass out.

Hindsight may be 20:20, but deadly for blood pressure.

Chapter 16: 90 km/56 miles
Day 10, May 29, Davidson to Outlook, SK

Depart time: 5:10 a.m.
Arrive time: 10:25 a.m.
Highways: 11, 15
Day – total km/miles: 90/56—1,184/736
Day average speed: (kmph/mph): 19.3/12
Day – total elevation gain (m/ft): 14/46—1,601/5,253
Calories daily/total to date: 2,564/31,528
Daily dangers/excitement: Offered place to sleep, Patricia made it to Bowbells, ND.

Begin blog:

Today's ride brought me from nearly all crop ground into rolling hills scattered by cattle and crops. At the speed of bicycling (approximately 10 mph) it is much easier to envision the past. Although I spooked an occasional antelope—curious, but too close, they would lope to a safer hill to view the strange rider. Hungarian partridge would flush—likely surprising me more. Vast herds of bison are now gone, but it was quite easy to envision them grazing the hills and creeks. (The Plains animal we call buffalo are bison but related to what are called the wood buffalo or mountain buffalo of western Canada.)

Why are there now tens of thousands of wild and confined buffalo in the U.S. and Canada?

Perhaps a hundred generations or two survived off the Plains bison meat and hides. It took only a generation or so to slaughter them. Norbert Welsh (1845-1932) is immortalized in book and bronze as "The Last Buffalo Hunter" (a book by Mary Weekes and monument by the Saskatchewan Historic and Folklore Society). Today's blog photo was of a roadside historic monument to a local historic notable, buffalo hunter Norbert Welsh. On this ride, I would rather see herds than monuments.

South Dakota rancher, Scotty Philip (1858-1911) is credited with saving the American buffalo on his ranch near Ft. Pierre. His original 83 turned into hundreds for others to reproduce, turn loose, or even add scenes to movies.

You may recall the 1990 Kevin Costner film "Dances with Wolves". We were living in Pierre when Costner rented a house during filming. The buffalo scenes were filmed on the Houck Ranch, and my brother-in-law supplied most of the horses.

So, rancher Philips a hundred years ago, rounded up some of the remaining buffalo and propagated them?

There is more to the story.

Philips bought his original buffalo (bison) stock from Pete Dupree. Fred Dupree, Pete's son, captured seven buffalo calves in 1901 during one of the last free-range hunting parties. Did young Fred come up with the idea to save the buffalo? No.

Fred's mother (Pete Dupree's wife) was both Lakota and French. It was no surprise to her the vast herds used by her ancestors would soon disappear. She encouraged her son to capture and raise some buffalo calves. He did. Two of the seven died in captivity. In a few years, the remaining five calves matured, populated, and were eventually sold to Scotty Philips with encouragement from Scotty's wife (also Lakota) who knew Mary Good Elk Woman Dupree—the woman who saved the American bison.

We live in an interesting culture. One man destroyed and is glorified; one woman saved animals from extinction and is forgotten.

-----End Blog-----

Gadgets are not reliable. I am not complaining, just acknowledging that my eyes can detect where water runs and my muscles can feel even slight rises and slopes. For example, today I down-geared four times to climb some hills while my Garmin's global positioning system never detected even a one foot rise.

Saskatchewan is flat. Actually, it is too flat for my Garmin® to pick up short rolling knolls. Likely, it detected elevation only occasionally to save battery.

Again, it sounds like a light bitch, but today I rolled over more hills in the last twenty miles than the previous hundred.

Sob. Sob. Sob. Not really. They were slight practice for what lie ahead. In hindsight those little inclines were far less annoying than even one motorcycle passing with noisy mufflers. Other times, motorcyclists passed with barely any noise.

On this journey, it amazed me each time a carefree, leathered motorcyclist approached. Some I could hear coming a couple miles behind which rattled me when they passed with undulating roar for unseen miles.

It is fine to be carefree, but fellow travelers including this bicyclist wanted to see area wildlife which were disturbed repeatedly by noisy motorcycles.

While some rode quietly, why would anyone ride in the great outdoors with intent to disturb everything around them? It reminded me of a saying meant to be a joke. What is the most annoying person in the world? Answer: The one that demands to be heard.

As a Vietnam Era serviceman who wore headsets intercepting foreign signals, upcoming vehicles actually enticed me into a hearing game.

Obviously, throughout the trip, I had to maintain constant vigilance of approaching vehicles in case they were over-width, or drivers were snoozing, texting, watching videos, eating, reading, or just wandering onto the highway shoulders. When shoulders were graveled or still littered with sand from winter, a swoosh of tiny particles would occasionally blast me from the side. Moving closer to the ditch was my escape. Never, was a full ditch diversion necessary.

For the next three thousand kilometers, the game converted to an unconscious routine.

The game started by trying to identify the type of approaching vehicle. Motorcycle, car, pickup truck, recreational vehicle, truck pulling trailer, truck pulling camper, empty semi-truck, loaded semi, etc. and etc. When they passed, usually within thirty seconds, I would confirm my hunch.

It was a game, but much more, a safety notice.

Today, I was planning to bike past the little town of Kenaston. A little gas station and a convenience store was just opening about 6:30 a.m. as I rolled in. Convenience is a bit of an exaggeration. The gas pump was self-serve and the inside was too small for aisles. It did have frozen sandwiches next to a microwave oven with pre-set sandwich buttons. The ultimate inconvenience food.

Like most upgraded 1960s gas stations, the place had no place to sit. Outside with my hot foiled sandwich, I sat on the concrete rim supporting a gas pump.

After biking well over an hour, I started feeling hungry—likely from my fifteen hours of biking yesterday.

I may have appeared shuffled if not just hungry.

An older gentleman, probably my age, pulled his aging pickup truck up to the pump, injected the nozzle, and came around to chat.

"You need a place to rest?" he asked.

"No." I said, " I'm just passing through and grabbed a breakfast sandwich."

"Well, if you need a place for a day or so, I have a camper you can use," he graciously offered.

"That is so nice of you, but I'm heading over to Outlook and should be there by noon," I responded heartwarmingly.

He finished filling and went into pay as I mounted with a warm departing wave.

This is rural Canada—friendly, amiable, and compassionate to a complete stranger. You have to love it!

I looked forward to tomorrow's ride. It was equivalent to biking from Philadelphia, PA to New York City, NY. Way too much traffic there. I would much rather bike rural Canada.

Each day I woke wanting to see what tomorrow would bring.

Chapter 17: 156 km/97 miles
Day 11, May 30, Outlook to Kindersley, SK

Depart time: 5:05 a.m.
Arrive time: 1:55 p.m.
Highways: 15, 4, 7
Day – total km/miles: 156/97—1,341/833
Day average speed: (kmph/mph): 19.3/12
Day – total elevation gain (m/ft): 158/518—1,759/5,771
Calories daily/total to date: 4,635/36,163
Daily dangers/excitement: Rain, cold, and wind from every direction, and Patricia catching up with me.

Begin Blog:

I didn't know the winds could shift about 480 degrees in nine hours! It started out from the ENE at 5:00 a.m. when I departed. Different rain showers moved through. While I headed 97 miles west, the winds made much more than a complete circle and when I arrived, they were back to the northwest. Luckily, they likely did not exceed 20 mph. Temperature at departure was 52°F (11°C) and likely went into the 60s and 97 miles later it was 59°F (15°C).

My delightful wife was my sag wagon this afternoon hauling all my panniers. Unloading the ~40 pounds likely saved me two hours of wet biking. I gave her a big hug before I jumped into the hot shower fully clothed. Hey, I was wet anyway. It just saved me an extra step washing my biking clothes.

Yes, I have biked 11 days in the same outfit, but laundered each night and they were dry by 5:00 each morning. When I came out from showering, a piping hot bowl of thick bean soup was waiting.

My sister-in-law, Sharon, sent a huge frozen container. Nothing better than hot soup on a cool rainy day.

This morning I started just before the sun appeared over the South Saskatchewan River. Today's blog photo was looking back east to Outlook. The most amazing thing biking at sunrise each morning was the wildlife just finishing a night of hunting or just getting out for an early morning graze.

Just past the river, a pair of deer slowly moved from the ditch to trees as I approached. Not more than a couple miles further a grey wolf was feeding in a slough along the highway. As I approached, it moved its prey away another 25 yards and continued feeding. I stopped and took iPhone photos but I feared getting too close to a feeding wolf.

A few miles further a pair of antelope were on the highway allowing me to coast by getting a nine second video. Soon thereafter, I passed an abandoned farmstead with two Canada geese roosting on top of the barn. They flew as I stopped to get a photo.

It is absolutely amazing the wildlife and morning beauty on a spring Saskatchewan sunrise —before cars, wind and a lone biker share the road.

-----Blog end-----

Before vehicles created roadkill, there was a reason for night feeding. Many animals are nocturnal: skunks, mink, porcupine, owls, field mice, fox, beavers, bats, badgers, weasels, wolves, possums, raccoons, rabbits, toads, crickets, and the list goes on. Wildlife are feeding opportunists. Why wait until daylight when your favorite food is available at night?

Coyotes generally are day hunters unless people encroach on their territories; then they will hunt at night. Females find night feeding easier to keep their bellies and litter happy. It was common to see coyotes during the day—indicating hunting pressure was light.

Wolves are another story. I find them a peculiar beast. They can hunt as packs during the day, but often come out at twilight (which means they are crepuscular). I wanted to see a wolf, but I certainly did not want to see a pack.

Wolf packs attack. For scary details read the old book, "*The Life and Adventures of Robinson Crusoe*" by Daniel Defoe first published April 25, 1719. It began with Crusoe's first sea voyage in August 1651. Decades after escaping isolation, Crusoe nearly perished when violently attacked by a pack of wolves in the mountains of France.

That reminds me of a cougar story. Some places they are called panthers, puma, painter, catamount, and jaguar. South Dakotans generally call them mountain lions and are not related to wolves.

In the Black Hills of western South Dakota mountain lions are hunted. They are sneaky, dangerous animals. They can weigh over 200 pounds (>90 kg.). Licenses are issued each year based on population counts. When over-populated, mountain lions move out of the woods to farms to find their own territory and when native food is not available, they feast on lambs, calves, people and other domestic critters.

Towns and cities are not exempt. Mountain lions encroach on new territories, populated or not, and will feed on domestic dogs, cats, and children. Adults and bicyclists are not exempt.

One day, my aunt was babysitting her youngest grandchild in a residential area of Rapid City, South Dakota. That morning, the five-year-old pointed out the window to show her grandmother the big cat that was laying by their garden fence.

My aunt, a portly lady, yelled! "You can't go out there. That mountain lion will eat you in one bite."

The child, obviously a quick wit, said, "Grandma. You would make a whole buffet."

I was not about to bike at night. You do not have to. Bike early. It was sure exciting watching wildlife finish their lasts meal at daybreak.

Luckily, a wolf caught its prey before I arrived. It no longer wanted me, but it did want to insure it took its food far enough from me that I would not fight him for it.

Wind. Distance. Cold. Sun. Endless Plains. River valleys. With mountains, permafrost, and wilderness ahead, some have questioned why I took a longer route through the Canadian Plains.

Bicyclists moving on roadways at about 15 percent of vehicle speeds assume the shortest route should be taken. There are several reasons. History and structural design are two.

The most direct and shortest route is generally taken by long-haul truckers. Bicycling on roadways is much more pleasant without traffic, especially noisy trucks. When heading to Alaska, Trans-Canada Highway 16 from Saskatoon on to Edmonton would have made logistical sense.

Alternatively, moving west from Regina bypassing Saskatoon angling on 4-lane Saskatchewan Highway 11 to Davidson saved miles and unfortunately avoided iconic Moose Jaw and their citizens (referred to as Moose Javians).

My level route looped east and north between Moose Jaw and Saskatoon. To avoid climbs, long-distance bicyclists seek level routes. I did. Believe me Saskatchewan is level—leveled by the most recent glacier ending about 11,700 years ago. Its compacted sand and clay molded today's shallow oil fields. Aerial dust particles in snowflakes and deposited on glaciers formed farmland. It is used in today's warm period--geologically referred to as an Arctic interglacial era.

Today reminded me of the glacial warming period. It was cool, overcast with a constant chill-penetrating wind.

My bright yellow water-resistant jacket was a must. Mornings, when temperatures were only eleven degrees Celsius (52°F), I used it.

It started raining before Patricia caught up with me. I had been watching for her. My clear light rain poncho covered my upper half as it whipped mist into the wind.

For ten days I biked alone. I missed Patricia. When she pulled beside me, waved and pulled into an approach ahead, I was relieved. She looked bright and cheery compared to the overcast windy drizzle.

Our vehicle was warm and cozy as Patricia.

After biking over seven hours already today, I knew I could not relax long before my legs would tighten and resist the next thirty plus kilometers.

After a couple of kisses and light snack she delivered, I unloaded about eighteen kilos (40 lbs.) of gear into our vehicle and took off.

Panniers and back rack bag were a part of me for the first 1,300 kilometers (~810 miles). I could not believe how fast and light I felt—even pelted by a cool rain and twenty-five-kilometer per hour (15 mph) winds.

I flew as the clear poncho was whipping in the open, then sucking toward big trucks as they passed.

Upon arrival, I quickly washed my grimy bike with rags from the Super 8 motel. More than helpful staff ran a garden hose out the laundry room window so I could pressure wash it onto their greening lawn. After drying it in their lobby and oiling the chain, I carried (the now light bike) into our room.

The Super 8 staff were so helpful. They were used to construction workers showing up muddy, head-to-toe. Prepared, they had a machine in the lobby each of us could insert muddy shoes into clear plastic booties without handling anything.

Around 1:00 p.m., hours before normal check-in time, the welcoming staff gave Patricia the keys to a freshly cleaned room. The smell of soup wafted through the hallway as I carried my bike to the open door.

I had no concerns about Patricia finding me or her abilities. Often she would produce a meal from virtually nothing.

Not only was I ready to hug my wonderstruck wife, but after 162 kilometers (97 miles), much of it battling a windy rain, I was salivating over the smell of fresh bean soup supplied by her sister, Sharon.

Life was good. Real good.

Chapter 18: 130 km/81 miles
Day 12, May 31, Kindersley to Macklin, SK

Depart time: 7:40 a.m.
Arrive time: 4:55 p.m.
Highways: 21/31
Day – total km/miles: 130/81—1,471/914
Day average speed: (kmph/mph): 15.1/9.4
Day – total elevation gain (m/ft): 62/203—1,821/5,974
Calories daily/total to date: 3,160/39,323
Daily dangers/excitement: Cold, cloudy, another double day's ride.

Begin Blog:

Today I woke at the normal time (4:00 a.m.) and checked the weather. Rain was forecast for early and late in day so I planned only a 30-mile day and ended up at 81 miles. The temperature, 8.3°C (47°F), when I departed at 7:40 maxed out at 12.2°C (54°F) in Macklin, SK in the afternoon. It was interesting that the day I left Pierre it was 47°F degrees at 6:00 a.m. and 12 days later my day started at the same temperature.

Macklin is the last town in Saskatchewan before biking mostly west across Alberta in the next few days. Winds from the east would be nice.

Today I passed through the most oil rigs I have ever seen. I counted as high as 19 in one square mile and up to 14 in a half section. I decided oil wells are drilled for convenience; otherwise it is an unusual quirk of nature. I am not a geologist, but 2500+ foot deep oil-bearing layers follow roads—usually wells are a couple hundred feet from roads. That seems unusual. As you will notice in today's blog photo, they are still drilling more wells. Look closely and you will see two drilling rigs—perhaps drilling laterally.

For my fellow agronomists, note the spring wheat in today's photo. That is about the tallest field. It is the last day of May. Some fields are not planted—likely canola was planned for them.

About seven hours into my cool ride, my tempting wife flagged me down to present a hot caramel roll from a local bakery. Small towns with local bakeries offer a service under appreciated by locals and missed by most of us. When I arrived 81 miles (130 km) later in Macklin, the ladies at our motel cheered as I approached, and Patricia had hot rice and thick beef soup waiting. What a treat!!! Great way to end a cold day....zzzz

-----End Blog-----

Before we left Mexico, I had planned for today's ride to be the shortest at thirty miles (48 km) from Kindersley to Kerrobert. Waking in morning's chill reinforced my decision of a month earlier. By the time I arrived in Kerrobert (~11:30 a.m.) the wind had gone down and it remained a cool biking temperature.

We had lunch as I stretched and flexed my fingers to regain semblance of normal composure. They were cold, stiff, and curled. Macklin, the last town in Saskatchewan, was doable that afternoon—another eighty kilometers (50 miles).

I felt good. A day was gained between Bismarck and Minot, North Dakota. Then two more days were skipped when I pedaled a three day ride in one from Weyburn to Davidson, Saskatchewan.

Stopping for a good Kerrobert lunch, made for area farmers and oil construction workers, accumulated calories spent in the short morning ride. By restocking calories lost a couple days earlier (6,823 calories—nearly three times my projected burn), I had no reason to quit at noon.

Besides, I figured riding in the cool, but damp, fresh air today for 130 kilometers should be good experience for the Yukon where that may be the minimum distance between lodgings.

It was so pleasant sitting down at noon enjoying a hot lunch with my wife.

Unbeknownst to me, after lunch she shopped in the local hardware store for a pair of leather gloves. My biking gloves were padded, but fingers were always exposed. If I needed full gloves today, she decided, I could certainly use them in the mountains only days ahead.

Within an hour after lunch, she pulled beside me and waved to pull over.

Not only did Patricia surprise me with gloves, she found, by smell, the Kerrobert bakery, and brought me the first Canadian sticky bun (a huge caramel roll in American vernacular).

Yesterday's blog described the pleasure of having my wife join me. She was far more than just a sag wagon to haul my supplies. She was my partner this whole trip just as she has been the past few decades.

We enjoy each other's company. Like everyone, we sometimes want our own space and want to do our own thing. We did on this trip.

If you plan a similar trip, remember it is not always about you, you, you.

If you are fortunate enough to have someone toting extra supplies in a vehicle, it would be a good idea to bicycle a few days alone as I did. Determine what you might need later. Decide what you do not need to carry daily.

Then notify your support. They can identify more closely with your needs, increase passion for your trip, and enjoy the solemnity of their journey without you in their vehicle.

My wife, Patricia, or anyone constantly following a dawdling bicyclist, would have been bored out of their minds.

Cars are not meant to drive with windows open on road shoulders at ten-miles-per-hour.

Although Patricia woke daily to see me off, she returned to bed, arose at will, enjoyed her morning tea, and mingled with locals before meeting up with me between 11:00 a.m. and noon.

Usually, we enjoyed a snack together before I stretched, remounted and rode off.

Sometimes Patricia took a short hike or investigated interesting shops.

In the early afternoon, she would catch up with me again to discuss our evening destination.

While I biked a few more hours, she would go ahead and find a motel, Airbnb, bed and breakfast, or sometimes a house with rooms for rent.

Always, she found a place to eat. Sometimes it was only a lunch table in the back of a gas station. Quaint places were easy to enjoy. They were far better than eating canned meat and crackers in a motel room.

Occasionally, after Patricia arrived at the day's lodging, she would hop on her bicycle and meet me a few miles outside of town.

Biking with her gave me renewed pleasure like we had experienced before bicycling in the Florida Keys, deserts of Arizona, mountains of eastern Alabama into Georgia, Tour da Kota, and pleasing times on rail-to-trails in the West Virginia mountains, Minnesota's lake country, or South Dakota's Mickelson Trail.

Having someone to dine with evenings allowed each to discuss the day's interesting experiences and plan for the next. Of course, I would order an extra-large meal and usually finish Patricia's. She had always shared her meals with me.

Restaurants serve the same portions to large men and small women. Alternatively, since food is less than a third of restaurant costs,[31] a standardized meal upsized twenty percent could potentially increase gross revenue twenty percent.

On this trip, I would have welcomed upsized meal portions and been happy to pay extra for those services. My waiter or waitress surely could have carried more potatoes or pasta without requiring me to order side items when all I wanted was more volume of the entrée.

---

[31] Restaurant Food Costs: "Food costs…should stay somewhere around 28-30 percent in order for the restaurant to show profitability." Ideal Software; https://idealsoftware.co.za/restaurant-food-cost/ (Sourced December 23, 2019).

Likely, that concept is not functional with standardized industrially packaged foods arriving by truck. Henry Ford's century-old assembly-line production system standardized vehicles, parts, foods, packaging, doctor visits, and education.

Likewise, the new normal is standardized climate-controlled vehicles, homes, and schools. Those are not normal as they replace the feel of nature.

Another example is standardized highway speeds to maximize safety. Bicycles have a right to use most highway lanes, but those lanes are not safe for cyclists. Forced to highway shoulders, everyone bicycles at a different speed.

Freedom abounds. A solo trip like this one allowed both my wife and me to stop whenever and wherever we wanted. Tentacles of each diversion were individual choices. Some good. Some bad. Some encouraged. Some avoided. We each made choices.

Non-competitive long-distance cycling should not be standardized. My daily charts of distances, elevation and calories burned can be an example, not a requirement.

Cycling pleasures are personal--kind of like eating octopus for the first time. Cooked and flavored right, it is fantastic. Sometimes the unexpected hairs between tentacle suckers are irritating.

Solo bicycling avoids irritation. Can you imagine having someone tell you how fast and how far to bike limiting where and when to stop?

Many drive on vacation that way. Sad.

If you let someone else, or wind, rain, noise or other irritations bother you when cycling, you might as well seek a meal with octopus' hair, ride without support, and have someone horse-whip you when you slow below expected pace.

This trip was just the opposite. It was planned and executed for both Patricia and me to enjoy. Otherwise, we could have been working (verses retired) and never vacationed.

Gary W. Wietgrefe

Chapter 19: First day off
June 1, First day of rest: Macklin, SK

Begin Blog:

A break is in order. Twelve days on the bike and after 914 miles, I am nearly a third the way through my trip. It started at 40°F (4.4°C) this morning with a high predicted at 47°F (8.3°C) and rain all day with a 11 mph (18 kmph) NNE wind. OK. I'm a wimp. Double lubricated chain and gears are now ready for the next few days heading northwest.

For you real bikers, here are a few stats in American and international standards: Average speed: 10.1 mph (16.3 km/hr.) over 914 miles (1,471 km). Average miles per day 76.25 (122.7 km/day). Average calories per day 3,277.

The Garmin® Edge 20 Cycling GPS ($99.99/Amazon) apparently uses my weight, 183 lbs. (83 kg), times bike speed to calculate calories consumed. My slowest day, fighting winds with fully loaded bike (79 lbs. or 35.8 kg.), I averaged only six mph (10 km/hr.) and consumed 36.3 calories per mile (21.8 cal/km); whereas my longest day with the wind behind me most of the way I traveled 166 miles (267 km) averaging 12.9 mph (20.8 km/hr.) and supposedly consumed 41.1 calories per mile (24.7 cal./km).

Obviously, calories consumed were estimated based on weight and speed. For closer estimates, I should have built into the original setup my pannier weight. Reality was I burned far more calories per mile fighting wind than with wind behind me. Likewise, I burned far more calories for 737 miles carrying an average of forty pounds (food, clothes, tire, tubes, etc.) in panniers for ten days than 178 miles during last two days without it.

As long as I am referencing my odometers, I find the $12.95 Walmart Bell Dashboard 150 quite satisfactory compared to the

Garmin® Edge 20 ($99.99/Amazon). The Bell system will operate all summer on one battery, but the rechargeable Garmin® will not last a full day (usually less than eight hours) which is not adequate for serious long-range bikers.

Since I am on statistics today, I had a few minutes in the past 12 days to count pedal revolutions. I am averaging right at 70 revolutions per minute. That means in 914 miles (1,471 km) the pedals have circled about 380,000 revolutions. Take that times two (knees), the body's natural lubrication is amazing...and I had to lubricate the bike chain and gears daily.

-----End blog-----End day of rest-----

Now that Patricia has caught up with me, this may be a good time to interject another alternative to bicycling solo with a support *sag* vehicle.

Since we are both avid cyclists, at one time we considered both biking and relaying the vehicle. We could have made Pierre-to-the-Pole in half the time and each of us only had to bike halfway.

An example would be that I take off in the morning at regular time. Patricia would get ready and depart at her normal time. Once she caught up with me, we would discuss how far I wanted to bike before a break. She would then advance the vehicle to that point—say another twenty kilometers, where she would park, mount her bike and ride on. All the extra weight would be carried in the vehicle.

Upon arrival, I would put my bike on the carrier, use my set of keys, and catch up with Patricia, and park the vehicle perhaps ahead at her twenty kilometers mark. The system could be repeated each day as long as both wanted to bike.

This was not a race. The trip was for enjoyment. Rest days could have been interspersed depending on how each felt and who wanted to bike.

Multiple cyclists, say four, that wanted to make this journey and only had a couple weeks off work, could also take one vehicle and relay with four bicyclists. It would take much more coordination and vehicle backtracking.

For example, one would depart lodging, the other three would be dropped off at designated spots. If thirty kilometer legs, the driver (rider two) would drop rider three at sixty kilometer mark and rider four at ninety kilometers; then return to the thirty kilometer mark to start his/her ride. Rider one would stop at thirty kilometers and take the vehicle to pick up rider three and advanced to the 120 kilometer mark to begin riding. Rider three would return to get rider two and four and then advance to 150 and 180 kilometers and drop off riders. Consider variations.

Relay planning, to minimize wait time and maximize daily distance, should consider strength of each rider, road and weather conditions, and elevation gains. Undoubtedly, segments would not be a uniform thirty kilometers.

Under the relay system, four riders could potentially cover 5,000 kilometers in ten days each cycling the same 125 kilometers-per-day that I averaged.

However, my biggest caution for bicyclists considering the relay system is the purpose. If the purpose is to cover the distance the quickest, without a doubt the benefit of peacefulness, serenity, casually observing nature, and biking at one's own pace would be compromised. Stress and strains would cause irritability defeating the purpose of this beautiful ride.

Chapter 20: 140 km/87 miles
Day 13, June 2, Macklin, SK to Sedgewick, AB

Depart time: 5:15 a.m.
Arrive time: 3:30 p.m.
Highways: 14/13
Day – total km/miles: 140/87—1,611/1,001
Day average speed: (kmph/mph): 14.5/9
Day – total elevation gain (m/ft): 555/1,820—2,289/7,509
Calories daily/total to date: 4,213/65,946
Daily dangers/excitement: White rainbow of hope.

Begin Blog:

Today's blog photo is a first for me—a white rainbow, so close I had to take two photos to get it all. After rain all day yesterday, the clouds were breaking up by 5:30 this morning, but still a brisk west wind at 3°C (40°F) made for a chilly start. With the sun behind me facing a west wind into a shallow cloud bank, the white rainbow appeared. Since I had just entered Alberta, I took the pure rainbow as a good sign of the next 2,000 miles (3,226 km).

Speaking of signs, about twenty miles (32 km) into Alberta, going through rolling hills with dense pockets of aspen there was a yellow highway warning sign. It was a moose sketch and below it "Next 25 km". The way the countryside looks on today's 87 miles (140 km), the sign could be accurate if it said, "Next 2,500 km".

Trees are already noticeably shorter, and cropped ground dwindling to non-existent for most of today's ride.

Riding so slow through the countryside, it was easy to absorb all the activities of cattle, horses, lama, brush cutting, oil pipeline construction everywhere, and wildlife (deer, partridge, ground squirrels, jackrabbits, etc.) always popping up unexpectedly. No moose sited yet. Stay tuned.

-----Blog end-----

Yesterday was my first down day--a rain-day. After starting this morning on wet roads and light mist, I expected to have more rainy days by now. I peddled on….

Planning a two month trip should always include a precipitation outlook.

The Dakotas' wettest month is June; so is Saskatchewan. The closer to June, the more likely it is to have rainy days. July is the wettest month in Alberta, the Yukon Territory and northcentral Alaska.

My initial plan was to leave May 20 and arrive in North Pole by July 20th. Rain was not only expected, the thirty-year average precipitation records suggested that I should have expected rain up to half my biking days.

Fortunately, today I did not have to hum the 1970 John Fogerty song "*Who'll Stop the Rain*" made popular by Creedence Clearwater Revival.

Did I have rainy days? Sure. This was not one of them. It cleared early with a white rainbow greeting my early morning. The sun quietly burnt off foggy residue.

I grew up in northern South Dakota—thirty-five miles from the North Dakota border. Each spring,
"Long as I remember
the rain been comin' down
Clouds of mystery pourin'
confusion on the ground," as Fogerty wrote.

Luckily, the spring of 2018 was drier than normal in the Dakotas and Prairie Provinces. The white rainbow, though very strange, encouraged me. I biked to it.

Every day I woke to ride—to see what was out there. I wanted to ride early. Early morning lingers with animals and weather not wanting to give up the night's "…*mystery pourin' confusion on the ground.*" Even some plants flower at night—nocturnal plants they are called.

If I was confused by mystery, it was by highway distance markers.

Macklin was only four miles from the Alberta border. As I looked out yesterday through rain-streaked hotel windows, the highway distance sign read "20 km to Provost".

It seemed longer than four miles (6.4 km) to the border, but after a day off, perhaps I needed mental recalibration. Within a kilometer after crossing into Alberta, the large highway distance marker read "19 km to Provost". My bicycle odometer had recorded 4.04 miles.

Confused?

Obviously, this is an extreme example of improper distance markings. In Canada I found few to be accurate, but I did not know to where they were marking. In the U.S. distance markers are from center of town to center of town.

After mentioning the confusing markers, an Albertan suggested the signs may sometimes measure to the edge of town. If that is the case, Provost suddenly became a thriving Prairie metropolis overnight as Saskatchewan and Alberta erected border signs. It did not.

About ten miles (16 km) into my ride (and six miles into Alberta), the sky started clearing. With the sun behind me itching to burn the remaining low thin cloud bank, a white rainbow appeared. I could see miles, and miles ahead.

A deer near a deer crossing sign was the first wildlife I observed in Alberta. Wow! That marker was accurate.

The next sign was a "(Moose sketch) NEXT 25 KM". Though I questioned distance markers, I never saw a moose near Provost, or for several hundred kilometers. However, moose are private creatures and elusive. Be alert! Drivers can be killed when hitting a moose, or moose can kill by hitting a bicyclist.

It is harder to bicycle in freezing conditions, especially on frosty roads. I intended to completely avoid freezing temperatures, deer, moose, or any other thing that got in my way. As you will read later, I did not.

113

Chapter 21: 🚲 132 km/82 miles
Day 14, June 3, Sedgewick to Wetaskiwin, AB

Depart time: 5:20 a.m.
Arrive time: 2:50 p.m.
Highways: 13, 2A
Day – total km/miles: 132/82—1,743/1,083
Day average speed: (kmph/mph): 17.2/10.7
Day – total elevation gain (m/ft): 93/305—2,382/7,814
Calories daily/total to date: 3,429/46,052
Daily dangers/excitement: Visiting friends.

Begin Blog:

Great day to be biking—no winds for the first five hours. What I found fascinating was how some businesses, farms, and ranches made their places welcoming. Others did not.

Today's blog photo was obviously an Alberta ranch. The horse, rider, cow and calf were silhouettes, but appeared so realistic on a pasture hill. Another place yesterday was an acreage, apparently an oil-field worker, who had constructed a huge archway of perhaps 12-inch black pipe. Without words, it was welcoming and showed pride in his and/or her profession.

Late this afternoon, we were invited to a farm by a couple we had met while wintering in Mexico. As an agronomist, I was thrilled to see their canola emerging and spring wheat attempting to establish itself in a cool spring.

However, the real treat was being taken to their private campground with a newer camper, expansive deck overlooking a small 28-foot-deep lake stocked with trout.

They are not large farmers and had allowed an area to be mined for sand and gravel. Rather than just letting weeds grow as if it was past usefulness, they asked their gravel contractor to reclaim an old pit by flattening an area for camper and parking. Then tapering the slope into the water's edge, trees and shrubs were allowed to fill in around the lawn that was well maintained. Even a playground was erected for their four grandchildren. What an enjoyable evening by being taken to a private family spot to enjoy peaceful conversation.

As I bike, I look forward to seeing businesses and farms that take pride in their place. We certainly found one this evening.

----Blog end-----

Dogs protect farmsteads along highways. Those that chase cars on the highway usually get killed. A survivor attacked me.

On a beautiful morning, as I was coasting down a small incline, my phone rang. I reached into my back jersey pocket to check who was calling. For two weeks I had biked and only answered calls from Patricia. Smartphone recognition indicated the call was from my nephew.

As I slowed to stop, I answered it while passing a farmstead. A second, maximum two, after "Hello" I fell over. I forgot to unclip my right shoe (always the first to unclip). This was the only time on the whole trip I fell over.

As I tumbled, still clipped-in, a large barking farm dog came running from the yard. It may have been a German shepherd/collie cross.

With barking dog quickly approaching I yelled, "I got to go!"

I hung up, pocketed the cell phone as I unclipped, and remounted. None too soon. The dog gained on me up the next incline, but before I reached the top, luckily it had turned back.

When we lived in the country, our son's border collie loved to chase cars. If cars slowed to avoid her, she would continue to chase them. If they sped away, she seldom followed beyond our property. Dogs are extremely keen on property lines. Likely, today's dog had similar instincts to our collie and turned back.

My nephew, David, knew I was heading to North Pole and just called to check in. With nothing but open road and emerging wheat fields, I stopped on the highway shoulder and returned his call. David was afraid he had caused an accident. I explained, it was not his fault, but all mine for foolishly answering a call while riding, especially near a dog-protected farmstead.

Next time my luck may fail. I no longer answered phones until I was stopped, unclipped, and stood in a safe area.

We had preplanned to see our friends and hoped to see their farm but we were running late. Wetaskiwin is a fairly large town, maybe even a city, by Alberta standards. Anyway, my route was five miles (8 km) longer than anticipated, because they have multiple exits into the Wetaskiwin. I was not sure where to exit, but our motel was on the last one.

As mentioned in today's blog, we were treated to an afternoon on Myles and Adel's small private lake after viewing their farm.

Thereafter, we were invited to their house for dinner. Not minutes, we were a day late.

Had we arrived the day before, we could have enjoyed fifty other family and friends for the farmer's seventieth birthday party. Instead, we were treated to the most bounteous leftover feast I have ever had. (Rewarmed) fried chicken, beef, multiple salads, and a huge slice of birthday cake.

They knew I had biked 132 kilometers (82 miles) earlier in the day, so I was not bashful in taking seconds of everything—maybe thirds on cake.

Chapter 22: 129 km/80 miles
Day 15, June 4, Wetaskiwin to Drayton Valley, AB

Depart time: 5:03 a.m.
Arrive time: 2:45 p.m.
Highways: 13, 20, 39
Day—total km/miles: 129/80—1,872/1,163
Day average speed: (kmph/mph): 15.3/9.5
Day—total elevation gain (m/ft): 154/506—2,536/8,320
Calories daily/total to date: 3,322/49,374
Daily dangers/excitement: Millet, more Alberta friends.

Begin Blog:

As mentioned yesterday, businesses and farms present an image for passerbys—good, bad, or who cares. People are the same. Likewise, towns and cities large and small either welcome or discourage outsiders. The small Alberta village of Millet is a good example. See today's blog photo as I approached town. (*Note: please check blog photos at https://www.relatingtoancients.com/pierre-to-the-pole-1.*)

With a few hundred residents at most, Millet had three blocks of active retailers—obviously catering to the passerby.

As an agriculturalist, millet is my favorite grain. Although I wrote two books about the crop (published in 1989 & 1990), I had no idea there was a village in Alberta named after the crop.

With antique grain drills and other old farming equipment displayed with fresh potted flowers surrounded with perennials in every park and public area, it was obvious farming had been the lifeblood of this village. Likely, the crop millet was the major crop in the area when the village of Millet incorporated.

117

Millet grain is not native to North America and was only introduced (by outsiders) about 150 years ago by German-Russians emigrating from the South Russia (now Ukraine).

For thousands of years a crop survived because enough producers and customers found it served their needs. Although small towns are dying daily as businesses close, never to reopen, the village of Millet survives because its image produces what attracts customers. It is an absolute pleasure to occasionally find a community as welcoming as Millet, Alberta.

My wife and I have been impressed with Canadians everywhere. For an example, a couple, Deb and Rob, we had met and befriended vacationing in Mexico drove four hours to join us for a wonderful welcoming of socializing and meal after a long day's ride. It was motivation in so many ways to be surrounded and encouraged as I biked north.

Businesses, farms, communities, and people have opportunities to feel welcome. We do in Canada. Thanks for making my ride even more enjoyable!

-----End Blog-----

The motel we left this morning in Wetaskiwin was clean, reasonably priced, and the front desk was manned 24-hours for security. We stayed in a small room on the second floor. A large maintenance closet was located just off the check-in counter. Courtesy of the manager, that was where I kept my chained bicycle overnight.

The wind, which was commonly out of the west in the Prairie Provinces, could make a long day for the planned eighty miles. A brisk wind was expected.

Long days, I had planned to start peddling about 5:00 a.m. Commonly rising about 4:15 would allow enough time to casually prepare for the day.

At about 4:50 I headed downstairs. Unexpectedly, the maintenance closet door was locked. That was good. At least my bike would not be taken while staff made their rounds.

A few steps back, I waited at the counter for the night clerk. Minutes passed. The sun had not risen yet, but dawn was approaching. Likely, the motel night clerk was delivering checkout receipts often slipped under doors. I waited.

Finally, I rang the counter bell. It brought unexpected commotion. I stepped back. Both of us were surprised.

A sleep-groggy clerk crawled out from under the front counter. Apparently, he had a comfortable nest and was not used to checkouts before 5:00 a.m. The location was sneaky if evading a burglar, but likely it was a place staff rested while being paid.

Quickly, he grabbed keys and tried them all on the maintenance closet door. None worked. I waited. Finally, after retrieving more keys from a back office, I was allowed to claim my bike.

For forty days, each morning I would anticipate heading out the door to see what the day would bring. Day 15 of biking was no different.

Anticipation is a good thing. It brings internal excitement that a few extra minutes in the motel lobby could not subdue.

Taking secondary roads usually require zigzagging to eventually get back to the more direct primary route. Northwest through central Canada from Regina to Saskatoon, Saskatchewan on to Edmonton, Grande Prairie, Alberta, onto Dawson Creek, British Columbia where the Alaska Highway began would have been logical.

Even though Saskatoon and Edmonton were avoided, the route to Drayton Valley (with an oil-town population of 7,235) would be a day with more highways, more turns, and more wind than normal.

At 9:25 a.m. I stopped to film a beautiful Canadian flag bristling in the strong west wind. It was whipping perhaps at thirty miles-per-hour (~50 kmph) in my face. I took a second video of its noisy demonstration—a prairie experience.

Luckily, this was the strongest wind so far. I geared down and biked into it.

My trusty sag wagon arrived about noon with Patricia unfolding a hefty serving of hot rice and sweet potatoes. Starches. Great starches!

Relying on advice gathered from road-biking friends a decade earlier, starch dishes, sandwiches, and pizza were my go-to meals. Heavy meals with lots of meat I avoided, especially when eating late evenings.

Starchy meals (reacting with saliva's amylase enzymes when chewing) immediately begin converting to usable sugars. Through digestion, starch is much slower than glucose and fructose which flow into bloodstreams almost immediately.

That is why diabetics drink orange juice to quickly revive after a spell rather than eating a piece of bread. It is the same reason bike shops sell sugary, pop-in-your-mouth energy boosters for reviving weary bikers rather than beef jerky.

Baked goodies, like sticky buns, are a biker's friend, especially if they are not too sweet...At least that was the excuse I gave Patricia.

Chapter 23: 95 km/59 miles
Day 16, June 5, Drayton Valley to Mayerthorpe, AB

Depart time: 5:45 a.m.
Arrive time: 1:30 p.m.
Highways: 22, 16, 22
Day—total km/miles: 95/59—1,967/1,222
Day average speed: (kmph/mph): 15.9/9.9
Day—total elevation gain (m/ft): 247/810—2,783/9,130
Calories daily/total to date: 2,487/51,861
Daily dangers/excitement: Spouse, friends, and continued enjoyment.

Begin Blog:

Today was back to my expected normal mileage at 59. I had been projecting 60 miles (~100 km). Three days in a row over 80 miles was enough (considering wind every day and rain late yesterday.)

This was logging and oil country and as I came north out of the hills and valleys it turned into cattle country and crops as landscapes flattened.

It was a cool 41°F (5°C) when I departed and I may have seen frost in the valleys. I did not confirm as it was very cool biking and I kept going to stay warm.

Last evening's rain softened the road ditches. Although highway was marked for moose, I did not see any yet. There were plenty of tracks.

After breakfast, our friends, Deb and Rob, and my wife, Patricia, came 40 miles further north to check my progress before they turned south again for Calgary. (Check out today's blog photo. My wife was on the right.)

I keep repeating it, but I really did have another wonderful bike ride and the countryside was beautiful.

-----End Blog-----

I hope it is becoming evident, but as I progressed into this ride, my attitude and judgements are becoming less critical. Blogs indicate the change.

My life has been one of blessing after blessing.

Troubles? Job stress? Losses? Sorrow? Sure.

Everybody has those.

If more hop on their bikes take a few days to ride to wherever, stress, ulcers, cholesterol, blood pressure, and complaints would likely subside into smiles.

Your ride does not have to be to North Pole, but it would be worth it!

I used to gripe on a detour when spots on our city bike loop were blocked for street construction. Life is too short to worry about detouring a few minutes.

Even many exercise buffs drive to their exercise retailer for gumption. Question the price? Is it worth it? Then, before and after using each machine, someone's sticky, disgusting sweat is scrubbed off handles and display screen. Usually it remains. Disgusting.

One does not have to have germaphobia to feel the need for change.

Nature is not clean. Germs are everywhere. No. My handlebars are not spotless. My gloves were washed at least weekly even if I only biked 500 miles (~800 km).

Germs are not the irritation to manage in the local workout center or on a long-distance ride. It is attitude.

With one event, some people explode, deteriorate, or are embarrassed into an attitude adjustment.

That reminds me of a story from one of my Canadian friends who was a grocery store manager.

A young cocky sale representative came in when another store manager had stopped by. The visiting manager asked if the sales rep had stopped into a certain town in northern Manitoba.

"Yes, I go there." The sales rep replied with a smirk, "The only women up there are hockey players or whores."

Calmly, the visiting manager said, "My wife was from there."

Without hesitation, the sales rep asked, "What team does she play for?"

Both managers quickly found out why that rep kept his job—quick wit, and ability to quickly change his attitude.

Chapter 24: 🚲 43 km/27 miles
Day 17, June 6, Mayerthorpe to Whitecourt, AB

Depart time: 7:40 a.m.
Arrive time: 10:30 a.m.
Highways: 43
Day—total km/miles: 43/27—2,010/1,249
Day average speed: (kmph/mph): 16.9/10.5
Day—total elevation gain (m/ft): 115/377—2,898/9,507
Calories daily/total to date: 1,180/53,041
Daily dangers/excitement: Relaxed.

Begin Blog:

This was the shortest planned day—27 miles.

Why? First, several days over 80 miles a day has worn me down a bit. Secondly, Whitecourt was an active commercial center—a good place to stay. Thirdly, this was vacation. Why rush?

Several friends and family have wondered if we are blowing our budget on lodging. Best answer: No.

Unbeknownst to me, this was very slow season in oil field country. Heavy drilling equipment got bogged down once the ground thawed. Consequently, the busy season for lodging in Saskatchewan and Alberta is in the winter, and again in the summer for tourist season. Fortunately, many rooms have kitchenettes and full breakfasts, like this place. Late spring was a great time to be slowly passing through.

Today's blog photo was our room in Whitecourt. It was $CA107.00 ($US83.07) with lodging and gross sales taxes included. The room had a full-size refrigerator, gas fireplace, king bed, huge bay windows, and biggest in-room whirlpool tub I have ever seen.

It certainly helped having a 24% U.S. favorable exchange rate, but this place was far above our expectations and below what we budgeted.

If you plan to vacation in Alberta or Saskatchewan, consider late spring. It is not only beautiful, but economical.

-----End Blog-----

The forty-three-kilometer (27 mile) ride was so short I started late. Pedaled slowly. Arrived early and relaxed.

Casually pedaling along reminded me of a sign on an island off the coast of Belize. We were there to relax after risky travel in Honduras. The island had cars and a few trucks but most locals commuted and shopped by bicycle.

As vehicles whizzed by me, I remembered the island sign: "DRIVE SLOW WE HAVE TWO CEMETARIES & NO HOSPITAL."

Most highway laws allow bicycles the same driving-lane rights as vehicles. However, many drivers get upset at bicyclists using the far right shoulder. One time I asked an irritated driver why he did not want bicycles on the road. He said, "**They** are going to cause an accident." Not surprisingly, he was annoyed at rubble-strips (which likely meant he crossed or drove on them too often).

On this trip, even though I biked on the right shoulder, I found semitruck drivers the most courteous by passing in the left lane— the same right granted when passing vehicles. Those driving RVs and pickups pulling campers seldom moved from me. When roads were damp, their wheel spray enveloped me in dirty mist.

Without options for lodging, my alternative today was to bike 216 kilometers (134 miles) from Mayerthorpe to Valleyview, or to break it into a short ride (which I did) and a more reasonable 172-kilometer (107 mile) ride tomorrow.

It was nice to have plenty of reasonably priced lodging options in Whitecourt. Places to dine were also plentiful with many catering hearty meals for oilfield workers—perfect for me.

The extra-large whirlpool hot tub was another unexpected treat.

Chapter 25: 172 km/107 miles
Day 18, June 7, Whitecourt to Valleyview, AB

Depart time: 4:40 a.m.
Arrive time: 2:10 p.m.
Highways: 43
Day—total km/miles: 172/107—2,182/1,356
Day average speed: (kmph/mph): 19.5/12.1
Day—total elevation gain (m/ft): 706/2,317—3,604/11,824
Calories daily/total to date: 5,296/58,337
Daily dangers/excitement: Cool valleys, favorable breeze.

Begin Blog:

One thing for sure, I'm getting experience biking in cool weather. For a week now it has been in the low 40s°F when I started. Check out today's blog photo. This is what happens when the creek water temperature is warmer than the air. Steam (warm air) rises into the cool morning.

The photo was taken a few minutes before 5:00 this morning with sunrise at 5:12.

This blog I have tried to keep numbers understandable for U.S. readers, but since ride-day 7 (May 26) I have been traveling in kilometers and biking in Celsius temperatures.

It can be confusing, but it should not be. All my published research and patents are in metric, but there is an easy way to estimate.

These conversions have been passed on by Dawn, our Canadian friend, who was going to school when Canada converted to the metric system. She simplified Celsius to Fahrenheit for me. Just take the Celsius times two, less 10%, and add 32. Example: this morning was 5C. Using the quick estimation method even I could do it in my head: 5 + 5 = 10, minus 10% is 1. Ten minus 1 = 9 plus 32 equals 41°F. (It is not perfect, but close.)

Quick kilometers (km) estimates are easier. Multiply them by 0.6 to get miles. With estimates, a 5,000 kilometer ride would be 3,000 miles. If a sign says 60 km to the next town, it would be about 36 miles. For more accuracy, add 2 miles for each 100 kilometers, or get out a calculator and multiply by 0.62137119224.

When biking, it was inconvenient to stop and calculate temperature or mileage. Those were just some of the ways I keep my mind busy biking. Your next question: What does your mind do the other 6 to 8 hours?

Stay tuned.

-----End Blog-----

Topography changed from flatland prairies to hills and creeks with natural trees instead of artificial shelterbelts planted by pioneers. Days started cold and remained so for the past several days.

Today's 172 kilometers (107 miles) would be similar to biking from the center of Washington, D.C. through hills to Richmond, Virginia. Added beauty--virtually no traffic here.

It was 5°C (41°F) when I departed before sunrise. Yes, I used my new leather gloves most of the morning.

If I had stayed at Fox Creek, it could have been a shorter day. There were plenty of lodging options halfway between Whitecourt and Valleyview. I arrived in Fox Creek at 9:50 a.m. with generally favorable winds. Valleyview, where a room was assured, was an easy ride through mostly wooded long sloping hills and open vistas.

For some people, elevation gain may be confusing. North Pole, Alaska was about 1,000 feet (305 meters) lower elevation than Pierre, South Dakota.

Why was I constantly gaining elevation if the trip ended closer to sea level?

Was it because I was gaining elevation approaching the mountainous continental divide?

No.

Today I am about halfway between Edmonton and Grande Prairie, Alberta. The airport at Edmonton has an elevation of 2,373 feet (723 meters) above sea level whereas Grande Prairie lies to the northwest, closer to the mountains and has a slightly lower elevation, 2,196 feet (669 meters).

To the best of my knowledge, bicycle metering devices count elevation gain because it takes more energy to bike uphill than down. Therefore, it is good to know accumulated elevation gain during a cycle ride to estimate the effort it will take compared to a completely flat surface.

Treadmills offer metered incline to convey the same affect.

Consequently, it was my belief that mounted elevation meters are a mind game for bicyclists. When I used Google® Maps to plan a bike route between Pierre and North Pole, elevation gain was around 65,000 feet (compared to my recorded total of 59,200 feet or 18,044 meters). Perhaps I found a more level route or Google® and Garmin® have differences.

Using today's final elevation gain in Alberta of 5,850 feet (1,783 meters), it appears I went up over a mile (5,280 feet). In reality my location in Valleyview was only a couple hundred feet above where I crossed the Canadian border.

Daily charts should be used to track distance, speed, calories, and location, but also effort (elevation gain). Unfortunately, I am not aware of any bicycle meter that accounts for total bike carrying weight and elevation gain totaled with a plus or minus wind factor. More metering would have been required.

It certainly takes more calories (effort) to bike uphill against a wind than a crosswind or wind from behind. The cumulative factor should have been registered as calories used. It was not.

Chapter 26: 126 km/78 miles
Day 19, June 8, Valleyview to Grande Prairie, AB

Depart time: 5:20 a.m.
Arrive time: 1:15 p.m.
Highways: 43, 670, Range Rd 51, Township Rd 712-68th Ave.,
Resource Rd-Range Rd 60a, Range Rd 62, Hwy 40
Day—total km/miles: 126/78—2,308/1,434
Day average speed: (kmph/mph): 17.7/11
Day—total elevation gain (m/ft): 286/938—3,890/12,762
Calories daily/total to date: 3,396/61,733
Daily dangers/excitement: Coyote, several deer, and arrived at
friend's place.

Begin Blog:

Often messages supporting my ride end with "Be safe". Yes, I try with lights on bike and helmet flashing and dressed in yellow and white with a red helmet. To comfort the many, I must admit highway shoulders are much wider and smoother in Canada than in the U.S. It is unusual to find a highway shoulder less than two-foot-wide, and major highways have ten-foot-wide smooth shoulders many of which have recently been swept clean. (I suppose to brush off the winter treatment of sand.)

In today's 5:00 a.m. blog photo I am making French toast as my wife prepares a peanut butter and jelly sandwich for my morning snack.

I made it to Grande Prairie in northwest Alberta today. Grande Prairie (pronounced "Grand") is the last expected stop in Alberta.

As I biked into Grande Prairie County, I was surprised to learn this was the first organized county in Alberta. It was not designated the first county until 1951.

Alberta did not become part of Canada's Northwest Territories until 1882 and did not become a Province (along with Saskatchewan) until 1905.

Alberta in land area is huge. It has rivers draining into the Hudson Bay and the Arctic Ocean, but only borders one U.S. state—Montana.

I look forward to my trip through the far northeast corner of British Columbia in the days ahead and I thank all who have checked these posts as I progress north.

-----End Blog-----

More trees interspersed with farm and pastures provided wildlife cover and year-round food sources. Hence, more wildlife, especially deer were seen. A lone curious coyote was a treat.

Others considering this route may not take all the roads I took today. The last twenty-five miles (40 km) was a suggested, more scenic, route by friends that lived south of Grande Prairie. I avoided the city.

Normally, a cyclist would remain on Alberta Highway 43, lodge and eat on Highway 43, and keep on Highway 43 until it changes into British Columbia Highway 2 near Dermmitt.

I called ahead to notify friends, Joe and Jan, of my approximate arrival time—between 1:00 and 2:00. Both were gone. Joe was at an out-of-town golf tournament, and his wife, Jan, was at a horse training clinic.

Like true friends any place in the world, they told me where they hid an entry key so I could get in and relax. They suggested, no demanded, that whenever I arrived, I should take a shower and grab a beer.

Maybe it had something to do with the 126-kilometer (78 mile) bike ride to their place. I would smell (and appear) better if I at least showered before they arrived.

I did. It was wonderfully relaxing—better than a motel. Afterwards, I relaxed on their porch with a beer.

All my clothes were in panniers packed in our vehicle. Joe's robe sufficed until my biking jersey and shorts had dried quickly in the sun.

When they arrived, Joe showed me his elaborate shop with an amazing display of unique coffee grinders, while Jan was organizing the preplanned dinner. Their son and daughter-in-law were also invited and showed up after work--just before Patricia arrived.

In another token of friendship, Jan made a massage appointment for Patricia. The long drive (2,308 km, 1,434 miles) from Pierre through two states and two provinces justified a long, relaxing massage.

Yes, I considered Jan a great friend, but she did not suggest I needed a massage after biking that same distance. She knows us well enough to know I do not get massages.

Her evening meal was very tasty. Though I was not paying attention, I likely ate twice as much homemade moose schnitzel as anyone at the table.

Tomorrow was projected to be raining. It gave us even more of an excuse to stay an extra day. We did.

Chapter 27: Second day off

June 9, Rural Grand Prairie, Alberta

Begin Blog:

A predicted rainy day was a good excuse to extend our stay at friends, Jan and Joe. It was a perfect way to enjoy locals in their environment.

Their quarter section of wooded ground was located on bluffs overlooking the Wapiti River a few miles south of Grande Prairie. Yes, I biked there and will make the long climb out by bike, but it was so worth it.

While my wife, Patricia, enjoyed Jan's indoor equine pole training with the local horse club, Joe and I checked out their rustic cabin. As one would picture from the old days, it was not plumbed or wired. Heat came from a pot-belly wood stove and the kitchen had the early 1900s white enamel wood cook stove. A table to eat and play cards had a few chairs. Beds allowed children, grandchildren, and friends to experience a day and night, or several, living rustic as centuries past. Fortunately, I could go back to their house for an extended steam bath to loosen my legs muscles after three weeks of biking.

As I stepped outside the hidden cabin to view the Wapiti River below, I had to step around moose dropping. This place was an unexpected treat to relax and allow my legs to recuperate.

Woods in this area, and likely most of Alberta, are surrounded by wild prickly rose just coming into bloom in late spring. With brilliance of reds and pinks, no wonder the wild rose is the official emblem of Alberta.

The Wapiti River (Cree for elk, wapiti) originated in the mountains of British Columbia. While at their cabin, viewing through poplar, pine, spruce, and tamarack, we could see the Wapiti was now carrying mountain runoff making it more difficult to navigate. Although we were unable to take their one-of-a-kind homemade boat into the river, it was relaxing just viewing the rippling water several hundred feet below.

It is no wonder trappers and fur traders of centuries past spent summer and winter making a living in this area. Now oil and timber are the base industries, but a city of over 60,000, with airport and all services is a great place to enjoy summers. Many retire here.

-----End Blog-----

Though I did not know it at the time, this was my second and last day break before North Pole. I had spent three weeks biking and I was not halfway.

Up to this point, gadgets claimed I had bicycled 2,308 kilometers (1,434 miles) of the projected 5,000 kilometers (actually 3,012 miles). Secondly, I pedaled climbs of 3,890 meters (12,762 ft.) with a cycling calorie burn of 61,733 in less than eight hours each day.

That was merely practice and conditioning.

More practice on climbs would have helped!

I may have downplayed potential blisters, sunburn, burnout, fatigue, dehydration, spasms, wind, aches and rain.

Intimate crotch chaffing (on narrow seat strenuously rotating over 600,000 revolutions--about seventy per minute--dawn to afternoon, from May 20 to June 8th) did not happen. No chaffing.

Hidden calluses? Maybe.

To my pleasant surprise, I had taken no medication and no pills—not even an aspirin.

Did I sweat? A lot.

In three weeks, I had already bicycled 594 kilometers (369 miles) farther than if I had driven from New Orleans, Louisiana (on the Gulf of Mexico) to Windsor, Ontario, Canada.

For Europeans, Pierre, South Dakota to Grande Prairie, Alberta would be like bicycling four times from Basel to Brussels—Switzerland to Belgium. Yes. Four trips! Plus I could have taken different routes to see more of Switzerland, Germany, France, partied in Luxembourg with a celebration in Amsterdam, Netherlands.

For my Australian *mates*, how *ya goin'*? *Gone walkabout*. *Wuckers*. *Yeah nah* longer an *ankle biter*, this *drongo ranga coulda* been *in the bush beyond the black stump* from Canberra and been a *banana bender* in Cairnes and *scab ya*. As a *Yank chat* saving a few *ticks* like an *outback bushie* in a *bugger*, I would have had to *grab a feed, sanger, snags* and *bangers, take-away* at *servos* more than once from Adelaide to Perth. An *ocker bloke* been there quicker if Spencer Gulf of *Australian Bight* hadn't been so big with more roads and fewer *roos*. Luckily, *nah yous* told me to *get onya bike*. It's been a *ripper!*[32]

The route to Grande Prairie was not too difficult to follow; beyond Grande Prairie an idiot could find his way—it's one road.

Rivers create hills and drain continents. Some of those hills and supplying rivers and creeks I had already passed including the Missouri/Mississippi, Saskatchewan, and Nelson River drainages emptying into the Atlantic Ocean's Hudson Bay and Gulf of Mexico.

Some of the biggest rivers in the world, draining into the Pacific and Arctic Oceans, lay ahead with Slave, Peace, Laird, Mackenzie, and the mighty Yukon Rivers and their mountain and hill drainage awaiting my two legs, pushing two peddles, moving two wheels over hundreds of bridges.

Real adventure had barely begun.

Was I prepared for the wilderness, the cold, and eight mountain ranges? The end came surprisingly quick.

---

[32] Australians have a special English slang and is more confusing in rural areas than cities. In order above: Mates has multiple meanings, in this case "friend"; Ya goin' means how are you?; Wuckers means no problem, and politely literal No f...ing worries; Gone walkabout means been traveling; Yeah nah means no; Ankle biter means child; Drongo means idiot; Ranga means red haired person (like me) as in red like an orangutan; Coulda means could have; In the bush means not as remote as outback; Beyond the black stump means an imaginary point beyond civilized; Banana bender means a Queenslander; Scab ya means scrounge off someone; Yank means American; Chat means an unclean person; Ticks means a short time; Outback means more remote than in the bush; Bushie means lives off the land; Bugger in this case means a non-offensive expression of damn; Grab a feed means get something to eat; Sanger means sandwich; Snag means sausage; Banger also means a sausage (in some places a different type than snag); Take-away means take out; Servo means service station or roadside convenience store; Ocker means an unclean crude Aussie (pronounced Ozzy); Bloke means a manly Australian; Australian Bight is the gulf or sea off southern Australia; Roos are kangaroos; Nah means no; Yous is plural of you; Get onya bike means get going, get out of here, or tell your story as we want you to be walking away; and Ripper means excellent, exciting, or sometimes meaning actively painful.

Chapter 28: 🚲 143 km/89 miles
Day 20, June 10, Grande Prairie, AB to Dawson Creek, BC

Depart time: 5:59 a.m.
Arrive time: 6:25 p.m.
Highways: 40, 43, 2
Day—total km/miles: 143/89—2,451/1,523
Day average speed: (kmph/mph): 14.5/9
Day—total elevation gain (m/ft): 555/1,820—4,445/14,582
Calories daily/total to date: 4,213/65,946
Daily dangers/excitement: Breakfast with friends, leaving Alberta, entering British Columbia to the Alaska (ALCAN) Highway.

Begin Blog:
This was an interesting day. I biked for an hour; had an hour breakfast with a couple of Canadian friends, Joe and Leif, biked out of Alberta into Dawson Creek, British Columbia which was Mile Marker One on the Alaska Highway.

As I was departing Grande Prairie, for the first twenty miles I had my first view of snow-capped mountains.

It was cool again this morning 6°C (43°F) with winds constant from the WNW as I was biking 89 miles (143 km) directly into it or a side-wind. Cloudy too—all day temperatures did not get into the 60s°F (not much above 15°C).

As today's blog photo indicates, I made it to Mile Marker Zero of the Alaskan Highway.

I departed Pierre, SD three weeks ago today. Based on my estimates, I reached the halfway point today.

The most unexpected treat was a hot caramel roll. This was no normal roll. A regularly scheduled community "garage" sale had vendors selling out of their car trunk (very similar to the "car boot sales" in England). Patricia found a family handmaking dough. Once rolled thin, butter and cinnamon were added then baked in an outdoor wood-burning oven. Texture and unique production were minor compared to the taste. I jumped off my bike, sat in our warm car with Patricia, and gobbled the tastiest caramel roll I had in years. What a great treat for a long, cold, windy ride!!!

-----End Blog-----

It may surprise some, but there are grain fields this far north. As an internationally Certified Crop Advisor (agronomist), I found it interesting to check fields along the route from the Dakotas through Canada. The last planted field in Alberta was last year's two-row barley stubble with spring wheat seeded without tillage (no-till).

Patricia, my wife, just finished reading a travelogue while I was writing today. She said, "Be sure to include personal information." Our daughter, Charmion Harris[33], currently cloistered in Guatemala finishing her second book, also pressed me to "Keep it personal."

This may seem to have nothing to do with a long bike ride, but being freed of gadgets, music, media, and daily news allowed my mind to settle into a pleasurable routine of self-study, watching nature and attempting to understand societal development. I was particularly interested in cultural practices—tillage and cropping systems, local economic development and culture.

I found changes fascinating.

After leaving South Dakota Governor's Office of Economic Development, I used my Commercial Economics degree to develop (at the time) our state's largest grain terminal. In order to train staff on purchasing, segregating, and selling grains, I attained a license as a Federal Grain Grader.

After wholesaling agricultural products for a few years, I started my own seed plant (mainly processing millet) as a Certified Seed

---

[33] Charmion Harris is the author of *East West Practical Guide, A Way Forward through Yoga*, and is currently working on her second book, *Journey through Critical Mass to Living True*.

Conditioner and introduced a crop rotation program in the 1980s using no tillage. At the time, virtually all crop ground was tilled. On this ride, tilled ground was a rarity, except for organic producers who still use tillage extensively causing wind, water and tillage erosion (pulling topsoil downhill).

Nature is unity. Tillage is not natural. Nature does not dig itself to reseed nor does it propagate erosion. Instead, natural processes are amazingly agile, first producing weeds to prevent erosion, then establishing permanent cover.

As a personal observation of labels, organic food consumers are not told if their food comes from unnatural tillage practices. Nearly all organic farmers till. Through tillage, air and water borne soil particles contaminate lakes and streams and cause respiratory issues in poultry, livestock and especially humans. A 1994 study in Ontario, Canada found that at least seventy percent of their farmland erosion was caused by tillage.[34]

My experience and presentations on environmental protection through reduced tillage led to a seminar invitation at Uludag University, Bursa, Turkey. That 1997 opportunity blossomed into a two-decade relationship of published (peer reviewed) crop research in a Mediterranean climate—much different than we had in the Dakota Plains.

OK! Enough of my interests.

However, I would strongly encourage anyone making this trip on bicycle to dive deep into their interests. Whether it be wildlife, flora, fauna, environmental, economic, engineering, or social observations, the mind gradually breaks free of pre-determined barriers.

Yes, bike and think clearly!

Having traveled five continents as a self-described societal explorer, you may also want to read my book, *Culture and the mysterious agent changing it*, I state "Ancient life followed nature. Stark reality of

---

[34] Gill Gullickson, Is Tillage Steeling Your Soil? Successful Farming, October 10, 2017, https://www.agriculture.com/machinery/tillage/is-tillage-stealing-your-soil.

ancient life compared to societies today is unconnected. [35] Technological gadgets have replaced intellect...."[36]

Wildlife on today's ride were frisky in the cool temperatures as they were still shedding their winter coat. Several deer were along the route with white on top of the tail and black the lower half with long dark ears. Deer tended to phase out as I progressed north on the Alaska Highway.

The Alaska Highway, often referred to as the ALCAN (Alaska-Canadian Highway), is the only highway from eastern British Columbia to North Pole, Alaska. It is also called Highway 97 in BC, Highway 1 in the Yukon Territory, and Highway 2 in Alaska.

Another Yukon highway (2) runs from Whitehorse, the Territory capitol, to Dawson City in the Yukon north only to drop down and meet Alaska Highway 2 (ALCAN) at Tetlin Junction, Alaska.

The most direct route, except by airplane, from Dawson Creek to North Pole was on the Alaska Highway. Even dog mushers used it.

Population along the ALCAN was sparse, very sparse, except for mosquitos, no-see-ums, and black flies. They obviously prefer reproducing in muskeg (bogs), bush, ditches, and marshes which bother the deer, moose, elk, wood bison, bears, and bikers, or anything else using it.

When did the Alaska Highway get built? Who built it?

It has a short, fascinating history.

Although Canadians and Americans had discussed building a highway to service northwest Canada and Alaska by vehicle in the late 1930s and early 1940s, it went nowhere (no) thanks to both countries isolationist policies against Germany's European expansion and Adolf Hitler's atrocities.

First to clarify timing and geography, Hawaii and Alaska were U.S. territories, not states, during World War II (1939-1945). In 1912, New Mexico and Arizona had been the last states to join the

---

[35] Gary W. Wietgrefe, *Culture and the mysterious agent changing it*, *Relating to Ancient* series, 2018 copyright, p. 53.
[36] Wietgrefe, Ibid. p. 77.

Union. Hawaii and Alaska were added as states fourteen years after the war--as I entered the first grade, 1959.

When Japan, a German ally, bombed Hawaii's Pearl Harbor December 7, 1941, the U.S. declared war on Japan and Germany. Canada quickly followed. By June 1942, Japan was attacking Alaska's Aleutian Islands of southeast Alaska—north of Japan.

An exceptionally long highway linking (contiguous) United States to Alaska required Canadian approval. That happened very quickly as American/Canadian war involvement began. Less than two months after Pearl Harbor's bombing, the U.S. Army Corps of Engineers approved a route (February 6, 1942), and five days later Congress and President Franklin Roosevelt authorized it.

Construction work began on the Alaska Highway the following month, March 8, 1942 at Mile Marker zero near a spot in the road called Dawson Creek, British Columbia.

In just over eight months, using 10,607 soldiers and civilian support, the 2,700-kilometer (1,700 mile) road was completed on October 28, 1942. Yes, eight months!

Terrain was brutal. Eight mountain ranges, over three hundred bridges, permafrost, rivers and muck challenged the Army.

Compared to other roads in human history, it was a monumental accomplishment.

After the war, in 1948, civilian use was authorized. Straightening curves, switch-backing mountain passes, improved bridging over streams, and shortening and paving the whole route was finally completed in 2012 to speed traffic.

The U.S. Army completed the hardest task in eight months. It took civilians with regulations, environmental studies, administration, and bureaucracy sixty-four years to upgrade it.

Hellish cold winters and constant construction are inattentive drivers' nemesis.

Today, the ALCAN has been shortened and reconstructed to about 2,232 kilometers (1,387 miles). Taking out curves and making shortcuts, original Mileposts are no longer accurate. Travelers need to be leery of kilometer, mile, and *The Milepost* markers.

If you are estimating time in each segment of the Alaska Highway, consider about eighty percent is in Canada with roughly half in British Columbia and half in the Yukon. The remaining twenty percent is in Alaska and ends in Delta Junction but is often grouped with the Richardson Highway from Delta Junction to Fairbanks.

The Alaska Highway I peddled was about 2,232 kilometers (1,387 miles) from Dawson Creek, British Columbia through Delta Junction, Alaska (officially the original Mile Markers Zero to 1,422).

Technically, the ALCAN ended 140 kilometers (87 miles) from North Pole. Also, please keep in mind, I bicycled to lodging that was not always on the Highway which accumulated a few extra miles.

Chapter 29: 🚲 74 km/46 miles
Day 21, June 11, Dawson Creek to Fort St. John, BC

Depart time: 5:40 a.m.
Arrive time: 12:25 p.m.
Highways: 97
Day—total km/miles: 74/46—2,525/1,569
Day average speed: (kmph/mph): 13.3/8.3
Day—total elevation gain (m/ft): 552/1,811—4,997/16,393
Calories daily/total to date: 1,853/67,799
Daily dangers/excitement: Construction, bridges, steep hills.

Begin Blog:

Seriously, I was not sure if I would bike today. High winds out of the west were predicted. Wind peaking by noon and sustained with showers was expected in late afternoon. It was cool again today, but my goal was under 50 miles.

I did not expect the first ten miles of the Alaskan Highway to be under construction. Actually, grinders stripped off the top few inches leaving a rough surface so the new pavement mix would bind. Shaking handlebars and slow progress made wind an added annoyance. Considering I had biked over 1500 miles, ten miles of construction were minor, but likely more would follow.

The new **wrist support bar** had been tested thus far for 2,500 kilometers. Today's construction was the ultimate test. It far exceeded expectation.

Two rivers had to be crossed today—the Kiskatinaw and the larger, Peace River. Both rivers have steep downhill grades on the south and long (very long) climbs out.

141

Before the Peace downhill, one warning sign stated, "Extreme Downhill Grade" followed by "6% next 5.3 km" and partially down the mountain was a 10% downhill warning.

Did today's blog photo come from the bottom of the Peace River hill? No! The pickup truck never made it to the second river.

Notice the rear driver-side tire was still smoking. Nobody was in the parking area, so I did check the burned-out vehicle for human remains. I found none. Everything that could burn apparently did. Interestingly, the fire likely started from overheated brakes, and the last thing smoking was what remained of one tire. Winds likely spread the flames quickly, and apparently the driver (and possibly passengers) escaped and were given a ride to safety.

One thing for sure, my bike has a better chance of reaching Alaska than that truck.

Another certainty on this trip—every day I have a new experience.

-----End Blog-----

As I stated in today's blog, I expected construction on the Alaska Highway, though I did not expect it to start at Mile Marker Zero! Later I learned the Alaska Highway was always under construction in some place. A few miles into construction, brief exasperation settled into just another challenging expectation.

Tops of paved highways were often roughly ground and a new layer of oil, tar, and graded gravel reapplied. Road shoulders have much thinner layers resulting in shockingly rugged riding when being constructed or reconstructed.

My wrists would determine if I could continue.

For years, on long bicycle rides, my main bodily irritation was sore wrists. Gravel, deteriorated pavement, even extra wide seams (expansion cracks) in concrete highway shoulders made my wrists ache for days.

Anticipating wrist problems, I had searched bike shops for years to find a solution.

Our friend, Harlan Krueger, was a bike expert in Sioux Falls, South Dakota. Not only did Harlan operate Harlan's Bike and Tour shop, he bought frames, built bikes to his specifications, and used them on long-distance road and mountain trails. Describing my wrist issue, his wife Donna spent an hour adjusting my riding stance to reduce weight on handlebars. Secondly, she fitted my bike with tapered rubber grips on the end of my handlebars. Padded gloves were also recommended.

Although my wrist tingling lessened the next two years, it did not prevent what experts refer to as compression of the ulnar nerve, wrist hyperextension, or handlebar palsy.

I was not the only one with wrist problems from biking, but I had fallen into the common human trap of relying on others to solve my problem.

A weather induced human problem, starvation, forced bicycles to be invented.

A worldwide famine of 1816 (known as the Year Without a Summer) was caused by the April 10, 1815 eruption of Mount Tambora (now part of Indonesia) and its continual belching. People starved for lack of food as crops failed. With sun blocked, weather (not climate)[37] froze struggling crops not allowing them to mature. Streams remained frozen in spring across Europe and the United States. Snow was reported June 6, 1816 in Albany, New York.

No fodder was available for livestock as the hungry ate horses—the draft animal and mode of transportation. Recognizing the human need, a German Duke, Karl von Drais, invented and eventually patented the *Laufmachine* nicknamed the "hobby horse" we now know as the bicycle to carry freight by two wheels with human power.

Mentioned earlier, the day before my ride began, desperate to try a wrist aching solution, I went to the Pierre Ace Hardware store and searched for options. I purchased four feet of PVC pipe, pipe insulation, endcaps, bolts, and tape to build a second, inside, bar to parallel my handlebars supported by an old handlebar stem.

---

[37]Weather refers to atmospheric conditions, whereas climate refers to average weather of a location.

Before returning to construct my vision, I stopped at Pierre's bike shop, *Pedal and Paddle*, and discussed with the owner, Tom, the best padded handlebar tape. I bought a roll.

The result was a flexible, padded parallel bar which could be used for steering, but was intended to support my wrists. Hence, I named it a ***wrist support bar***.

As an inventor, I have a design and several utility patents. This bike accessory could have been potentially patentable. To help all long-distance cyclists with wrist issues, rather than going through the patent application and registration process, I decided to openly display it. Others cannot capture value from my design or functionality. Bicyclists will find it helpful.

Every day I used the **wrist support bar**. Today's first ten miles of construction reconfirmed its usefulness and practicality.

Normally, handlebars are held to steer and allow quick switching of gears and braking. That was how I biked--all the while resting my wrists on the support bar.

Anticipating rough areas, my hands were moved unto the **wrist support bar**. In areas that severely vibrated my bike, like today's construction, I moved my hands to the far end of the **wrist support bar**.

Amazingly, I never had sore wrists today, or on this whole trip.

After ten miles (16 km) of construction, another of today's tests was crossing the Peace River just before Taylor. The bridge, the longest river span of the whole Alaska Highway, was constructed of welded steel in uniform vertical cubes which allowed snow, ice and rain to fall through into the river rather than accumulate on the bridge decking. It was a bike-vibrating nightmare.

Although temperatures were in the 40s-50s Fahrenheit (4-10°C) today, fear was not ice, but wind and drizzle down the sand-strewn shoulder with a 5.5-kilometer 6% grade. That was followed after a curve with a sign, "Extreme 10% downhill grade 5 kilometers".

Fright continued with braking downhill ten kilometers, approaching the Peace River bridge. It was initially built in 1942 and replaced with the current bridge in 1960 and was only one of over three hundred bridges on the ALCAN. Steel bridge cubes were extremely smooth and slippery from over five decades of wear.

The area was stunning.

Constantly flowing blue water between wooded mountains with a peaceful town nestled a step above the river was breathtaking.

I was in trouble. More dangerous than wildlife, every bridge was different.

Sandy pavement was tricky. Careening down, at nearly forty kilometers per hour (24 mph), toward a steel guardrail was threatening as the highway shoulder narrowed into sand-covered rumble strips.

Hitting the well-worn, traffic-grooved steel grated bridge decking across the Peace River was draining. Adrenaline sapped rebelling synapses. Hair follicles on my forearms and neck were irritated as my watering eyes blurred cold steel cubes over fast flowing water.

At the bottom, across the Peace River's north side, lay the small town of Taylor (site of the first Army road-construction camp). After quickly passing Taylor with an unsettled stomach, I had plenty of time to sooth titillated nerves gradually climbing for miles out of the Peace River valley.

Face-to-face with merciless reality, for some reason a cemetery scene popped into my brain. Did I have enough nerve endings for the last half of my journey? Now, looking back after a year has passed, the Peace River had affinity to be called a dead end.

Life is too rushed—like going down a mountain too fast. Passing slowly, surroundings are cherished.

Chapter 30: 89 km/55 miles
Day 22, June 12, Ft. Saint John to Wonowon, BC

Depart time: 8:03 a.m.
Arrive time: 1:40 p.m.
Highways: 97
Day—total km/miles: 89/55—2,614/1,624
Day average speed: (kmph/mph): 15.9/9.9
Day—total elevation gain (m/ft): 667/2,189—5,664/18,582
Calories daily/total to date: 2,373/70,172
Daily dangers/excitement: Rain, cool.

Begin Blog:

Some things are natural; others are not. Phone and Internet services are not. Such communication is only a recent phenomenon. Many have come to expect it. My point is that I am biking into an area that is more natural than synthetic.

For the past day, I have been generally without phone service. Internet has been accessible at lodging sites. Following telephones, Internet has become a lodging standard feature, like bed, towel, and pillows of the past.

My daily bogs may become less frequent. It does not mean I am incapacitated, but more likely closer to nature.

For example, I woke this morning, checked the weather and winds on my smart phone as I normally do and prepared to ride. Weather this morning showed expected winds less than 10 mph all day and zero percent chance of rain. I took the bike to the hotel lobby as I was going to pick up a light breakfast. It was raining—and did so until 8:00.

Rain is natural, weather predictions are artificial.

Fortunately, on this trip I am getting to become more accustomed to nature again. As my photo today indicates, I brought my bike into our room daily. Thievery and rain are natural. I want to protect my transportation from both.

I appreciate my followers, but I may be closer to nature than Internet the next couple weeks. Keep checking. Thanks!

-----End Blog-----

Life, full of opportunities, is best lived free.

Isn't it sad that many people restrict themselves to climate-controlled rooms? They are losing touch with nature.

Minds at all ages need stimulation even if muscles do not move. When they do, it stimulates the body and brain.

I am not saying I somehow got smarter biking to North Pole. It made me think differently.

All my senses were stimulated—sight, hearing, touching, smelling, and tasting the environment. Black gnats and mosquitoes offer all, including smelling their breeding beds.

Inactivity slows minds and mechanisms.

Renowned transportation authority and author, Samuel I. Schwartz' 2018 book, "*No one at the Wheel*", connotes health effects of self-driving vehicles. He wrote, "Worldwide, inactivity kills more people than smoking does."[38]

Invited to speak at a transportation conference of tech experts, Schwartz found himself dazzled by wiz kids' gadgets and thing-a-ma-jigs though, he claimed, they knew virtually nothing about transportation. Baffling them with simplicity, Schwartz expounded how people can be moved within a mile of home or office at no additional cost by a 3000-year-old invention—shoes.

---

[38] Samuel I. Schwartz, transportation engineer and author of "*No one at the Wheel*", quote from page 212.

Rain subsided this morning as I left. Puddles slowed me a bit. Drivers sped by enveloping me in a cloud of cool mist. Using a cliché, *adding insult to injury*, I was tire-splattered from the side.

Did drivers consider my insult-to-injury? Some did. They moved to the far lane when passing.

Driver insult-to-injury would be more like adding cholesterol to veins, donuts to diabetes, caffeine to hypertension, cigarette smoking to lung cancer, and salted chip to blood pressure while listening to screeching music and reading irritating news—sometimes all in a mile.

Eating is easy in a vehicle but hard on a bike. Stopping for a snack was something I looked forward to. It was enjoyable, just visiting my surroundings in complete peace.

My wife would sometimes surprise me late morning by passing and motioning to stop ahead on an approach or intersection (which are rare the farther north you get). Biking a mile, two or more to reach her was not unusual. I salivated for sticky buns. Farther north, opportunities became fewer.

During the trip, I ate large, high starch, high calorie meals in the evening. During the day, I usually ate sparingly. Usually I had a peanut butter sandwich, a protein bar or two but four or five times Patricia delivered a large sticky bun to me.

Come to think of it, I have never seen a marathon runner swallowing a gut bomb halfway through a run.

I was at peak weight, 205 pounds (93 kg.), anticipating retirement. My wife and I considered joining the Peace Corp[39] although they rated me physically obese. I certainly did not feel like it. I was active, walked and biked regularly, but ate too much fast food while driving and consumed steaks too late in the evening on business trips.

Retirement allowed me to get off cholesterol and blood pressure meds within six months by eating healthier and getting more exercise. I dropped to 195 (88.5 kg.)—still considered obese at my annual medical physical. Over the next couple years, I dropped to

---

[39] Peace Corp is a volunteer organization sponsored by the United States of America started March 1, 1961 under the direction of President John F. Kennedy to support social and economic development in foreign countries. See https://www.peacecorps.gov/.

about 185 (84 kg.)—the same weight as I was when I left Air Force Basic Training at age 18.

In the last few decades, an increase in physical immobility resulted in insurance and government subsidized walkers and battery powered mobility scooters. Some are certainly needed. However, it has been culturally acceptable to drive everywhere rather than walk. Two blocks to the local drug store used to be a walk, now it generates stress and frustration driving around the block until a parking place opens near the door.

What's the cure? It is not medication? Read labels…as I will explain later in this book.

Weight gain is a side effect of taking popular antidepressants, antihistamines, birth control pills, pain medications, and those being treated for allergies, depression, inflammation, and diabetes.

It is interesting that diabetes caused by excessive weight, treated with insulin causes more weight gain—an oxymoron that makes pharmaceutical marketers smile.

I left Wonowon, British Columbia heading northwest. Words like obese morph. So did Wonowon as words and definitions changed.

Wonowon, I thought was a First Nation name. It is not.

I biked on the shoulder of Highway 97, better known as the Alaska Highway from Dawson Creek into Alaska. Settlements are few and place names more practical.

Wonowon used to be a settlement called Blueberry—a place to gather wild blueberries. As the World War II Alaska Highway progressed north, Blueberry settlement was at the highway mile marker 101. Pronounced one-oh-one, hence Wonowon.

How things change.

While writing this book, I looked out the window and saw sidewalks empty and traffic, usually one person per vehicle, passing by. Lately, drivers have looked at me as if I was homeless when walking with recycled bag a mile or two to the library, grocery, fishing dock, and recycling center.

I was not always this way. In midlife, I drove everywhere. Bicycling to North Pole renewed my boyhood desire when I used to walk the mile-long pasture to get milk cows or run through wheat stubble to take dad fresh water, sandwich or a wrench.

With fresh air in my face, this part of northern British Columbia was beautiful. More mountains await. There was more space to enjoy, fewer people to enjoy it, and a time and place to think about life's changes.

I want to encourage others to go for a bike ride or walk. If able, go somewhere under your own power if only to your local store. You will have fuller appreciation, physically and mentally, for your purchase.

Look forward to going farther tomorrow. I did.

Chapter 31: 🚲 119 km/74 miles
Day 23, June 13, Wonowon to Buckinghorse River, BC

Depart time: 5:25 a.m.
Arrive time: 2:15 p.m.
Highways: 97
Day—total km/miles: 119/74—2,733/1,698
Day average speed: (kmph/mph):15.8/9.8
Day—total elevation gain (m/ft): 1,288/4,226—6,952/22,808
Calories daily/total to date: 3,371/73,543
Daily dangers/excitement: Braking downhill.

Begin Blog:

Amazing day. No wind but overcast and cold. At 39°F (3.9°C) when I started, it likely never got out of the 40s°F. Hills! And more hills! Seventy-four miles (123 km) of them. Snow was in the mountains to the south most of the day. This was the first time when my ascent (4,226 ft./1,288 m.) exceeded calories (3,371). At thirty miles (48 km) into the trip, I figured feet elevation could not continue to exceed calories. (See today's blog photo.) I was proved wrong.

One downhill outside of Pink Mountain had an ominous warning sign in *The Milepost*: "Suicide Hill, one of the most treacherous hills on the original Alaska Highway noted for its ominous greeting: 'Prepare to meet thy Maker.'"

I had to use both front and back brakes off-and-on all the way down. One stretch had narrowed the shoulder for a half mile with concrete abutments on my right and rumble strips. (Note: bike and rumble strips are not compatible.) This downhill was worse than any uphill!

The Milepost guide of services and points of interest has been published annually since the 1940s and covers Alaska highways and roads into and around the state. Heed their warnings! Suicide Hill is a non-fiction fact. Such allegories ought to scare drivers. It did scare this biker. I experienced it!

The most amazing part of this ride was a cow moose with very young calf at her side that came out of the woods about a 100-yards (~90 m) ahead of me. The tiny calf could not have been more than a week old.

The pair came up on the highway shoulder (my shoulder) and was trotting toward me. I stopped to grab my phone/camera when I first saw them. My phone battery was dead. I could have been, too. The cow moose came towards me.

At most she was forty yards in front of me trotting, face-to-face. I did not move as I straddled my bike. The cow stopped with calf by her back legs. She looked at me, puzzled by a strange object.

Realizing I was not threatening, she trotted across the highway, down the opposite ditch and disappeared into the woods. Luckily, there was no traffic on the highway.

As a farm kid raised around cattle, I have been chased by a cow protecting her calf. Fortunately, the moose did not find me offensive.

Today's moral: On the Alaska Highway there is more than one way to "Meet thy Maker."

-----End Blog-----

As I have mentioned before, *The Milepost* mile-by-mile directory of Alaska Highways was a must when traveling this remote area. See themilepost.com. It does not have all the retail shops listed—that would be an hourly directory.

Most shops open when they want, close when they want, shut down for the fall when they want, and open in the spring if they want. If they run low on supplies, they shut down to make a trip which could be hundreds of miles.

Surprisingly, trucks became rarer farther north. Opposing traffic was less as I progressed north. When trucks passed me, most were extremely courteous by pulling to the far lane. Unfortunately, I had no way of showing appreciation.

Apparently, it is more economical to ship supplies by ocean-going container into Canadian and Alaskan ports and truck them north than to bring them over highways from lower Canada or the contiguous United States.

Note Mile Marker 145. Today's memorable climb and freewheeling down was—Suicide Hill. Advise: Do not use graveled truck turnouts—you will not have time to zip your fly or swallow a sandwich fleeing from a brake-burning truck or RV.

To minimize road building and repair, gravel mines were usually close to the Highway. An exception, "The Cut" (Mile Marker 124.3) was the Highway. Excavation likely provided surface gravel, but more importantly made the mountain pass more doable with loaded Army trucks.

With a cold morning drizzle, Pink Mountain did not display its glistening feldspar, but that did not diminish its beauty. Chain-up parking lots were a great place for breaks and enjoying scenery.

Sometimes I would stop just to look at what I had passed. Amazingly, things looked completely different from the other direction.

My journal had a special note worth repeating:

"After I left Pink Mountain, there were two steep hills to descend. One had concrete abutments for about a half mile rather than cable guard rails."

I cannot over-emphasize caution. Look for hints of danger.

For example, to keep from catapulting into the unseen unknown, safety experts occasionally required expensive downhill concrete barriers. When you see them, rather than more economical cable, use extreme caution as sand builds along the concrete and wind creates little sand eddies on road shoulders. Whirling bicycle tires on downhill sand was "touch-and-go" into the unperceived.

Like yesterday, today seemed to have more wildlife crossing signs—usually a symbol of deer, moose, elk, bear, or wood bison. *The Milepost* gave special warnings to watch for wildlife "…especially at dusk and at night."

May I insert "…also at dawn!"

Two reasons I jumped on my bike so early was first to see the sun rise, and secondly to see nature finishing the dawn of another cycle as wildlife moved to daytime shade. Even after spring shedding, these heavy-coated animals get too warm during spring and summer days. So, they feed at night.

No degree of caution can protect you, or me.

Biking early morning was beautiful, no doubt.

Animals were abundant—traffic was not. Danger abounded.

In the late 1800s, high wheel bicycles were the rage before chain-driven ones hit the market. They were dangerous.

Excessively outgoing and willing to try anything, Samuel Clemens (a.k.a. Mark Twain) commented: "It was on the 10th day of May 1884 that I confessed to my age…by mounting a bicycle for the first time."

Clemens like most men (they were not for women) found bicycles, the first mode of personal mechanical transportation, dangerous to mount and to ride. He wrote, "Get a bicycle. You will not regret it. If you live."[40]

If for some tragic reason I would have been stomped to death by a moose, eaten by a bear or molested by a wolf, later that day my wife likely would have spotted my bicycle, blood and helmet before finding my strewn body in the bush. Right-of-ways were very wide, but regrowth could easily hide danger only feet from the highway.

Too obvious, recovering remains was not one of the follow-up protocols my wife and I discussed.

Again, I caution cyclists and vacationers—this time about moose. They are unexpectedly tall with long legs. Maybe I could have ridden

---

[40] Samuel Langhorne Clemens, November 30, 1835-April 21, 1910, a.k.a. Mark Twain wrote *Taming the Bicycle*. His short story was featured as The Short Story of the Day, May 21, 1919 (nine years after Clemens' death). See https://americanliterature.com/author/mark-twain/essay/taming-the-bicycle.

under the mother moose's belly. Munching in marshes they seem like cattle. Be careful. What makes moose so dangerous is their unpredictable temperament.

Humans have always sought beasts of burden. Reindeer are Santa fantasies. Caribou were fare (as in sustenance, not for transit). Moose are powerful and could have certainly pulled more than dogs, but moose have never been domesticated. Mankind has learned never to trust a moose. My nephew, an avid hunter in North Pole had advised me, "Moose injure or kill more Alaskans than bears."

Chapter 32: 87 km/54 miles
Day 24, June 14, Buckinghorse River to Profit River, BC

Depart time: 7:25 a.m.
Arrive time: 12:35 p.m.
Highways: 97
Day—total km/miles: 87/54—2,820/1,752
Day average speed: (kmph/mph): 18.8/11.7
Day—total elevation gain (m/ft): 311/1,020—7,263/23,828
Calories daily/total to date: 2,557/76,100
Daily dangers/excitement: Don't feed the bears.

Begin Blog:

What was one clue I was in a rural outpost? When the lodging (cabins), cafe, and fuel pump's only source of electricity was a shedded generator—running sometimes.

Another clue was the highway sign just before entering Buckinghorse River: "Check your fuel 174 km to next station".

According to *The Milepost* directory, there was no lodging reported between Buckinghorse River and Fort Nelson. Without knowing the terrain or weather before I started, I figured I would have a tough ride, or luck out and find a place to stay. Thanks to the Internet, I found a bed and breakfast halfway to Fort Nelson and entered the phone number in my "Pierre-to-the-Pole" trip guide. Anticipating today's ride, I called the phone number last night and was pleasantly surprised that not only was the bed and breakfast open (for the past year), but the owners asked if we wanted them to make us supper.

What an offer to a hungry biker! The owners had been living in Vancouver for seven years, before buying and remodeling the spacious place. Originally, she was from China and he was from Tibet.

The hardest part about making a homemade Chinese meal in this area was getting customary spices. Otherwise, they picked up supplies once per week in Fort Nelson—a 112-mile (180 km) roundtrip.

By the way, wildlife highlight for today was a marmot watching from his rock pile perch next to the highway as I stopped and took photos.

-----End Blog-----

As mentioned in the blog, distances to services here are measured in hundreds of kilometers. For non-bicyclists, that was a long way.

This country is big. As I wrote in my journal:

"Everything was farther than it appeared. The hill outside Buckinghorse River Lodge appeared to be a mile climb. It was foggy so I could not quite see the top. It was actually just over two miles (2.06) to the crest. In another place, a long flat low area with a few minor hills, I estimated the next bigger hill to be about three miles where I would take a break. Actually, it was just over five miles."

As mentioned during my Saskatchewan travels, I grew up in open spaces where mirages gave me anticipation of sights over thirty miles (50 km) away. That gave me confidence over the years to judge stamina. Mental example: "Can I make it to that hill before I take a break?"

Rather than being disappointed, it put life more in perspective. Distances, or life, are not always what you expect.

My journal continued:

"Sun came out in mid-morning—made for a pleasant ride. Wind, when there was any, was less than five-miles-per-hour. Main wildlife, birds…and bears."

How can you not enjoy this area?

Realize though, some people cannot help themselves from being fools.

Pull-outs beside this Highway are few. After very long distances, drivers need a safe place to take a break. There are few approaches and virtually no sideroads. Grizzly and black bears are everywhere.

Pit toilets and solid steel trash containers with self-locking bear-proof covers provide convenient disposal at some graveled break areas. Signs were always posted not to feed or leave food for bears.

Really, how dumb would someone have to be to slice apples, oranges, even onions and lay them next to an open can of tuna in designated parking areas with signs "DO NOT FEED THE BEARS"?

Are those signs hard to misunderstand?

Unfortunately, some people either cannot read, stupid, or blatantly ignore the signs. That is tragically dangerous! Do they realize a child can be grabbed, bitten with bear teeth puncturing their brain before the parents could open the vehicle door and get in?

When I stopped to rest, I picked up nincompoops' litter. I ask followers to do the same.

A crime worse than littering, why would someone deliberately display litter with potential to injure a follower?

Stops along the Alaska Highway are few where children can get out and run and adults can stretch leisurely. Others can ruin it. Can anyone really think a can of tuna will save a bear from starvation?

Rest areas were few; bears were many. I certainly did not want bears hanging around rest areas searching for food—neither did the highway department erecting the signs. If a vehicle was attacked, drivers could speed away faster than the bear. Meanwhile, bicyclists have little or no protection and certainly cannot outrun a bear.

Bears forage and will attack people where food has been available. Bear warning signs were erected to protect the public. A few people could ruin a relaxing rest for others.

I could imagine a spousal conversation.

Him: "Honey. What do we have to feed the bears?"

Her: "Let's see….*The Milepost* shows the next rest stop is 50 kilometers. I know. We have an onion smelling up the camper."

Him: "Onion? Bears need a full meal. I saw someone left orange and apple slices at the last rest area. Bears need protein. We're heading to Alaska to get salmon. Let's attract bears with our can of tuna and the onion."

Obviously, bears out here do not hunt for fruits from the south, canned fish from the ocean, or onions from gardens, but they will eat nearly anything—and kill people to get at it.

What are bear-feeding, rest stop visitors thinking?

Are they diabolical nature terrorists—bringing bear terror to their followers? If compassionate morons, the dimwits may attract bears while they are waiting for a photo-shoot. Bears have great noses. They can track a scent ten miles or more.

If a tuna can would attract a bear, had feeders considered the fish scent would likely be on their hands, car handle or camper door? Had they realized black bears or grizzlies could slash open a car or camper easier than a senior pensioner, like me, can open a bag of potato chips?

Bears, especially those foraging in spring after a long hibernation, will kill nearly anything for food.

At various stops, I noticed some numbskulls even placed food items on perimeter rocks surrounding parking spots so bears would not have to stoop as far to feed. What do imbeciles think? Do bears get bad backs stooping?

I will give them a break. Likely bear-attracting tourists are innocent of malice. Unknowingly, they are conditioning bears to hang out at rest areas. When biking solo, like me, one of two things are needed—a break or toilet, not a bear!

Scat evidence was obvious. Wittingly, or unwittingly, bears had been attracted to rest areas. How could a cyclist rest after a long day of peddling? What if a break-down or exhaustion required camping for a few hours?

After seeing hundreds of bears, I was lucky and never attacked. Followers beware!

I had to be extra alert of bears coming out of the toilet.

No. I was not afraid they were taking a crap and did not lock the door. (I am serious. Some people may think bears use toilets.)

I feared when I came out, a snarling grizzly may have been rummaging for my peanut butter sandwich.

Some people are innocent or so simply unaware, you just have to laugh at them.

Tourists feeding bears reminded me of an American standup comic, George Carlin (1937-2008) who once cracked, "Think of how stupid the average person is, and realize half of them are stupider than that."

Chapter 33: 92 km/57 miles
Day 25, June 15, Profit River to Fort Nelson, BC

Depart time: 7:15 a.m.
Arrive time: 12:55 p.m.
Highways: 97
Day—total km/miles: 92/57—2,911/1,809
Day average speed: (kmph/mph): 17.9/11.1
Day—total elevation gain (m/ft): 372/1,222—7,635/25,050
Calories daily/total to date: 2,593/78,693
Daily dangers/excitement: Crane.

Begin Blog:

The sun popped out after an early morning drizzle (<6:30)—the first day of sun for over a week. With a new bike chain and sun, I seemed to bike faster.

Today's most amazing thing was going to be the black bear that rambled across the highway a couple blocks in front of me. I slowed allowing it to enter the bush on my side of the highway. As I passed, I could not see it, nor did I pause to take a closer look.

Now for the once-in-a-lifetime event: About a half hour after I had seen the black bear, I was peddling smoothly about 12-13 mph with a slight northwest wind as I was headed north about 25 miles south of Fort Nelson.

I am not sure if I heard, saw, or felt something to my right (ditch-side). As I turned my head to the right at 90-degree angle, I looked blue eyeballs-to-orange eyeball (black pupil) at a sandhill crane. (At least that was what I would call it.)

Its long head was about two to three arm lengths away. It's long neck and wings were behind me. After it saw me turn my head, it landed in the ditch and walked into the highway ditch bush.

I cannot spot the crane in the blog photo, but at least you get an idea of the four to five foot-tall bush along the road where the bear and crane found refuge.

My reasoning--the crane was drafting behind and to my right. (Remember, I was cutting the northwest wind for it.) I have no idea how long it was there. My large round mirror was on my left so I could see traffic approaching in the driving lane.

On our farm in northern South Dakota, each fall and spring I used to hear sandhill cranes pass. Constantly squawking, they fly in group formation about a mile high.

I have never been so close to a wild flying bird before. This crane was huge. After it landed and went into the bush, I stopped. It squawked; waited a half minute or so and squawked again. Occasionally, it would pop its head out between the bushes. I ate my peanut butter and jelly sandwich waiting to get a good photo. It may have been bored with me, as it quit squawking and maybe moved into the woods or sat nesting. After seeing the bear earlier, I did not have the guts to walk in after the crane.

I will end saying that this crane was big. Standing in the bush with head up, it seemed like five-foot-tall with red crown on its head and brown body. It was truly a once-in-a-lifetime experience.

-----End Blog-----

My breakfast of two poached eggs, links of boiled sausage, orange juice and two apple rolls were delicious and prepared me for the once-in-a-lifetime event. Having, what I believe was a female Sandhill crane, draft beside and slightly behind me was an indescribable feeling.

Birds and bikes seem to have little in common; but one spring, Patricia was hit by a flying Canada goose on the Sioux Falls twenty-mile bike trail along the Big Sioux River. The gander was likely protecting goslings. It smacked her hip. Luckily, she did not fall but it left quite a bruise.

163

Please do not limit your imagination to my blog description of this crane event. It cannot be duplicated. My journal notes:

"About 9:30 a.m. a black bear walked across the highway (to my side) about two blocks in front of me. I was going into the wind, so I don't think she saw me as she was on all fours with head down and nose a few inches off the highway. As I went by, I could not see her when I passed as the bush in the wide ditch was about four to five feet tall.

"About a half hour later, I was biking into a 12-13 mph wind (19-21 kmph) with slight wind to my left/front. I am not sure if I felt, heard, or saw something out of the corner of my eye, but I looked to my right straight into the left eye of a crane. Apparently, it was drafting me….

"About a half hour before I arrived in Ft. Nelson, going downhill a big bug hit me between my nose and mouth. It smarted. I was going ~25 mph (40 kmph) and could not wipe it off (at least the impact) until I was down the hill--another reason to wear sunglasses all the time."

Was the crane courting me? I admit my bright yellow jacket would have been flashier than her other choices.

Today's events are clear-cut. You cannot understand this area until you experience it on a bicycle.

Chapter 34: 109 km/68 miles
Day 26, June 16, Fort Nelson to Tetsa River Lodge, BC

Depart time: 4:45 a.m.
Arrive time: 1:20 p.m.
Highways: 97
Day—total km/miles: 109/68—3,021/1,877
Day average speed: (kmph/mph): 15.8/9.8
Day—total elevation gain (m/ft): 1,115/3,658—8,750/28,708
Calories daily/total to date: 3,157/81,850
Daily dangers/excitement: Long mountain pass.

Begin Blog:

Today was wildlife day throughout. The second highlight was a five-mile stretch going up over a mountain pass into the Northern Rocky Mountains. My ride was completed by a blown rear tire (today's blog photo).

Nothing can compare to a crane drafting behind/beside me (yesterday's experience), but today I confirmed the crane's existence with photos of three feeding near the highway. A herd of five elk passed across the highway a quarter mile in front of me and a small black bear was feeding in the ditch. That was the first ten miles. A bull moose (still in felt) was feeding along the road as were a large black bear and deer. Numerous bear scat on my highway shoulder provided evidence I missed many.

Patricia kept checking and offering food and encouragement as I climbed (in my lowest gear) the 3,500 ft. Steamboat Mountain summit (Alaska Highway pass) overlooking the Muskwa-Kechika (Rivers) Management Area (an environmentally managed multi-use

165

area for resource and recreational development while maintaining natural beauty).

So far on this trip, I have not had to stop, or walk, my bike up a climb. Today was by far the longest and toughest. My leg stamina was certainly tested, but the half hour break at the top overlook was well worth it. While there, we first visited with an RVing couple from South Dakota, and completed our break by visiting with two couples from Switzerland. One made their wedding trip 40 years ago over Alaska Highway's gravel roads. They were happy to share their repeat visit with friends this time in a comfortable RV.

My seventy-one mile ride today was cut short by about three miles after I blew my rear tire (blog photo). This trip went so well. Who would be the first vehicle that came by after I started walking my bike?

If you guessed a professional who makes a living helping and protecting people, you would be correct. It was a Coastguardsman who was also a bicyclist!

He and his family were being transferred from Washington to

Juneau, Alaska. Since I had only about three miles to go to the cabin Patricia had found, we loaded my bike in the back of their pickup topper which had four bikes on top and a carbon road bike packed in shipping blankets in the box.

Their moving trailer had no room, nor was there any room in the backseat with their three children (one in a car seat). To make room for me in the front, their border collie crawled into the back.

Before leaving for Alaska, the Coastguardsman was advised to offer support to stranded vehicles. He said, "After hundreds of miles, what are the chances the first person we could help was a fellow bicyclist?"

As an Air Force veteran, I am so proud to know our servicemen and women are still helping others wherever they are needed.

-----End Blog-----

For a while today, I paralleled the Muskwa River (meaning Bear) the lowest point on the Alaska Highway (around 305 meters/1,000 feet) as it mostly dodges mountains for the next couple hundred miles into the Canadian Rockies.

Long days cast long shadows, especially in the early morning. Since I was not biking near midnight, I did not get a night version of a bicycle shadow projection across the Highway.

Up here, distance signs are warning signs. A blue one stated: "*Check your fuel. Next service 188 km.*" Canada law also requires the French version, "*Verifier votre carburant prochain service 188 km.*"

Today, the road just kept winding with a few dips and small hills mile after mile. The vistas were always beautiful with meadows, streams, woods, and wildlife.

Ahead, I could see the ALCAN curve after curve to the top of Steamboat Mountain summit (3,500 ft./1,067 meters).

About forty miles (64 km) into today's ride, Patricia pulled ahead—indicating a short water and snack break. Departing, Patricia said "Meet you at the top."

Distance was deceiving. With some level areas, I covered a couple upsloping miles before the serious climb.

Going nearly all the time in my lowest gear trying to keep speed at least five miles-per-hour (8 kmph), I kept inching my way up…and up…and up….

Looking beside me were a host of beautiful flowers--sometimes remnants of last year's weeds. It made me feel like I was going faster, much faster than staring at the continuous uphill road ahead. Sometimes I would watch road pebbles closely. They too would zip by.

For well over an hour I kept pedaling. Cars, RVs, and motorcycles that had passed me were parked at the top. Good. Patricia would find a place to park, and I could take a break.

When I arrived, several mountain and valley gazers cheered me to a stop. The view was gorgeous—I, a spectacle.

It was not until I looked at our trusty guide, *The Milepost*, that I realized I had biked uphill "… 6.7 miles (10.8 km) northbound; winding road, 8 percent grades" without stopping.

Going down was also eight percent grade with some rough spots. That was where I maxed out at 34.5 miles-per-hour (55.5 kmph).

Many times I have said the three hardest parts about biking are: 1.) Biking uphill against the wind; 2.) Slowing going downhill; and 3.) Stopping going uphill and trying to start again.

Point three, a short break may feel good for a few minutes, but reacclimating your leg muscles takes a lot of convincing.

It was easier to keep biking. I did. Never once on this whole trip did I stop going up a hill, pass, or mountain. I never walked my bike except once with a flat tire.

Until I wrote the last paragraph, I never realized I did not run out of breath. Apparently, lung capacity built on level prairies prepared me for the mountains.

Clarification on today's blog was best answered by a few questions.

After you got a flat, why didn't you call Patricia and have her pick you up?

For the next eleven hundred miles (1,800 km), cell phone coverage would be very limited. There was no cell phone coverage when my tire blew.

Patricia had just stopped and seen me a few miles earlier. Since I had mostly downhill remaining, she decided to go to the lodge where she had booked our room an hour earlier.

Following up: How did you get your blog sent?

That evening, I did not. We had no cell coverage or Internet at our cabin. I wrote the blog, but it was posted the next time we had Internet.

Little was written about the blown tire. Notice the tread (today's blog photo) was somewhat worn in the middle. It should have been. Not only had I put 3,021 kilometers (1,877 miles) on it since starting this trip, but I put those tires on in Arizona in the spring of 2017.

That summer over a thousand miles were logged on boiling hot pavement and quite a bit on gravel.

Someone asked, why didn't you put on new tires before you left?

Without a doubt, the tires were in good shape. Otherwise, I could not have ridden 1,341 kilometers (833 miles) loaded with 285 pounds (129.3 kilos) to begin the trip. Then, after Patricia arrived, I biked another 1,680 kilometers (1,044 miles) before the back tire blew.

Just for the record, I finished the trip with 4,823 kilometers (2,997 miles) without changing my front tire which then had over 6,500 kilometers (4,000 miles) on it.

A question-and-answer section was included in this book because people are curious how I did it.

Several people have asked, "Why didn't you bike a few more minutes and get exactly 3,000 miles?"

I have a degree in Commercial Economics and Agricultural Business. Early in my university economics classes, a professor said, "You always have a choice to be honest, or shade the truth. Once you start shading, you will never recover."

Why would you read this if I am not honest with you?

It was not until I developed a spreadsheet to write this book that I realized, the unique distance. Recording to the tenth of a mile, my trip, including all the side diversions to eat and lodge, actual distance totaled exactly three miles short of 3,000 miles.

Had I not survived a blown tire going downhill in excess of fifty kilometers an hour (~30 mph) and took the opportunity to ride about three miles into Tetsa River Lodge, my trip would have totaled 3,000 miles. Converted at the rule-of-thumb of 0.6 km/mile, I would have biked an estimated 5,000 kilometers.

Those three miles, not ridden, added to my ALCAN experience. Subtlety. It was help when none was expected. Thanks again to the Coastguard family that stopped for me.

Throughout this ride, sights, sounds, smells, thoughts and feelings are trying to be expressed in words. Being now in Canada, hence, I will rely on the German-born Canadian, Eckhart Tolle, who wrote:

"Words reduce reality to something the human mind can grasp.

"Your entire life journey ultimately consists of the step you are taking at this moment. What the future holds for you depends on your state of consciousness now."[41]

Your ride physically or mentally will be different than mine. Enjoy it!

[41] Eckhart Tolle, (1948-), *A New Earth, Awakening to your life's purpose*, Penguin Books,(2005), p 27, p 271.

Chapter 35: 77 km/48 miles
Day 27, June 17, Tetsa River Lodge to Toad River Lodge, BC

Depart time: 6:50 a.m.
Arrive time: 12:25 p.m.
Highways: 97
Day—total km/miles: 77/48—3,098/1,925
Day average speed: (kmph/mph): 15.8/9.8
Day—total elevation gain (m/ft): 714/2,342—9,464/31,050
Calories daily/total to date: 2,085/83,935
Daily dangers/excitement: Snow-covered mountains.

Begin Blog:

The whole ride today was on a stretch of the Alaska Highway designated as a Scenic Highway by AAA. Barren mountains with snowpack were either before me and occasionally on both sides throughout the day.

Two passes I had to bike over today allowed me into four river basins (one glaciated with its creamy water). A major clue I was near the top was Summit Lake. Where else would it be? The second clue was four rivers draining different directions.

A couple days ago, I was advised by my niece who lives in the Denver area, that the tree line is 10,000 feet elevation. That was likely the case in the Colorado Rockies, but not the north end of the Canadian Rockies. All the barren mountains appeared glaciated in the recent past.

What a beautiful and peaceful ride.

Just a short update on my new tire and tube: working well. In case you are wondering, I have three spare tires and four tubes, plus a repair patch kit for the last 1,100 miles (1,800+ km).

-----End Blog-----

Today's accent of 2,342 feet (714 m.) exceeded calories of 2,085. That day's-end clue was not needed. Obviously, when crossing from one river basin into the next clearing mountain passes was required.

Secondly, when a river (North Tetsa) flows under the ALCAN through concrete culverts, it must be high in the mountains and runoff consistent and fairly low volume. Bridges, huge bridges in valleys were generally required on these massive rivers often a kilometer wide. Now, in late spring, most were way below capacity when I crossed them near their source.

ALCAN bridges are designed to handle not only melting snowpack and rains, but are extremely sturdy, high, and wide enough for trees and ice-jams to clear underneath without destroying the bridge. That happened many times during initial construction in 1942.

Today, I distinctly breathed cool mountain air from the Stone Range, Muskwa Range and upcoming Rocky Mountains. It must down-draft cold convection currents through the river valleys during the day as it does overnight.

Seldom did I see fishermen casting streams for Arctic grayling and Dolly Varden. There are far too many places to fish to worry about seeing another fisherman.

Classification of various fish in this area has been going on since the 1700s and reclassified into the late twentieth century. Colorful and spotted northern trout are often referred to as Dolly Varden— as described by the nineteenth century literary genius, Charles Dickens (1812-1870).

Up here fish are grouped into common names. Dolly Varden, for example, are colorful spotted trout. Whether they are an actual Arctic char or some other subgroup of bull trout, who cares. They are fun to catch and great to eat.

I like to fish.

My rod and tackle were packed in our vehicle. My intention was to use them once I arrived in North Pole. I did.

As you will realize toward the end of this book, my intentions of taking side hikes with my wife and fishing these mountain streams on the drive home did not happen.

Before departing Alaska, I did crawl from our vehicle once, using a folding chair for assistance, I made it to a lake—where I could not stand. It took nearly a year before I used my fishing gear again.

Gary W. Wietgrefe

Chapter 36: 🚲 117 km/73 miles
Day 28, June 18, Toad River Lodge to Liard River Lodge, BC

Depart time: 5:05 a.m.
Arrive time: 12:35 p.m.
Highways: 97
Day—total km/miles: 117/73—3,217/1,998
Day average speed: (kmph/mph): 17.5/10.9
Day—total elevation gain (m/ft): 953/3,127—10,417/34,177
Calories daily/total to date: 3,449/87,384
Daily dangers/excitement: Beauty and bears.

Begin Blog:

This stretch of Alaska Highway, a AAA designated "Scenic Highway", really deserves its designation. Passing through the Northern Rockies, across three river drainage areas, and mountain passes with limited traffic was a great experience.

One key was to travel it in early morning. Only two vehicles passed me the first hour. When I arrived at Muncho Lake (30 miles after departing) the lake was still—completely calm. (See today's photo.) The couple that took a photo of me by float planes arrived the previous afternoon. They could not believe the difference between a windy rough lake last night and a flat, calm, dark blue lake this morning.

There were several reasons I rode early morning: 1. No wind; 2. No traffic; 3. More wildlife; 4. Arrive early; and 5. Made a much more pleasurable ride.

Why ride if you do not enjoy it?

-----End Blog-----

Total distance today, 117 kilometers (73 miles) was two miles (3.2 km) less than my whole trip's average distance. Ease between nightly stops meant endurance was building.

Before I detail descriptions of today, I must first reveal how it ended.

As is normal, Patricia met me late morning bringing me a snack. Thereafter, she drove ahead and secured our room for the night at the quaint Liard Springs Lodge. Across the Highway, natural hot spring pools fed by springs drained from a hillside.

Since Army Highway construction workers used them in the 1940s, permanent walkways have been built through the approaching areas around the hot pools. Clothes changing areas, blocked by bear gates across the walkways, provide modern, unexpected conveniences.

Normally, while washing my daily garments, I took a hot relaxing shower or soaked in a tub of Epsom salts to rejuvenate tightening muscles. Fortunately, before slipping into swimming shorts, I accomplished my chores of washing my biking uniform so it could dry.

Today, Liard Hot Springs far surpassed any shower or tub soak.

Upon returning from the Hot Springs, we relaxed for a scrumptious dinner.

When you make this trip, no matter what time of the day you pass through, take time to enjoy at least an hour in Liard hot springs.

Throughout the day I stopped to take photos on this "Scenic Highway" through three river basins. One of the mountain passes (I think it was between the Trout and Smith Rivers) was a bit more than exercise.

While rolling to a stop to film a feeding bull moose, a semi-truck flew by. As I videoed, the moose meandering into the woods. It would have been much better as I coasted closer if the truck had not frightened him. There were other moose to film, but I was leery of getting too close.

My first mountain sheep was seen today.

I figured most bear did not pay attention to me. They went on feeding—usually on dandelion blossoms in ditches.

One bear was more curious. It made me a bit uneasy. Sitting on the ditch bank, watching maybe a hundred feet (30 m.) from pavement, the bear gradually turned his head from my approach to when I passed.

(The following incident will be described further on day thirty-two.) One time I saw another bear ahead. I slowed.

A large RV flew passed me. Then, slammed on their brakes to film the bear. I quickly switched lanes and passed in the left lane while they were filming through their passenger-side window.

Two motorcyclists passed me up the following hill. When on top, they stopped, waited, and wondered what was going on. As I arrived, they had only stopped to ask if I was ok. This was a caring example of quiet motorcyclists and their concern for fellow travelers.

Watchful. Concerned. Caring. That was what I came to understand as the ALCAN culture.

"No worries," I said. "I just let the RV block that bear for me."

"Really!" One replied. The motorcyclist had not seen the bear.

Departing, they warned me, "Be safe!"

Their heartfelt attentiveness made me realize obnoxious travelers do not fit in up here.

Assuming no traffic, and there was little, generally, I would move to the far lane, pass the animal obstruction and return to the right road shoulder.

One time, Patricia had stopped and we chatted while I took a break. After pedaling a few miles, we agreed to take another joint break. We did.

When I went to her window the second time, I said, "Did you see those three bears in the bush?"

"Three!" she exclaimed. "There were five!"

A bit rattled, I was attracting more attention than I realized.

On a nearly level stretch, casually approaching a brush-laden streambank, I noticed an off-colored spot. Brush of various species were a bit twisted and regreening after apparent spring flooding.

Trees of multiple species provided pleasant background. A low-sided metal guardrail channeled traffic over a large metal culvert.

Sounds of the creek rippling through culvert and over rocks backgrounded by multi-flushed greenery were pleasantly deceiving. I slowed to a stop. As I grabbed my phone for a video, the spot moved. It was a huge black bear coming to cross the guardrail and road with both eyes on me. Without time to click my phone off, the video turned out mostly road grinding under my shoes and tires as I tried to frantically reclip to pedals with the bear approaching through the brush.

Apparently, bears near the road, or in bush clearings, were visible to me. Those missed likely were only a few feet away camouflaged, but always ready for another meal—especially in spring. Attracting some bears' attention allowed others to notice me.

Over the years, I have noticed good political leaders, whether I liked a particular candidate or not, were great at using decoys. Sometimes it was diverting the press to a non-relevant issue. Firing high level staff always created a flurry allowing the leader to enact a more fundamental issue with less scrutiny.

Likewise, countries' leadership, facing internal unrest, have used the common historical *modus operandi*. They make audacious invasion claims or assertions of being threatened by a foreign military. Unsuspecting citizens, unified for domestic protection, have allowed dictators to retain power.

The same principles can be used with tame or wild animals. A potentially cruel example would be when a vicious dog threatens, call your tame dog. Your dog will distract the vicious as you move to safety.

Such tactics work bicycling.

One day Patricia caught up with me in late morning. I could see her following slowly on the highway shoulder in my mirror. She watched me slow as we both had seen bears near the highway ahead.

As I slowed, she reacted.

Pulling past me, as normal, on the left, she moved ahead to distract the bears. While playing decoy with our vehicle, I passed her and the bears on the left.

Every situation, especially with bears, has to be handled differently. Be careful.

Growling stomachs after hibernation provide quite an aggressive incentive to feed on you or something. Sadly, not all travelers fear bears.

Another day, Patricia noticed a white car ahead of her had slowed and pulled to the highway shoulder as a bear entered the highway. The bear slowly approached the car from the left. A hand appeared through the driver's window apparently holding out food for the bear. Likely, the driver did not realize the bear could have severed a hand or arm with sudden clinching teeth of its ripping muscular jaws.

Patricia waited for the expected attack and prepared to be a decoy. Fortunately, seeing the next car (Patricia) approach, the bear was wiser than the driver as it meandered into the ditch.

Later, at one lodge an older couple (older than me) pulled in with a white four-door pickup pulling a camper. Both doors on the driver's side were red. They had reservations two weeks earlier but were delayed by a bear—not just any bear.

While staying in a cabin the wife got up at night to go to the bathroom and saw a huge grizzly bear in the living room picture window. At her scream, the bear scurried away.

You have likely heard the saying, "She was so scared she peed her pants." Apparently, she was not wearing any.

The bear did not scurry too far. In the morning, they found it had ripped a hole in the side (not door) of their camper to get at food. Not satisfied, the grizzly was so strong and hungry his ~~fingernails~~ claws wedged between the glass and metal on the driver-side door and backdoor. With incomprehensible might, it stripped the metal sheeting on both doors of their large 4-wheel drive truck to gain entrance.

Reading before this trip, bear avoidance, bear interaction, and reacting to a bear attack were part of my study.

My maximum speed on this trip was 68.7 kilometers-per-hour (42.7 mph). Twenty-nine days I recorded my maximum speed with an average top speed at 52.6 kilometers-per-hour (32.7 mph).

Of course, my maximum speeds were all achieved going downhill. Was that too fast for a bear to catch me?

NO!!!

Black bears reportedly peak out at about 56 kilometers-per-hour (35 mph) and grizzlies could pass them as if they were standing still. Top speeds of grizzly bears are around 90 kilometers-per-hour (~55 mph).

WARNING! If you take this route to North Pole, beware of bears. You cannot always see them, and you certainly cannot out bike them!

I saw hundreds of bears. At my average biking speed (16.9 kmph/10.5 mph), grizzly or blacks could have caught me without darting.

That reminds me of a Canadian bear story.

A bear walked into a bar and with a gravelly voice said, "This bear wants a beer."

The bartender glanced up and mumbled, "We don't serve beer to bears in this here bar."

The thirsty bear howled, "This bear wants a beer! If you don't give me a beer, I'm going to eat that barmaid over there."

As if a bear wandering in was an everyday occurrence, the bartender said sternly, "Get out! I told you before. We don't serve beer to bears in this here bar."

The bear, without hesitation, scrambled over, ate the barmaid, came back, slammed his paw on the bar, and growled, "This bear wants a BEER!"

The bartender, used to the rowdy, said, "We don't serve beer to bears on drugs."

The bear asked, "Eh?" (Remember this is a Canadian story.)

The bartender replied, "That was a barbiturate."

Chapter 37: 🚲 209 km/130 miles
Day 29, June 19, Laird River Hot Springs Lodge, BC
to Watson Lake, YT

Depart time: 4:15 a.m.
Arrive time: 6:25 p.m.
Highways: 97, 1
Day—total km/miles: 209/130—3,427/2,128
Day average speed: (kmph/mph): 18.3/11.4
Day—total elevation gain (m/ft): 1,240/4,066—11,657/38,243
Calories daily/total to date: 5,530/92,914
Daily dangers/excitement: Distance, wood bison racing.

Begin Blog:

At 130 miles (209 km), I will admit this (bike day 29) was my third toughest day. Day 6: Minot to Bowbells, ND for 71 miles (114 km) fighting wind was worst. I averaged only 6 miles-per-hour (10 kmph). The second worst was Weyburn to Davidson, SK, 166 miles (267 km) when I averaged my fastest time so far at 12.9 miles-per-hour (20.8 kmph). Remember Day 9 was also by far my longest day (15 hours, 15 minutes) and I was still carrying full panniers. Heat and wind (whatever direction) were wearing.

Some have asked about my progress. This was day 31 (including 2 break days). Today started at 1,998 miles (3,219 km) and ended at 2,128 miles (3,427 km) which put me over two-thirds of the way.

Never have I seen so much wildlife in a 50-mile (~80 km) stretch. Wood buffalo (bison) were the most numerous. Individuals and herds up to 50 or so were feeding. They seemed to ignore vehicles but were not sure about my bike. Their two choices were to defend their grazing area or run.

Once I realized that my front brake screech causes them to run, I used it as an approach tool. However, a small herd (dozen) decided that they needed to cross the highway in front of me.

I picked up the pace to keep bulls from turning around. Moving at about 15 miles-per-hour (24 kmph) does not allow much escape time.

A herd running moves at about 15 mph. (They can certainly run faster.) The 50 or so I mentioned earlier gradually grouped over a mile and a few young bulls, a couple times stopped, turned towards me. Front brake taps persuaded them to keep with the herd. Four camping rigs were on the left side of highway. As the herd slowed, I sped past as they found refuge through a thinned area of the ditch-lined woods.

Today's blog photo was of a bull that decided to run as I was going to sneak past as he had been calmly grazing.

Another thing, as I approached the Yukon Territory and passed the border, the buffalo were larger. They seem to resemble our Plains bison in size. Years ago there was an attempt to increase the genetic base cross-breeding from the limited numbers that had survived hunting a century ago. Perhaps, these herds are segregating again.

-----End Blog-----

Had I been in Brussels, Belgium an equivalent ride would have been like biking to Amsterdam, Netherlands (220 km/137 miles). For American readers, that was the same distance as biking from Seattle, Washington 137 miles to Vancouver, British Columbia.

Today was a long day—like biking 139 miles (224 km) from Washington, D.C. to Philadelphia, Pennsylvania. Fortunately, I did not have to bike though those six population centers.

In hindsight, it was the second largest accent after Wonowon to Buckinghorse River a week earlier. Elevation gain that day was 1,288 meters (4,226 ft.) in 119 kilometers (74 miles). However, today I biked further (209 km/130 miles) and recorded uphill pedaling of 1,240 meters (4,066 ft.).

Each of these two days I biked more than two-third of the combined elevation gain in the first 1,471 kilometers (914 miles) across the northern Prairies. There are certainly other routes, like through Montana, to get to Dawson Creek (the start of the Alaska Highway). I planned the flattest route.

Even though the ALCAN followed level areas along rivers when possible, pedaled elevation accumulated as hills turn toward mountains. To put distance and elevation gain in perspective, total distance biked in South Dakota, North Dakota and Saskatchewan was 1,471 kilometers (914 miles) with elevation gain in those thirteen days totaling 1,720 meters (5,974 ft.). Today alone elevation gain was 1,239 meters (4,066 ft).

Interestingly though, by the time I got to North Pole I would be about a thousand-foot lower elevation than when I started in Pierre, South Dakota. I just have to climb a few more mountains to get there.

Today, I started in British Columbia (a Province) and ended in the Yukon Territory.

There are many Territories in the world. The Yukon, Nunavut, and the Northwest Territory are Territories of Canada. Canada's First Nations government or bands are similar to Native American Indian Reservations in the U.S. They are not considered Territories.

I have been to many dependent and independent territories around the world. Puerto Rico, Washington, D.C., Okinawa (now Japan), Republic of San Marino (an independent hilltop state within Italy), Canary Islands (an autonomous Spanish archipelago off the west coast of Africa), and Transnistria (a breakaway republic of Moldova), besides many Native American Reservations where I have worked. All are different than the Yukon Territory.

A bit of history:

Territories, through world-acceptance, are officially "owned" by a country. For example, Greenland appears as a Territory of Denmark. Functionally, Greenland remained an "autonomous constituent country" of the Kingdom of Denmark.

Puerto Rico (a Caribbean Island), Guam and American Samoa (in the Pacific) are "unincorporated" Territories of the United States.

Guantanamo Bay (on the island of Cuba) remains an "extraterritorial holding" of the United States, whereas Washington D.C. is a "federal district" of the United States.

At the close of World War II in 1945, the Ryukyu Islands (often referred to as Okinawa) were a "military government" of the United States until 1972 when administrative rights were granted back to Japan, although China still expresses historic interest.

On July 1, 1997 Great Britain's "lease" of Hong Kong and surrounding area was repatriated to the People's Republic of China, under assumption of Hong Kong's home rule (independent of communist China's National People's Congress).

Enough!

Suffice it to say, some Territories, like the Yukon, operate paralleling a related province or state. Some have near independence. Others are ruled as ugly stepchildren, whereas some simply are military holdings.

The spacious Yukon Territory was different than any place I have been exposed to.

It is big, size wise—about halfway between the size of Texas and Montana, but it has the smallest territorial population (35,874) of Canada equaling only one tenth of one percent of the country. In most countries a population of under 40,000 would be called a town—not even big enough to be called a city.

Whitehorse, Yukon's capital and surrounding villages make up three-fourths of population with Dawson City the second largest "city" at 1,300 people. No other Yukon town has more than a thousand people.

My point is—unless you are near Whitehorse, do not expect to find many places to get food, lodging, medical care, or other services.

Bike, or drive! Enjoy the scenery, wildlife, and open (and I mean very open) spaces. If solitude is desired, you will find it in the Yukon.

Chapter 38: 🚲 24 km/15 miles
Day 30, June 20, Watson Lake to Nugget City, YT

Depart time: 11:45 a.m.
Arrive time: 12:58 p.m.
Highways: 1
Day—total km/miles: 24/15—3,449/2,143
Day average speed: (kmph/mph): 16.7/10.4
Day—total elevation gain (m/ft): 205/673—11,862/38,916
Calories daily/total to date: 622/93,536
Daily dangers/excitement: Relax, visit with bikers.

Begin Blog:

My shortest day—15 miles, gave us time to sleep in, eat a leisurely breakfast, wash the car, stock up on groceries, head to the next stop, enjoy lunch, and relax all afternoon.

We were in the Yukon. There would be lonely stretches ahead.

For over 2,000 miles (>3,200 km) I have only seen two other couples long-distance biking (in South Dakota, and Alberta going the opposite direction). Four cyclists were at today's stop. All had different plans and directions.

Check out their bikes in today's blog photo. Specifically, check out their loads.

My stripped bike was in the foreground. The three loaded bikes are hard to see under all their gear.

One guy started in Utah in March, another was a guy about my age who had made three trips across Canada, and the third recently finished a bike tour in Japan and was heading from the Pacific Coast to Calgary, AB.

The photo puts into perspective how my wife, Patricia, and I can enjoy this trip without the "camping experience".

Patricia woke every morning to send me off. After her morning exercise, she repacked our vehicle, restocked supplies, and usually caught up with me by noon.

After a break or two together, she moved on to get our next lodging. By the time I arrived, all I had to do was clean up, wash my jersey (unless a washer was available), oil bike chain, and prepare for the next day.

Us five long-distance bikers had each gone over 2,000 miles (>3,200 km) this year. With my three 40+ pound bags (panniers) carried the last couple weeks in our vehicle, I was glad we chose this method for our North Pole adventure.

-----End Blog-----

My second longest day was yesterday (850 minutes)—about a half-hour less than day 9 in the flat country of Saskatchewan. (All Saskatchewan is flat compared to southern Yukon!)

Before, I had mentioned my destinations were based on available lodging. Today was no different.

If we would not have stopped in Nugget City (really just a gas station with cabins), I would have had a projected 138 kilometer (86 mile) mountainous journey to the next lodging. After the previous day of biking from British Columbia, I was ready for a short relaxing day.

A Norwegian archeologist arrived late in the afternoon, booked a cabin next to ours and we enjoyed an evening beer as we discussed our rides. He had flown a small plane and his bike into Prudhoe Bay in the far north oil fields of Alaska and biked south five hundred miles (800 km) to Fairbanks before heading east on the Richardson and Alaska Highway.

His European style distance bike was well packed and looked rugged. He had repaired his last rear innertube several times and asked if I had seen a bike shop. No wonder he was concerned; the first half of his route was gravel.

"Yes." I reported " There was a small bike shop shortly after entering Saskatchewan. You are about 2,500 kilometers away (~1,500 miles).

"I'm going south at the next junction." He asked, "Have you seen it?"

"Yes. It is a couple more kilometers. The intersection, on your right, will be evident," I explained.

My fellow Norwegian cyclist wanted a new backup innertube before heading south to Prince Rupert 927 kilometers (576 miles).

Although he was carrying shelter, food, and a water purifier, it was extremely unlikely he could find bicycle parts on the unpopulated Dease Lake Highway (37) or Canada Highway 16 before Prince Rupert.

"I have several extra tubes. They might fit your bike," I said and quickly went to our vehicle, pulled out a new boxed spare and handed it to him.

"Yes. This size will work, but I have Presta valves," he said with concern.

Most road bikes come equipped with metal Presta valve stems. Schrader rubber valve stems like I was using, are mainly used for bicycling around town. Fortunately, his air pump fit both types, but his next issue was rim hole size.

I explained, to my knowledge rims with steel Presta valve stems were designed large enough rubber Schraders would fit.

Satisfied…we had another beer.

The next morning, I headed west an hour before he finished restocking supplies. Water bottles sold at Nugget City were $2.50 (Canadian) for their small private-label brand bottles. His new food purchases cost less than water had he refilled all his containers.

Patricia refilled all his containers from our large 23-liter jug.

Happily, my new Norwegian friend confidently headed south. Several months after returning home, I received an email reporting details of his trip and he asked if I made it to North Pole.

Try to realize how much food and water was packed in that European bike. Consider what I ate and drank each day.

Eating pattern: My daily vitamins (taken only before ride included one glucosamine/chondroitin tablet, on krill oil capsule, one magnesium/calcium/zinc tablet, one multivitamin tablet) were standard. When available, I ate a banana one hour after starting followed by a couple peanut butter/jelly sandwiches spaced an hour apart. Snacks during the day (generally supplied by my wife) included a bakery roll or two, boiled egg(s), milk, snack crackers, candy bar; one to two protein bars and any other food that came my way during the day. I ate a huge meal in the afternoon or early evening (two meals if I completed the day by early afternoon). Generally, meals were very generous portions of pasta, potatoes, or rice. For speedy digestion, carbohydrates were the main calorie source with small meat portions.

Liquids consumed: I averaged two to three gallons (4-12 liters) of water each day. Before departing each morning I would drink twelve ounces of fortified water (as was recommended by Scheels® All Sports store in Sioux Falls, SD).[42] Those were supplemented with one to three bottles of mixed electrolyte drinks; a protein drink after completion, glass(es) of milk during meals, a beer and sometimes a glass of red wine evenings, and the normal few glasses of water (taking morning vitamins, during meals, and before bed). I tried to avoid all caffeine.

---

[42] Scheels® All Sports, now over 115 years-old, is an employee owned chain of twenty-seven retail sporting goods stores headquartered in Fargo, North Dakota. My experience shopping at Scheels® has been that they selected employees for various sports departments based on their personal experience and knowledge of that sport. After testing several models, my Trek bicycle was also purchased at Scheels® a decade earlier.

Chapter 39: 🚲 114 km/71 miles
Day 31, June 21, Nugget City to Continental Divide Lodge, YT

Depart time: 6:30 a.m.
Arrive time: 2:10 p.m.
Highways: 1
Day—total km/miles: 114/71—3,563/2,214
Day average speed: (kmph/mph): 15.9/9.9
Day—total elevation gain (m/ft): 830/2,723—12,692/41,639
Calories daily/total to date: 3,042/96,578
Daily dangers/excitement: Mountains divide water, past tunes.

Begin Blog:

Today I crossed between two of the largest river drainage systems in North America—the Mackenzie (and its tributaries which flow northward 2,650 miles eventually flow into the Beaufort Sea/Arctic Ocean) and the Yukon River drainage (after 2,300 miles empties into the Bering Sea/Pacific Ocean).

After a 70-mile ride, I am on the Continental Divide in today's blog photo.

The best way so far to describe my opinion of the Yukon is vast.

----Blog end-----

Sometimes, when a déjà vu memory occurred, or when I saw a sign like "Yukon River", or saw white-capped mountains, a lyric would repeat through my brain. Constantly repeating catchy music is called a brainworm or stuck song syndrome.

For miles, I would hum a little tune or ditty from some song of years past. That's because I really do not know lyrics of current songs. As I weaned from television the last ten years, radio and music also faded away. Hence, I had no electronic static on this trip.

When people are happy and at ease, they tend to sing, hum or whistle. Tunes were whistled when I knew only a few song lines. It was hard to whistle bicycling so I made up song lines.

While in high school, every morning and evening we listened to the radio milking cows—by hand (now a lost talent). Hand milking cows since I was six-years-old makes squeezing handlebars easy. Oh, and some study said cows liked music. At least to justify a radio in our barn, that was a good disclaimer for a teenager.

Back then, tilling summer fallow fields, dirt would fly and precious moisture would evaporate from our semi-arid fields. I would sing, hum or whistle lyrics of a current popular song. Singing was easy going into the wind and every half-mile, I would hum when dirt whirled with dust engulfing from behind.

Without a tractor cab, hot, sun beating down, with sweat collecting black dust in every follicle, sweat stream, and seam, I would hum.

Farming was often too dirty to open my mouth to sing or whistle with dry lips. Today, like nearly every day bicycling, fine dust absorbed into my sweat filled pores, and jersey.

After centuries of dust-laden snow, now I understand why glaciers melt creamy water into streams and rivers.

My body must have magnetized and collected road dust from passing vehicles—something like tilling fields. Each evening, I was always amazed at the dirty bath and shower water melting away after each ride.

Bicycling solo mile after mile, especially in the Yukon, was similar to farming by sitting on a hard tractor seat hour upon hour. It was far more beautiful than a flat dirt South Dakota field…and it can be as lonely.

One can be surrounded by all the beauty in the world, but if not loved back, it is lonely. It is nothing. Nothing! Someone to share it with makes all the difference.

Approaching four decades of marriage, I have been so fortunate to be accompanied by Patricia on this ride.

Sure, she refilled our bulk water containers along the way and restocked our groceries, especially fruits and vegetables when available. Those kind of things men often take for granted as wives organize daily living. She kept our SUV nearly full of fuel, which was normally my task. My appreciation for her goes far, far beyond those things. Patricia is a joy to be around!

Trips like this can bring out the best in people. If you make a trip to North Pole, please consider taking a loving companion along.

Personal safety was always a concern. If not a bandage to cover a gash, there was comfort knowing Patricia would have general knowledge where to look for my remains.

At the hint of a bear, buffalo, moose, wolf, or dog…a black flash, a swoosh, a feeling of being looked upon, something would trigger an adrenaline rush to quicken my pace.

Occasionally, a childhood tune would pop into my helmeted head as soft earplugs kept distractions at bay.

I could only remember, like a scratched record, a few words as Johnny Horton's voice would pop into my head and keep repeating, *North to Alaska.*[43]

For miles, I sang it this way:
North to Alaska, goin' north the rush is on.
Big Sam left Seattle in the year of ninety-two
With George Pratt his partner and brother Billy too.
They crossed the Yukon river and
Found bonanza gold
Below that old white mountain
Just south-east of Nome….
North to Alaska go north the rush is on
North to Alaska go north the rush is on.

There was one verse that I could not quite remember. It emphasized that gold in this glorious beauty was worth nothing but loneliness only solved by love and companionship.

---

[43] *North to Alaska*, the song made popular by Johnny Horton, was written by Mike Phillips with John Wayne staring in the 1960 movie.

While writing this, I searched the Internet and confirmed stale memory.

"…George turns to Sam with his gold in his hand
Said Sam you're lookin' at a lonely lonely man
I'd trade all the gold that's buried in this land
For one small band of gold to place on sweet little Jenny's hand
'Cause a man needs a woman to love him all the time
Remember Sam a true love is so hard to find
I'd build for my Jenny a honeymoon home
Below that old white mountain
Just a little south-east of Nome.
Where the river is windin' big nuggets they're findin'.
North to Alaska go north the rush is on."

Interestingly, as the song explained, George Pratt gave up Seattle with two other guys. Later, after living in the north, he was willing to give up all the gold in the land for his sweetheart, Jenny', but where did he want to live? Right here searching for big nuggets…below snow-capped mountains with the love of his life.

Time and space coaxes the mind to wander where it wants to be.

Too many people are conditioned to live where they do not want to be. Bicycling long distances identifies possibilities to reposition mentally and physically.

Horton's duplicating ditty led me to another of his songs (not necessarily the correct version) as I peddled north to the rhythm of *Battle of New Orleans*[44].

"In 1814 we took a little trip
Along with Colonel Jackson down the mighty Mississip'.
We took a little bacon, and took a little beans,
We caught the bloody British in the town of New Orleans….
We fired our guns and the British kept a-comin'.
Wasn't nigh as many as there was a while ago….

---

[44]James Corbitt Morris (aka Jimmy Driftwood), a high school principal, wrote the lyrics to *Battle of New Orleans* to get teenagers interested in history. Johnny Horton's version was the number one Billboard song of 1959.

191

They ran through the briars and they ran through the brambles,
They ran through the bushes where the rabbits couldn't go...."

My version gradually developed into this:

In two thousand eighteen I took a little trip,
With a Trek bicycle down the mighty Takhini.
I took little crackers and I took Sports Beans®.
I caught a bloody bear in my sight at least it seems.
Well, I fired up the Trek and the bears kept a comin'.
There wasn't nigh as many as there was a while ago.
On dandelions they're munchin' as I kept a runnin'
Down the Yukon River to the North Pole.

Well, I biked past the briars and I biked past the brambles
And I left the bears in bushes where the rabbits couldn't go.
They ran so fast that the flies couldn't catch 'em,
As I biked the Yukon River to the North Pole.

It is amazing how many miles can be covered by blindly occupying the mind.

Patricia took a photo today at 11:18 a.m.—the longest day of the year. Overcast sky did not emphasize the summer solstice, but as I approached the Arctic Circle, there was plenty of day to sing as I pedaled.

For hundreds of miles I focused on tall brush ahead in highway rights-of-way. It reminded me of our old work horses that were not allowed to see off to the side—only straight ahead.

Rights-of-ways were not cleared but a few feet beyond the shoulder in upper BC[45] and the Yukon Territory. Maybe every ten years or so the wild bush was wacked back to the forest line.

Up close and personal, the wilds in nature heard a strange sound going by....though singing badly. Three meters from pavement, what was lurking beyond the brush? A bicyclist?

---

[45] BC is an oft used abbreviation for the Province of British Columbia.

What's that? What flavor would it be? Would it make a good meal? Ah, maybe not worth the effort.

With excitement and wonder, I found my venture to North Pole a rush, a rush of emotion.

I biked on.

Chapter 40: 🚲 126 km/78 miles
Day 32, June 22, Continental Divide Lodge to Teslin, YK

Depart time: 5:40 a.m.
Arrive time: 1:05 p.m.
Highways: 1
Day—total km/miles: 126/78—3,689/2,292
Day average speed: (kmph/mph): 17.5/10.9
Day—total elevation gain (m/ft): 742/2,435—13,434/44,074
Calories daily/total to date: 3,585/100,163
Daily dangers/excitement: Traveling protection.

Begin Blog:

Timing is everything, especially spotting and avoiding wildlife.

I had not biked ten minutes when I began crossing a bridge. There was a multi-colored fox (mainly dark with patches of red). Likely, it was a silver fox (part of the red fox species). Later, I spotted three snowshoe hares in their brown summer coats, and a moose swimming across a lake.

Bikers try to avoid bears. Travelers in vehicles feel safe enough to stop and take photos. That brings me to today's story—timing is everything.

My total ascent today was only 2,435 feet—meaning on this 78-mile ride there were not too many hills compared to the BC Rockies. As I was part way up a long incline, I spotted a large black bear crossing the highway to my side about a half mile in front of me.

(Side note: Yukon ditches are not maintained like the rest of Canada. Trees and shrubs, up to twenty-foot tall, have regrown since the ditches were cleared and mowed several years earlier. They are much more dangerous since wildlife can suddenly appear on the road without warning.)

Back to the bear on the hill story: With all the trees and shrubs in the ditch, I lost sight of the bear. As I rode closer to where the bear had crossed, I moved to the oncoming highway shoulder. I spotted the bear walking along, head down feeding (likely on dandelion-a typical bear food this time of year). As I was anticipating sneaking by, a huge, fancy Class A RV approached from behind me and pulled into position between the bear and me. Shielded from bear, I peddled uphill as the RV stopped to take photos of the bear.

As I neared the top of the hill, two motorcyclists pulled ahead of me and waited until I arrived. They had observed the RV/bicyclist interaction and wanted to know if anyone needed help. One had not seen the bear and I explained that they thankfully stopped for a photo shoot as I escaped. He said: "Be safe" and moved on.

I had ridden for perhaps ten minutes without a vehicle passing me. At rest stops I hear people complaining about the volume of motorcyclists and campers heading north on the only highway to Alaska. I am not complaining, as one acted as my protector and the other offered help. We share the road. In this remote area, I consider them my protectors.

-----End Blog-----

The nineteenth-century classic non-fiction book "*Walden Life in the Woods*" by Henry David Thoreau (1817-1862) fell from use during the late twentieth century. His story of a simple life has been revived and touches pent-up desires for gadget-free time.

Thoreau was born only forty-one years after America's thirteen colonies declared independence from Britain. To put location, timing, the mechanical and electrical revolution, literacy and gadget-living in perspective, my disabled grandfather, born twenty-nine years after Thoreau's passing, lived with our family until I was twenty-three. Grandpa enjoyed listening to radio and what he called "figuring."

Also, like Thoreau, my grandfather enjoyed reading and drove the ten-mile roundtrip to Ipswich to get the daily newspaper. It was placed in our post office mailbox each day after it arrived by train. Reading it was grandpa's ritual—just like listening to The Old Redhead's (Arthur Godfrey) morning show on the radio.

My mother married my father at age nineteen after teaching a year in a one-room country school; then they moved to my grandfather's farm. My father passed at age 51. When mother retired from farming, she moved to Ipswich. In her eighties, while watching television she complained about the *Aberdeen News* (paper) being thrown from the vehicle onto the driveway rather than her porch. She said, "We've been getting that paper for well over sixty years; they could at least throw the paper on my steps."

In order keep the farm viable, my grandfather and father had to quit school at age ten and fourteen, respectively. Likely, they had been reading the same daily paper well before my mother arrived. The *Aberdeen News* was founded as a weekly newspaper in 1885—four years before South Dakota became a state and twenty-three years after Thoreau's passing.

Writing about life in a lone cabin on Walden Pond, Thoreau, like centuries passed, produced his own food and considered himself isolated in his remote cabin. Even in the 1800s, Thoreau was not isolated by today's Yukon standards. Occasionally, he took a day off from gardening and walked to Concord, Massachusetts for supplies and walked home. Now, two hundred years later, Concord is considered part of the heavily populated greater Boston area.

The Yukon is different than Thoreau's isolation. Even now, walking to a neighbor in the vast Yukon is measured in days.

Can you imagine heading to the Yukon or Alaska in 1896? Besides scattered natives, the interior was generally unpopulated except a few eccentrics and trappers—usually the same person. Woods. Snow. Ice. Glaciers. Unknown beasts. No roads. No bridges. No caches. No lodging. Where could food be found? How about repairs? Innovate, or…die!

August 16, 1896, my grandfather had just turned five years old when miners discovered gold in the northern Yukon. The Klondike Gold Rush was on, partially driven by the severe and continuing depression of the 1890s. To prevent starvation, Canada required a year's supply of food be carried by those heading north.

Between 1896 and the turn of the century an estimated 100,000 gold seekers, roustabouts, tradespeople, and a collection of hooligans, ruffians, and criminals found it easier to swindle than mine. Cold, food shortages, and difficult transportation were serious deterrents that returned many south.

Before the first mode of personal mechanical transportation, the bicycle, beasts of burden were dogs in North country. There were no facilities to greet prospectors or get resupplied on the way. Upon arrival, except mountains, they experienced frozen ground, snow, cold, ice, rain in spring and a chance find of gold. In summer there was no night, but hungry wolves, bears, biting flies, and mosquitos were bigger than gold nuggets with rocks to sleep upon dreaming with gold fever.

Today, all I had to do was follow a well-oiled path and cross rivers and streams on bridges. Signs directed the way. Light clothing and snacks were carried. If I biked far enough each day, hot food and hot bath awaited each evening.

With all modern transportation and communication systems, twenty-first century travelers are pampered--wussies compared to adventurers of centuries past.

Bicycling gives hints of past efforts, but easier than hiking this lonesome area. It takes far more energy, planning, determination, and stamina than driving.

My goal was to present this trip as a doable challenge for many.

When our children were given challenges as teenagers, they responded: "The time of suffering is over." Their meaning was to take the easy way. Drive to school or work--not walk or bicycle the four blocks or so. Opulent lives have blinded many to the struggles of the past or the drudgery of others trying to provide daily food, clothing and shelter for their family.

Eight decades ago for a year-and-a-half, my father bicycled ten miles roundtrip through dust, mud and frozen ground to high school, until he, at age fourteen, had to quit high school because he could no longer keep up with demands from the farm as the sole son of my disabled grandfather.

After all, this is the twenty-first century. Yes, the time of physical suffering may be over for those that will never experience physical adventure. Yet, opportunity exists.

Those trapped in a synthetic world are oblivious to nature. Fortunately, today all our children and grandchildren enjoy outings, seek nature, and plan challenging activities with their families and friends. We are so proud of their exemplary lifestyles.

Yesterday, for the third time, I crossed a continental divide. Before arriving at North Pole, I peddled in four continental drainage areas.

Continental divides are determined by water flow.

My trip originated in Pierre, South Dakota, on the Missouri River. The Missouri and Mississippi River watersheds run south eventually emptying into the Gulf of Mexico and Atlantic Ocean.

In northcentral North Dakota, south of Minot, I crossed the North American north/south continental divide. It was generally flat with a few rolling hills.

Continental divides, with water flowing in different directions, was not noticeable, even on a bicycle.

Some days I crossed up to five river systems. Most drained into a common river. They did not the last couple days. Each time I crossed passes between river systems the road lead me up then down, only to be led up and down into the next drainage area.

I found I had to save my legs advancing each mountain pass, because I did not know how many more I would approach the next hour or the next day.

Beginning in Pierre until day five of my trip, waters flowed south—eventually into the Gulf of Mexico. After leaving Bismarck before I reached Minot, waters began flowing northeast and eventually emptied into the Hudson Bay on to the Labrador Sea.

The next water system divide (continental divide) was near Lonira, Alberta. As I pedaled northwest of Mayerthorpe beginning day seventeen, waters accumulated and flowed into the

Saskatchewan River basin and eventually into the massive Hudson Bay of the north Atlantic Ocean.

As I approached Whitecourt, later that same day, water flowed into the Athabasca River. That drained into the tundra laden delta of the Mackenzie River and eventually emptied into the perpetually frozen Beaufort Sea of the Arctic Ocean.

Yesterday (riding day 32) I crossed the mountainous continental divide that separated the Mackenzie River system and the Yukon drainage area. The Yukon River and its tributaries drain northern parts of British Columbia, much of the Yukon Territory and virtually all of central Alaska.

With global warming, the last ice-age subsided. Glaciers receded to the north. A flat glaciated plain drained its discharge south, north, east and west. However, glaciers remain in the upper elevations of northern mountains and are still changing water flows as I will detail on cycling day 36.

Glaciers are minor today compared to the last Ice Age when glacial ice sheets were a couple miles (3000 meters) thick as they moved across North America.

Glaciation is still noticeable on my farm in northern South Dakota.

Massive global warming changed centuries of global cooling and melted all ice sheets in the far northeast tip of what is now South Dakota, North Dakota, and most of Canada.

Our farm, for example, is littered with well-rounded rocks smoothed and strewn by the last glaciers—remnants of massive melts a few thousand years earlier. To the south and east of our farm glacial moraines pushed soil and rocks hundreds of feet high.

A few thousand years ago, before people claimed to change climate, a very quick climate change forced glaciers to melt and send water south. Fast melting caused glacial moraines blocking south flows. Glaciers continued to melt and recede. Remaining North American glaciers melting ice and releasing water continues to this day by either draining north to the North Atlantic, Arctic, northern Pacific Oceans or their supplying seas (Labrador, Beaufort, and Bering Sea).

As you will read later, the glaciers have not completely disappeared. I rode over many, many miles of their remnants. If you make this trip, you too can actually feel the glaciers melting below your tires.

Divide after continental divide, all forty days of this trip, were impossible to replicate from a vehicle.

Freedom, pleasantries, exertion, adrenaline peaks, sights, sounds, smells, satisfaction, interaction with nature, wind, mist and bugs in face, all are unfortunately avoided in an enclosed vehicle.

Loud vehicles and louder motorcyclists may be attempting to see the freedom of nature, but they scurry wildlife miles ahead of them. Is that riding in nature? Far from it! Fortunately, bicyclist and hikers actually see, smell, hear, and touch nature.

Combustion engine technology, pollution control systems, and quiet mufflers have made it a pleasure to drive from place to place with very little noise or disturbance. Electric vehicles are even quieter without noise pollution. However, it may be years before northern British Columbia, the Yukon and much of Alaska has reliable electrical recharge stations at intervals adequate for electric vehicle owners.

Battery (electric) assisted bicycle owners need to seriously consider vast distances, and many mountain passes before attempting the Alaska Highway. Before departure, I was encouraged to use an e-bike. My ten-year-old Trek was adequate and I did not have to worry about finding electricity and charging its battery.

Explorers of centuries past would have considered it preposterous to assume bicycling on paved roads to North Pole was challenging or dangerous.

Early American explorers ventured into Alaska to get rich or be isolated. True fools wanted both. Opposing original intent, most flocked to settlements or created them. Were most different from today's travelers who drive to Alaska expecting adventure?

You know what I saw passing me?

Some were job seekers. Most sped through the Yukon towards Alaska because they had little money and sought higher paying jobs. Others went because they could afford hotels, fancy RVs, or trucks pulling monstrous campers. Many annoying decked-out motorcyclists were seeing how many miles in a day they could cover. I talked to many checking into lodging or while dining.

Most are really, really good people.

Adventure, like money and fame, are fleeting. It is not around the next corner or over the next mountain. It is in the heart and mind, not vehicle. Few stop for hours just to see, hear, smell, and feel nature. You cannot avoid nature on a bicycle, but you can pity those with earbuds.

As a societal explorer, I love to see new places, new sights, new cultures, new things, and have new experiences. One is truly blessed when doing such with their spouse.

The Yukon Territory is vast. Vast. The best way to describe it is probably with stories, legends and songs, like Jonny Horton's *North to Alaska*.

As an older guy on a bicycle, the rush was no longer a search for gold but a rush to get up the next morning and a rush of excitement, learn new things, to see sights and sounds of what the new day would bring.

Yukon and Alaska compound the rush. Reality was truly strange when heading north to Alaska.

Chapter 41: 🚲 117 km/73 miles
Day 33, June 23, Teslin to Marsh Lake, YT

Depart time: 5:01 a.m.
Arrive time: 12:55 p.m.
Highways: 1
Day—total km/miles: 117/73—3,806/2,365
Day average speed: (kmph/mph): 17.9/11.1
Day—total elevation gain (m/ft): 656/2,152—14,090/46,226
Calories daily/total to date: 3,398/103,561
Daily dangers/excitement: Local's survival.

Begin Blog:

Wildlife can be a term applied to people living in remote places, like the Yukon. Today, I will relate a couple stories of how society changes with development.

Normally, I take a few short breaks during the day. Seldom are they over 15 minutes. On a cool, but sunny, day at a rest area surrounded by snowy mountains, a local older gentleman started visiting with me.

Besides asking where are you going and coming from, he said he had visited the Dakotas when he was younger and living in Saskatchewan. He moved to the Yukon Territory in 1986. He said, "Once you get settled up here you can't go back."

He went on to tell me how things are changing. I want to relay his points.

He started explaining, "Things are changing up here. There are 35,000 people in the Yukon and 20,000 live in Whitehorse. It's growing. People are bringing their ideas on how to change things." He continued, "A while back, a landslide closed the road (Alaska Highway) between Teslin and Whitehorse. What do you think was the first thing the stores ran out of?"

I responded, "Likely toilet paper."

"No," he said, "Bottled water. Can you believe it? Bottled water!"

He went on to show me a phone-type gadget (today's blog photo) he was using when I arrived. He was sending a text to a friend a couple hundred miles away. He said, "Satellite phones are expensive. You can burn up 200 minutes quickly, and it costs $300 a month. The thing costs $400 plus $70 a month and I can send a text to anybody in the world who has a cell phone with one of these (InReach®[46] Explorer, by Delorme).

"It works off satellite and, in an emergency, you just hit this button and someone answers and sends help. My buddy had to do it and they sent a helicopter in after him. Cell phones don't have much coverage up here, but anyone with one of these can track me wherever I go. You need this for your bicycle. That way your wife always knows where you are at."

It was very obvious to me, this older guy found, and was using, technology very appropriate for his environment—the Yukon.

As we were finishing our visit, a fully loaded bicyclist pulled up to visit. He had made eleven trips across Canada and last year biked across Australia. He said he was heading to Whitehorse tonight (another 50 miles). I mentioned I was going there tomorrow. He said, "At least we will have good roads the rest of the way. All countries in the world have good roads into their capital. Roads are a political thing."

It is amazing what one can learn at a Yukon rest stop in an hour about the world's changing culture.

-----End Blog-----

Looking at today's total accumulated distance of 3,806 kilometers (2,365 miles), I realized it was as if I bicycled 3,934 kilometers across

---

[46] InReach® is a trademark of DeLorme and Garmin Ltd. Company.

Australia from Sydney to Perth. Though I have over a thousand kilometers remaining, I have gone about as far as it is from Mexico City (in southcentral Mexico) to Estevan, Saskatchewan (3,972 km) where I spent my first night in Canada.

Each biking trip is different.

To get a feel of how some mornings begin, perhaps the best explanation was described in my daily journal:

"I thought I saw a part of a blown tire on the opposite side of the Highway ahead. As I got closer, it moved. The porcupine fanned out its quills with back toward me. Spines were tall on top rear and got shorter in a circular, more whitish, pattern near the anus.

"A few miles later a roadkill porcupine was killed overnight with a black raven pulling out its guts.

"A beaver was walking beside the road as it followed above Nisutlin Lake.

"Patricia began following me early, around 9:30. She noticed a small black bear in the ditch that I did not see."

Patricia was earlier than normal. I departed at 5:01 and did not think about why she caught up with me so early. I should have. With many bears in the area and little traffic very early mornings, maybe she thought a rogue grizzly was on the prowl.

Teslin had many places to lodge, but a music festival scheduled for the weekend filled all rooms by noon. Before I arrived 1:05 p.m. that Friday, Patricia had asked multiple establishments for any possible lodging. Based on a tip, she found a sparse room in the upstairs of a homemade cabin. I reported in my journal, "Very rustic room; plywood frame around tub and sink."

It was not until later Patricia revealed a morning conversation with the owner. The Yukoner related how his wife had left him and she could take advantage of an opportunity to stay in the Yukon. Patricia could not get packed and on the road fast enough!

In a rush to depart, she left our small cooler on the makeshift porch. A few miles down the road, Patricia realized her loss and seriously considered abandoning the cooler. Perhaps the guy would think she was returning for a Yukon opportunity.

Patricia turned around; dashed back; grabbed the cooler; threw it in our vehicle and took off before another kind of prowler reappeared.

Bare is spelled two ways and I should have been concerned about both.

Fortunately, having grown up on a ranch, Patricia, though petite, could handle herself. Her parent's Dakota ranch was so remote there were no school buses. She had to work for room and board in town during her high school years.

So many things happened on this trip—it is mind-boggling.

Most of the time we did not report viewings, because such events were happening all the time—usually with bigger animals. Up to this day, I had not seen a porcupine or beaver on the Highway. Today, they justified journal entry.

A guy with a loaded bicycle at a nice rest area showed me his map with markups of all the long-distance rides he has taken in Canada. Obviously, he was prepared for the trip.

For over two thousand miles, having a loving companion to carry my gear (maybe a tenth of what he toted), I was able to travel many more miles per day. Luckily, I did not have to camp, cook meals, carry as much food, bear protection, nor solar panels to charge gadgets.

Look closely at today's blog photo. You can see a bike under his stuff—someplace.

As a former corporate safety administrator, he designed his outfit to be viewable.

This fellow basically carried everything he needed--tent, sleeping bag, cooking gear, days of food, water purifier, tools, tubes, even toilet paper.

Compare his needs with someone living in a house or apartment in the Territorial Capitol, Whitehorse. Their daily services (electricity, running water, sewer, garage, police, fire, medical, and etcetera) were supplied by those I term the Faceless generation[47].

---

[47] Gary W. Wietgrefe, *Learning as it influences the 21ˢᵗ century*, *Relating to Ancient* series, copyright 2018, pp. 117-118, 121, 397-398.

205

Before I left this rest area, a gentleman arrived in a pickup truck, and described current Whitehorse. He was upset describing newcomers who call Yukon home.

A few months earlier, a landslide blocked the ALCAN preventing supply trucks from arriving. As soon as that news was reported on radio and social media, Whitehorse residents flocked to the stores to get bottled water.

Are they any different than in your town or city?

They should be!

First, Whitehorse in the Yukon is remote.

Secondly, one would expect rational adults would have their homes supplied with necessities—at least for a few days because of their remoteness and no sun in the dead of winter.

Thirdly, it has only been one, or at most two, generations since all Yukon residents were responsible for all their food, clothing, and shelter. Recent social engineering programs provide a crutch not only for the poor and destitute, but to the general public.

That brings me to point four—the main question: Why was bottled water the first thing in Whitehorse to run out?

Some of the most abundant and freshest water in the world is in the Yukon and northern Canada. The mighty Yukon River runs through Whitehorse. Incorporated towns and cities throughout Canada have drinking water piped to their homes.

Someone a few years ago pointed out Canada and the United States were the only countries in the world where all toilets are flushed with drinking water.

Survival is at stake.

The old guy (maybe my age) had lived in the Yukon thirty-two years—since 1986. He feared for the livelihood of his fellow citizens. That was why he related the mudslide and road closure before asking: "What do you think was the first thing the stores run out of?"

He was afraid Whitehorse residents could no longer survive there.

How could a simple thing like bottled water be a necessity when millions of gallons of free-flowing water were going by every hour?

His one question did raise a series of others.

Were Whitehorse residents no longer drinking tap water?

Were they so affluent they could afford bottled water?

Did people really think bottled water was safer and fresher than boiled water dipped from the Yukon?

Is transportation fuel and labor so cheap that a readily available commodity, water, can be bottled and trucked from some distant industrial purifier?

Was there no concern about Yukon trash dumps being filled with plastic water bottles (that would take centuries to decompose—if ever in the permafrost)? Alternatively, does plastic now require a two-way freight and labor bill to recycle?

If demand was really so high for bottled water, wasn't there an entrepreneur in Whitehorse competent to identify the desire for commercially purified water? Or, has laziness, or inability to innovate, permeated developed society now unable to purify water like the world's poorest countries?

Have mega-corporations manufactured disposable containers, including water, and promoted them to the point consumers believe they are a required purchase?

Has society become so economically affluent that wants are confused with needs?

These fundamental questions have threatened my confidence in twenty-first century culture and our ability to learn, rationalize, and react based on reality rather than marketing.

That gentleman hit a fundamental point of modern society. Have people in cities and even small towns, like Whitehorse (population 25,085 in 2016), lost their survival skills?

When a naturally occurring mudslide can cause irrational reactions, what is next?

A required 5,000-kilometer bike ride?

Gary W. Wietgrefe

Chapter 42: 🚲 68 km/42 miles
Day 34, June 24, Marsh Lake to Whitehorse, YT

Depart time: 9:40 a.m.
Arrive time: 12:35 p.m.
Highways: 1
Day—total km/miles: 68/42—3,874/2,407
Day average speed: (kmph/mph): 19.2/11.9
Day—total elevation gain (m/ft): 297/974—14,387/47,200
Calories daily/total to date: 2,201/105,762
Daily dangers/excitement: Yukon Capitol City.

Begin Blog:

Today's short ride was quite enjoyable for several reasons: First, I was able to sleep in and enjoy the breakfast at The Old Screen Door B&B on Marsh Lake; second, the proprietor sent me off with four fresh oatmeal/chocolate chip cookies; third, I had wind to my back which made the 42 miles seem short; and lastly, my wife and I got to spend several hours walking around and enjoying the quaint little city of Whitehorse (the only city in the Yukon Territory).

Today's blog photo is of the Klondike. It was one of the last paddleboats hauling ore and supplies on the Yukon River. It operated into the 1950s with two 500 horsepower steam-driven piston motors powered by a huge boiler requiring a man to feed it a five-foot log every 30 seconds. Each worked four-hour shifts and were paid $25 monthly.

It took a day and half to go down river (north) to Dawson City and six days to return to Whitehorse. Loggers built stations along the route to reload the 240-foot ore boat.

208

It could operate in very shallow water with three-and-a-half-foot draft. In today's blog photo notice the top cable supports. They operated like a cable suspension bridge with the cables tightened or loosened to keep the boat bottom from sagging to minimize how deep it sat in the water.

Canada Parks conducted tours on the dry docked Klondike during the summer which we greatly enjoyed.

Just a brief background on the Yukon Gold rush of 1896-1899. The North American economy was in a depression when gold was discovered at the confluence of the Klondike and Yukon Rivers August 16, 1896.

The Yukon Territory had very few people back then and no organized transportation system. Yet, that fall when news of the Klondike Gold Strike hit the daily papers in San Francisco and Seattle, it created up to 100,000 "Klondikers" to head into the unknown.

As the rush built, the Canadian government stepped in to require each prospector to bring a year's supply of food to prevent starvation. Gold made some rich, but hand mining was tough even in summer picking into permafrost.

Latecomers, with government requirements of volume and weight, arrived by 1899 when gold was discovered in Nome, Alaska creating the Alaska Gold Rush.

Dawson City boomed with an estimated 30,000 population in 1899 which soon crashed as heavier mining equipment moved in, and Klondikers moved out.

In 2016, Dawson City had an estimated population of 1,375.

Before I started my bike journey in May, I read the 1990 book by Harry Gordon-Cooper called "Yukoners True Tales of the Yukon."

One such story was of Fred Guder a seventy-eight year-old who annually carried his tent, small stove, clothes, blankets, and food the 300 miles from Whitehorse to Dawson each spring. For 14 straight days he walked about 20 miles a day on the Dawson Trail sleeping and eating at roadhouses along the way.

Guder, who died in 1984, credited his long life and "abundant good health" to "...the simple rigorous life he had." This is a great example of living in the Yukon where Guinness Book of World Records now rates Whitehorse the city with the world's lowest air pollution.

-----End Blog-----

My yesterday's reproof questioning the rationale of bottled water may make more sense after reading today's blog.

An old guy, a little older than me--in his seventies, annually walked three hundred miles carrying his shelter, clothing, cooking equipment and stove for an opportunity to live "...the simple rigorous life...."

We all should take opportunities when they are available. Old Fred Guder slept and ate in roadhouses that for decades catered to the needs of Yukon adventurers traveling north.

My readers may rightly ask, "OK smart guy, what would you have done if a landslide, or other calamity prevented you from reaching food and lodging each night?"

Great question.

As previously mentioned, we carried no tent, but every day I carried a very light emergency sleeping bag (bivy) on my bike. In case of a blown tire or other reason Patricia could not meet me, I wanted to be protected from the elements.

Mosquitos and biting flies were always pests. Nights were cool—sometimes cold.

Although only a couple times did I see snow flurries where I biked, fresh blankets of light snow covered mountains during some days. Mountaintops were especially brilliant in morning after fresh snow.

My emergency rolled bag was adequate and soon proved useful. I kept it in a four-inch (10 cm.) diameter roll on the back rack behind my seat. Fortunately, I did not have to use it, my nephew did.

The following fall, on an elk hunting trip in the mountains of western Colorado, my nephew backpacked into an area with a friend carrying hunting gear, food and sleeping bag—no tent. Weight is always an issue backpacking, but I sent my emergency sleeping bag with him. Fortunately, it was waterproof! He used it inside his sleeping bag sleeping dryly each night in misty ice and snow.

What did I do for food when none was available?

See Appendix 2; especially note the categories Nutrition, Backup Supplies, and Emergency Protection.

From a practical standpoint, we consumed from vehicle supplies I had planned, purchased and packed before departure.

For example, Patricia and I stayed at a bed and breakfast overlooking Marsh Lake last night. Our room was immaculate, our hosts were very gracious, and the breakfast fantastic. Did I mention dinner? NO. It was a bed and breakfast.

Upon arrival, we visited with our hosts. While I cleaned up and washed my daily uniform, Patricia, using our hosts kitchen, prepared an early dinner from supplies we carried in our vehicle—vegetables, pasta, canned meats, and fruit which Patricia resupplied when available on our journey north.

Our vehicle contained sleeping bags and a padded futon in case we had to sleep in our vehicle some nights. Besides a couple boxes of food, a compact stove, two chairs, and fishing gear were also packed in our vehicle.

Day after day I biked consuming 3,312 calories on average—plus probably another 1,200 to 1,500 calories when not on the bike. I was maintaining my weight, though my muscles were in a different shape than when I departed May 20th.

Had we been trapped, unable to travel for a couple weeks, I believe we could have survived off our packed food supplies, and maybe even supplemented them with a few fish I would have hoped to catch.

Next question: Where would we get water if remotely trapped?

Daily, I consumed about two gallons of water while biking, but I only carried just over half that amount. In our vehicle, before departure I had filled a six-gallon (23 liters) jug of drinking water besides two individual gallon (each 3.8 liters) containers. During the day, I refilled from the gallon jugs.

In case of emergency, like being abandoned on the road, or trapped for a week, I carried a bottle of iodine tablets. Concentrated iodine purifies. I never wanted to run out of water. Remember my story, day 9, running short between Weyburn and Davidson, Saskatchewan?

Some may ask, "Can't water contaminated with iodine hurt you?"

Yes. In heavy concentrations iodine can cause loose bowels but drinking water straight from even fresh Yukon streams can infest your system with parasites, like the protozoa, giardia. Not only does iodine kill bacteria, it also purifies water containing protozoa and viruses.

I carried iodine tablets and would have used my handkerchief or jersey to filter water before adding iodine.

Every organ and tissue in the human body contains iodine. It was less than a century ago that iodine was commercially added to salt to prevent goiters. Besides the leading cause of goiters, iodine deficiency lowers mental capacity (IQ). A 1990 report from the United Nations World Summit for Children found that two billion children worldwide were iodine deficient enough to affect their learning abilities. [48] People, especially children, should not avoid iodized salt.

There is a twenty-first century "health" fad away from using iodized salt. Apparently, iodine abstinence has caused mental lapses. Yes, people get permanently dumber when not consuming adequate iodine.

Fear exists. People love fear. Radio, television, news, and social media feed fear to sell products few need.

When I typed "Should I drop use of iodized salt" in my Internet browser, 59,100,000 responses were available. You can spend the rest of your life reading those. Wherever you live in the world, I would say yes, keep using iodized salt.

Excess salt is not good for you, but if you are active, especially a long-distance cyclist, absolutely keep your sodium intake up. I nearly passed out (day 9) because I did not.

---

[48] Frank Fournier, Sustainable Elimination of Iodine Deficiency, progress since the 1990 world summit for children, UNICEF/HQ098-0761/Frank Fournier.

Four propane gas cylinders were also in our vehicle for our compact stove which could have been used to cook and purify water by boiling.

Since we were in the biggest town, only city, in the Yukon Territory, soon after arrival I enjoyed a family sized pizza and a tall beer at Boston Pizza (a Canada based international restaurant chain). That was followed by an early relaxing dinner with Patricia in another pleasing street-side cafe.

In the afternoon, we took a tour of the Dawson City to Whitehorse 240 foot (73 m) paddlewheel boat. We walked throughout Whitehorse. Especially enjoyable was the (Yukon) River walk—a great walking and bicycle trail.

Whitehorse was appreciated because it was the last population center for restaurants and supplies until we reached Fairbanks, Alaska 950 kilometers (590 miles) northwest.

In case of an emergency, remember Whitehorse has a hospital and medical facilities. There are no others until Fairbanks.

Renewed, I was ready the next morning to bike the long hill out of Whitehorse as most of the town lies in a valley tucked along the Yukon River.

The ALCAN is an international highway. Those Australian visitors, especially children, by this time may be asking, "Are we there yet? How far is North Pole?"

For two winters since retirement my wife and I stayed on the east coast of Australia--about halfway between their largest and third largest cities (Sydney and Brisbane). My remaining distance is like biking between those two cities—daunting.

Chapter 43: 🚴 156 km/97 miles
Day 35, June 25, Whitehorse to Haines Junction, YT

Depart time: 5:53 a.m.
Arrive time: 3:33 p.m.
Highways: 1
Day—total km/miles: 156/97—4,030/2,504
Day average speed: (kmph/mph): 17.4/10.8
Day—total elevation gain (m/ft): 510/1,674—14,897/48,874
Calories daily/total to date: 4,238/110,000
Daily dangers/excitement: Ancient history.

Begin Blog:

Too many times Yukon history begins with the 1898 Yukon Gold Rush. In fact, human artifacts here date back thousands of years.

Stopping at rest areas (about half even have pit toilets) proved a good break for my legs and mind since I do not listen to music or radio while biking. I can hear traffic coming and it is becoming a personal contest to identify the upcoming vehicle without looking in my mirror. Good ear training—kind of like I did in the military 45 years ago.

Anyway, Yukon rest area signage is being developed to relate more to natural habitat, wildlife migration, and human history of the Yukon.

In today's blog photo I zoomed in on a small part of First Nation cultural history. If a bison rib was found incised (etched) 2000-4000 years ago, there is much history to discover in the Yukon besides repercussions of gold fever.

-----End Blog-----

For this long ride, I left early. Not too far out of Whitehorse, I saw a woman running her sled dogs in the ditch. Based on the well-worn trail, this must have been a regular year-around exercise path.

These were work dogs. To keep them in shape and to keep them from overheating, she likely trained very early on summer mornings.

All dogs have a purpose— cattle and sheep herding, guarding, hunting, drug sniffing, cadaver searching, to annoy and be pets.

In the north, they now mainly guard property. Historically, dogs, like Siberian huskies, were used as the main mode of winter transportation. Even in the twentieth century, dogs were used to haul mail and supplies to and from remote settlements.

To keep up the tradition, The Yukon Quest Sled Dog Race has been held annually since 1984. Simply called Yukon Quest, it is roughly a thousand mile (~1,600 km) race each February between Fairbanks, Alaska and Whitehorse, Yukon Territory.

Dogs can be dropped at checkpoints (roughly every two hundred miles—320 km) where veterinarians check the well-being of the dogs and medical staff check mushers.

Bitter, bitter cold, mainly along the frozen Yukon River, a dozen dogs or so pull a loaded sled of up to 250 pounds (113 kg) and musher following an historic, pre-selected route. Even if the trail passed remote outposts, teams would be disqualified if assisted or resupplied. All the dog food, clothes, shelter and other gear must be carried by each participant between checkpoints.

It is not a race for the timid, or those (like Patricia and I) who seek continuous summer.

Training new dogs is done year-around. Perhaps I biked by a Yukon Quest team training this morning.

Regarding remoteness, hopefully readers are not bored with my bear stories. If you do not want them, do not take this ride! It may be best to quote from my journal:

"One bear crossed the Highway about a quarter mile in front of me. I pulled to a stop and waited. When a vehicle approached from the opposite direction (a lady in a pickup truck), the bear ran to a large rock overlooking the ditch. The lady opened her window and asked if I had seen the bear. As she pulled away, I went to the opposite side of the road and the large black bear watched as I passed."

In these situations, I constantly had to make decisions whether to stop, advance, or wait for a vehicle to assist in distracting the bear. I NEVER turned around. The last thing I wanted was a bear chasing me when I could not see it.

The right response would be the one where you did not get mauled or killed.

Dressed in a flashy yellow jacket or, when warm enough, a chartreuse jersey, I would stand by my bike to look large and always prepared to raise the bike over my head to appear even larger. Never did I want to appear distracted, and I deliberately avoided eye contact.

This was a very long stretch. Maybe you would be interested in other journal notes from today's ride:

"There were lots of large gophers, maybe a half pound each. They weighed more than our South Dakota pasture gophers, but smaller than prairie dogs.

"Nine miles of road construction. Quite rough. My mirror fell off.

"Took lots of flower photos."

This country is not all trees. Actually, they struggle to survive at higher elevations where shrubs are more prevalent. In places soil (accumulated since the last glacial period) was sparse, or it has eroded. Flowery weeds seem to survive best attracting and supporting bees and birds.

As mentioned in today's blog, this area has been settled for thousands of years. Ancient residents hunted caribou among other game. Artifacts, over 9,000 years-old, have been found intact from melting ice and excavated including decorated, hand-thrown wooden arrows with sinew, feathers, and stone points.

Roughly halfway between Whitehorse and Haines Junction was a cosmopolitan sounding spot called Champagne Landing. It had a handful of people—sometimes. That was where I read markers about First Nations' heritage.

Champagne was a resupply site Jack Dalton established in the late 1800s on his namesake, the Dalton Trail, from Haines, Alaska to the northern Yukon gold fields. Haines was the shortest port with access to the Pacific Ocean.

As I approached Haines Junction, over roughly a forty-mile arch, the Highway gradually turned following its northwest path; then it bent west with the last few miles going directly south—toward glaciated mountains.

Haines Junction functioned as a major supply intersection between what is now the Alaska Highway and (Yukon) Highway 3. From Haines Junction, Highway 3 surprisingly heads almost directly south 238 kilometers (148 miles). Through mountains of extreme southwest Yukon and extreme northwest British Columbia, it ends in the deep fiord tipped town of Haines in southeast Alaska. We took that route on the way home.

Chapter 44: 156 km/97 miles
Day 36, June 26, Haines Junction to Destruction Bay, YT

Depart time: 5:40 a.m.
Arrive time: 5:35 p.m.
Highways: 1
Day—total km/miles: 156/97—4,186/2,601
Day average speed: (kmph/mph): 18.3/11.4
Day—total elevation gain (m/ft): 950/3,117—15,847/51,991
Calories daily/total to date: 4,498/114,498
Daily dangers/excitement: Glaciers.

Begin Blog:

I checked weather before I departed each morning. Today it was 35°F (1.7°C). That's the coldest morning so far. What should I expect? The clue: We stayed at the foot of Canada's tallest mountain (Mount Logan) in the Glacier View Motel.

Notice in today's blog photo my early morning shadow (lower left) stretched towards the mountains. Also, notice a faint glow above my head. I'm obviously in God's country.

I dressed in my usual gear, including my yellow jacket which I planned to wear rarely. Patricia bought me winter gloves in Alberta, and I have worn them five days. Today, I wore them all morning.

Until I read signs for helicopter and plane rides "Over the world's largest ice field outside the polar regions", I had no idea this part of the Yukon was so mountainous.

Not only is Mount Logan Canada's highest at 19,541 feet, but it is second in North America to Alaska's Denali. Mount Saint Elias at 18,009 feet (in this same range) straddles the Yukon/Alaska border and is the second highest in both countries.

Biking below majestic mountains and glaciers makes the eight Dall sheep, a black bear beside me popping out of the roadside brush and waiting for a small grizzly to cross before me seems minor by comparison.

-----End Blog-----

Today's distance matched yesterday's long day (156 km/97 miles). It was the first, and only time during the whole trip back-to-back days had the same distance. Today started with a climb out of Haines Junction about seven miles (~11 km). It was gradual but certainly noticeable on a bike.

Going uphill to transfer power to pedals, my hands had to grip the handlebars tighter than normal riding. Doing so, at about eight-miles-per-hour (13 kmph), converted to a windchill of 28°F (-2°C). Even with thick leather gloves, my hands got cold and stayed cold most of the morning.

Patricia caught up with me around 11:00 a.m. She then went ahead and reserved a room at a wide spot in the road, Destruction Bay, overlooking Lake Kluane 106 kilometers (64 miles) from Haines Junction.

It is hard to remember all details, but according to my journal, some of today's bear hid in the roadside brush and waited for three vehicles to pass it and me. I think we surprised each other as it rushed across the road, then turned and watched me as I picked up exit speed hoping vehicles remained a diversion.

About ten miles (16 km) further, a young (yearling?), perhaps a grizzly bear, crossed the Highway while I watched. It was lighter color—kind of golden.

Destruction Bay, I hoped had some rooms remaining when Patricia arrived about noon, which had a small store, gasoline, and a few rooms behind it.

This was the only day on the whole ride where I biked past lodging; returned to it and picked up where I left off the previous afternoon. Another blessing of having a companion.

After nearly a hundred miles (160 km) I was starting to wear down due to distance and construction. Cold, the distracting beauty of flowers, wildlife, lakes and rivers below snow-covered mountains kept me serene.

Patricia met me at day's end and hauled me and my bike back through patch-after-patch of muddy construction to Destruction Bay lodging. The next morning she packed early and returned me through the muck where I had left off.

As you will soon read, it was a full day.

Sorry for getting off on a day's end tangent, but I thought it was important for you to understand how the rest of my day progressed.

About ten o'clock this morning, I stopped about thirty miles short of Destruction Bay. Sitting on a dry log amongst glaciated rocks I peacefully reminisced my trip thus far in two short videos.

Silver Creek was notable for its short-lived gold rush in 1903-1904. (Those dates reminded me that my grandfather had completed his formal education in 1901 when he graduated fourth grade.) Although about a hundred meters across (560 ft), the flowing Silver Creek crossed under the Alaska Highway through a large culvert into Lake Kluane.

Alaska Highway skirts the south side of the 30-mile (50 km) Lake Kluane then crossed Slims River Bridge. It was very evident Slims River drained glaciers, or at least it did until glaciers melted enough to divert the flow away from Slims River which was the major water supply for Lake Kluane.

This area is a geological and climatological wonder.

Throughout pre-history and history, massive ice fields including Kaskawulsh glacier drained southeast into the Pacific Ocean through what we now call the Alaska panhandle (southeast Alaska). However, the last three centuries, Kaskawulsh drainage flowed northwest ending in the Bering Sea through Lake Kluane and extended drainage system.

Scientists believe the Slims River, now basically dry, is only about 300 to 350 years old.

Around the year 1700, commonly referred to as the "Little Ice Age", the Kaskawulsh glacier advanced diverting summer drainage from the Kaskawulsh River. As the seasons cooled, drainage eventually formed the Slims River filling Lake Kluane.

Through climatic cycling, it warmed again. Glacial movement slowed with melt gradually diverted back to the Kaskawulsh River reducing Slims River flow and hence less water to maintain Lake Kluane.[49]

As Lake water dropped, glaciated clay island sediment has formed on both sides of the Slims River Bridge.

It was windy today (and apparently not unusual) as downdrafts swept through the Slims River valley. Dust clouds engulfed my bridge crossing.

With wind pushing me, I arrived earlier than planned at the Thachal Dhal Visitor Centre a mile past Slims River Bridge. Not only was this a good place to rest, it had a small inside display, a helpful guide, outdoor restrooms, and on the visitor's deck were two spotting scopes mounted for visitors to view Dall sheep on Thachal Dhal (formerly Sheep Mountain) meaning "skin scraper mountain" in native Tutchone.

Fortunately, using the scopes, I was able to spot young nestling Dall lambs high on the mountain beyond bears as adult sheep grazed sparse vegetation.

Before departing the visitor's center, a group of six bicyclists, packed for long distance, stopped for a needed break as they had been fighting the 25 to 30-kilometer (15-20 mph) wind pushing me. The group started a week or so earlier in Anchorage. They had flown in with their bicycles and gear intending to take advantage of Canadian cycling with predominantly westerly winds. Not today. Wind caused a detectable bicker.

Their wind obstacle was a pleasant blessing pushing me as I pedaled on the highway channeled between Lake Kluane and Thachal Dhal (mountain) to Destruction Bay.

Tailwind, half-hour videoing, and a half-hour visitor center stop still allowed me to arrive our Destruction Bay lodging at 12:35 p.m.

---

[49] Jillian Rogers, Retreating Yukon glacier makes river disappear, June 22, 2016, https://khns.org/retreating-yukon-glacier-makes-river-disappear.

Since Patricia had already confirmed and paid for our lodging, I had a snack and decided to keep biking north in the afternoon, ending twenty miles or so (30+ km) past Burwash Landing while taking advantage of the tailwind.

Construction was a mess. Permafrost heaves and regular repair were bad enough. I found commiserating with vacationers enjoyable during waits for pilot cars. Meanwhile, construction crews constantly pumped water from the lake and spread it on the Highway to ensure an adequate pack before gravel was reapplied.

Cars, RVs, and campers were muddier than my bike. Likely, because construction delayed their arrival, all drove even faster after construction spots which varied from a hundred meters to several miles.

At one stop, I was third in line behind a camper and a car waiting for the construction pilot car. As we departed behind the pilot vehicle, I could not keep pace with vehicles behind me. Ignoring my safety, they had to pass forcing me to the muddier, loose gravel shoulder. Splattered? Surely!

Worse, some campers and RVs passed so close through muddy gunk that I could have punched the side of their vehicle. Not just one!

They were literally inches from my left **wrist support bar**. Because I was only going about twenty kilometers-per-hour (12 mph), twice I was tempted to punch the soft RV/camper siding just to get their attention.

After 2,600 miles (4,186 km) of solo conditioning, my road-rage temptation was not flamed—well, maybe a pilot light, though a bang on the side seemed appropriate.

After returning, again through miles of construction, to Destruction Bay, we dined in their small café overlooking mountain-lined Lake Kluane.

I slept well.

Chapter 45: 140 km/87 miles
Day 37, June 27, Destruction Bay to Beaver Creek, YT

Depart time: 7:22 a.m.
Arrive time: 2:47 p.m.
Highways: 1
Day—total km/miles: 140/87—4,326/2,688
Day average speed: (kmph/mph): 21/13
Day—total elevation gain (m/ft): 501/1,644—16,348/53,635
Calories daily/total to date: 4,460/118,958
Daily dangers/excitement: Permafrost.

Begin Blog:

We arrived in the most western town in Canada, Beaver Creek, Yukon Territory. If biking goes as planned tomorrow, I will depart Canada after 2,284 miles (3,676 km) peddling through Saskatchewan, Alberta, British Columbia, and the Yukon Territory.

Why do you think today's ride on the Alaska Highway had the most construction and patched spots?

If you guessed "lack of effort or money", you would be wrong.

The correct answer--permafrost.

It costs about four times as much to maintain a highway overlaying permafrost as other highways.

After taking today's blog photo of an international highway research project over permafrost, I inquired at the Beaver Creek Information Center. This town, with a population of 112, had one of the best information centers I had seen. For the last twenty-five years, the manager ran the place and had her main wall dedicated to permafrost.

After three years of highway permafrost research on a mile stretch outside of Beaver Creek, all solution attempts were considered failures. Why?

Although permafrost was defined as ground frozen for two or more years, permafrost underlying this part of the Yukon was buried layers of ice from the last glacial period—likely thousands of years old. When trees, vegetation, dirt and rock are cleared to put in a highway, the buried layers of ancient glacial ice melt randomly. As the ground warms over time, lack of permanent vegetative insulation and black pavement accentuated permafrost heaves.

For those with fancy cars, motorcycles, trucks pulling monstrous campers, and million-dollar RVs, I doubt they allocated time saved speeding for more satisfying purposes. Recklessness in construction could have allowed them time to stop at the Beaver Creek Information Center and learn about highways over permafrost. Next time maybe they will bicycle across the Yukon and enjoy it.

-----End Blog-----

Had permafrost affected the ALCAN for many miles? Yes.

Surrounding mountains slid. Landscape dipped and lakes appeared randomly. The Highway buckled and had sunk strangely in spots. Pavement crumbled. In hindsight, most, if not all were caused by ancient ice melting under dirt and rock.

So enamored with details of permafrost when we arrived in Beaver Creek, I did not blog many details on what transpired my last full day in Canada.

Here are details from today's journal:

"Patricia got up early to pack and take me for the thirty-mile drive where I left off yesterday. She followed me and wrote in her journal; then catching up with me about every half-hour.

"Today was what I pictured the Yukon to be—scrub trees, minimum hills between river valleys with mountains in the distance.

"The temperature started cool, about 49°F (9°C), likely got to the mid-60s (18°C), and it was cloudy most of the day. A random rain showered before the sky showed sun. Long days seem to increase the sun's intensity when blocked from the light breezes.

"Wind pushed me most of today—that was why my average speed was so high…."

Perhaps some of my readers likely track daily data beginning each chapter. If you are one tracking speed, you will notice today was my fastest average speed of thirteen miles-per-hour (21 kmph) and my third fastest maximum speed at 56 kilometers-per-hour (38.4 mph).

With the fastest average speed, near maximum downhill speeds while gaining elevation over 140 kilometers (87 miles) took more than luck after thirty-seven days of continuous biking 4,326 kilometers (2,688 miles).

After biking a couple hours to start the morning over mountains and valleys I was about ready to take a break. Before declining from the last plateau, I could see for miles. A vast, empty, beautiful water and scrub-wooded valley stretched as far as I could see. No towns, no houses, nobody. I coasted down and started peddling—looking for a safe area to stop.

What a pleasant surprise! A folded plywood sign adjacent the Highway shoulder read; "5 km Bakery".

At about 9:30 a.m., with no breakfast, my month started watering as I picked up speed toward my reward.

There had been no town since Burwash Landing, eighty-two kilometers (51 miles) behind me. On a graveled cut-out below the Highway sat several log cabins centered by an office, which I immediately assumed was the bakery. The entry sign read: "Pine Valley Bakery Creperie".

What! There was a red pipe across the entry. It was locked. Maybe they kept this entry locked; so I pedaled to the north entry. A locked pipe crossed that entry, too. No smells. No bakery. My nose deflated without bakery sensations.

I biked on.

In five kilometers, sure enough there was another plywood sign on the opposing (south-bound) shoulder stating, "5 km Bakery".

Had I missed the first sign, and pipe closings, I would have turned around. Instead, I stopped and ate a protein bar. For the next twenty miles (32 km) I thought about all the disappointed travelers seeing the signs and no bakery. No smells.

As I continued north, the pine trees seemed to get bigger. I rounded a corner and to my surprise, an extremely well-maintained camp appeared. Patricia arrived just behind me as I rolled into Discovery Yukon Lodging and RV Park.

We took a break. Patricia grabbed an ice-cream bar from the glass-topped chest freezer while I bought a few homemade chocolate covered peanut butter cereal bars and in full sun ate them on the deck.

"I wished we had known about this spot before," Patricia said. "We need to stay here on our way home."

Later, we would be delayed here several days on our troubled return.

We met the owner/manager, a British lady that had moved here a decade ago. She was trying to make a living serving Alaska Highway customers during the summer. Tough living, but she was surrounded by mountains and bordered by the White River. With tough economics, where could she behold more beauty?

Local labor was non-existent. For assistance during the summer, she recruited a young, ambitious college-age guy from Hungary.

When we told her about the closed Pine Valley Bakery, she said they likely needed supplies and headed to Whitehorse.

I said that is 250 miles away (400 km).

She went on to explain (or complain) Canadian and Yukon regulations and taxes prevented them from getting supplies from Fairbanks, Alaska. Fairbanks, she claimed, had fresher fruits and vegetables.

After a very refreshing break, I biked across the magnificent White River bridge and through mountains, woods, and permafrost—destined for Beaver Creek.

Yes, I had a favorable breeze. Perhaps more importantly, even through permafrost construction, my legs were strong, body conditioned, weight maintained, and breathing light.

I have never considered myself a true athlete, though occasionally an amateur participant.

Definitions have been watered by hyped abilities and often steroids.

Sure, I messed around in school sports (basketball, wrestling, cross country, and football). Thereafter, I wrestled representing Air Force Europe while still a teenager and set an unofficial world record playing continuous softball for seventy-four hours and five minutes raising money for helping the blind in Japan. Since, I hiked. I biked.

Observing recreational activity for six decades, it seems many have played those sports—I was one. Most were participants, like me. Few were true athletes with special gifts trained for physical prowess.

My physical abilities have likely peaked on this trip. More importantly, by my age, many realize where their strengths were, and maybe still are. Individually, our efforts are piddly.

One day realization hit me.

I was in my late twenties working in a government office with the objective of promoting our state's agricultural products. After months of demonstrating what piddly effort I did was worth little. To the contrary, if I could get hundreds of people in their organization promoting their products, they would get the credit; they would be motivated; and with self-pride they would continue helping their industry.

By backing off government product-focused efforts and by communicating with hundreds of businesses and organizations, I produced my first two books (more like booklets), The South Dakota Agricultural Export Directory, and the South Dakota Agricultural Organization Directory. Result: Everyone benefited from the supplier to the producer to the processor to distribution, transportation, organizations, the consumer and the state's economy.

Since then, I looked at system changes rather than trying to focus on an individual, especially myself. System changes take years, sometimes decades. I love to see people changing and taking self-pride in helping their business or organization as the new system ecologically and economically improves for everyone.

At age 65, I am likely in the best shape of my life. So what?

If this book gets more people physically active, thereby healthier, weeks of pedaling and writing will be even more satisfying for me.

All I did was ride bicycle on a highway shoulder and write a few words.

Perhaps some can reach their peak with home exercise equipment, in a local workout center, or be guided by professional coaches. Great! That was not my way—never has been.

My peace of mind may have also peaked. Did it aid my endurance? Likely.

We all take different routes through life. Often, we need a pilot. Look for one. They are likely in uncommon places.

I reminisced today preparing to leave Canada. It has been an eventful experience in a marvelous country. The end was a state away. If anything like my trip so far, I would make it to North Pole in a few days.

Dangers? I have had many.

Wildlife encounters? Absolutely. Errant drivers? No question! Luckily, I avoided downhill mishaps at sixty-five kilometers-per-hour (40 mph).

Accident avoidance certainly was not just skill or luck.

I prayed every morning and every night that God provide me with protective angels. With human frailty, likely I wanted to insure He had replacements should the assigned need backup on some of my stupider moves.

Speaking of pilots, today I had to negotiate more permafrost construction areas. As mentioned in yesterday's summary, I would wait in line with other vehicles waiting a pilot vehicle to escort us through.

After I had passed many such areas, I noticed the pilot vehicle (a pickup truck) waiting for me to clear before she returned. I thankfully expected that. Whoa did I get an earful!

As soon as I was within earshot of her (and other construction workers at that end), she started yelling at me from her pickup window.

"What are you doing? You are supposed to wait your turn! Just because you are on a bicycle you just can't go through a construction area any time you want! You need to follow the rules!!!" She went on and on, without taking a breath or waiting for my response.

It probably infuriated her even more when I said, loud enough for others to hear, "I was in line and followed as fast as I could, but everybody passed me."

As others looked and listened to her hollering, it became apparent she did not see me amongst waiting vehicles.

I asked somewhat smugly, "I have been going through construction areas for days. What was I supposed to do?"

As she was ready to lead another group the opposite direction, she pulled her pickup closer to me, with a more calmed voice said, "After this, you bike to the front of the line. Put your bike in the pilot vehicle and ride with them."

Happily, I said, "That's great! I wished someone would have told me days ago."

She was my pilot for a safer ride. Thankfully, she gave me unbeknownst rules. For the past several days, they would have made my ride safer and easier.

After that episode, I biked a few more miles. As I approached the next construction area, which happened to be the last pilot area in the Yukon, I slowly biked past a few cars, campers, and a couple motorcyclists to the front of the line. The pilot driver likely had received a radio message from the last pilot gal.

As soon as he turned around, he jumped out of his pickup, lowered the tailgate, and let me lay my bike over the spare tire, some heavy-duty chains, and other stuff. He closed the tailgate as we both went to the cab.

That piloted area was short—not over a kilometer. He waited for a few more vehicles to fall in line.

Meanwhile, he asked about where I had biked from and where I was going. Then he went into a bitch session about the idiots that were making them tear up this perfectly good stretch of the ALCAN.

"Why are you doing it if the road is good?" I asked.

He transitioned to a more active voice. "For some f…ing reason policy requires every bit of this Highway to be torn up and reconstructed every twenty years. Rather than spending our time fixing permafrost, we have to do sections like this that are perfectly good. Hell, if they lasted twenty years and are in this good of shape, why the f… are we wasting time on it?"

To which I thought he had a good point. Pilots, even managing superiors, are not always good pilots. Often listening to a simple, practical pilot's messages can be worth millions.

"We're fifty kilometers from nowhere and wasting our time," he summarized as I was ready to bike on.

When he pulled to a stop, I jumped out, retrieved my bike, and peddled on thirty kilometers or so toward Beaver Creek.

This was likely not the "nowhere" the pilot driver was referring to. For many miles, I had noticed construction equipment heading back to Burwash Landing. A huge fenced construction area lay on a hill on the edge of town. When finished each evening, my pilot driver and other workers likely had to return to Burwash Landing.

Only a couple miles out of Beaver Creek, an international permafrost project was well recognized and signed briefly indicating each experiment.

I rolled into Beaver Creek's welcoming center (south side of town) at 2:47 p.m., Patricia was already there. She had secured our room in a small cabin behind Buckshot Betty's.

Like every successful town, business owners make it so. Buckshot Betty was a more ostentatious one. Highlight Buckshot!

After showering, washing and hanging to dry my now well stained jersey and white (or it used to be)[50] long-sleeved undershirt, padded pants, socks, and handkerchief, we walked around the well-maintained café.

The café was full. Like normal, I was not. Ready to load up. I did.

Two other bicyclists came in. We chatted. They were from Europe. Like most others, they had flown into Anchorage, repacked their bikes and just arrived in Beaver Creek after clearing Canadian Customs on the north end of town.

Like me, they were excited to reach the first town in Canada, Beaver Creek. A mile or so north of town was the Canadian

---

[50] Water quality at many nightly stops was very poor—rusty, not potable, sometimes dirty, and reacted with soap to stain anything—especially a white undershirt.

Custom's station which was twenty miles from Alaska's international border crossing.

That stretch, which I will describe in more detail tomorrow, was kind of like no-mans-land. No other roads. No people. Some hills. Muskeg. Mostly marsh. No way to get in or out of that area (except dog sleds or snowmobile in the winter).

Anyway, the European biking pair were planning to bike the ALCAN. They were pleased knowing I had just made it. Both appeared in great shape, an expectation of European cyclists.

Buckshot Betty was busy waiting tables.

When she finally found time to ask the European cyclists what they wanted, they said two loaves of bread. Disgusted, Betty hobbled away. (She was wearing a leg cast and had apparently injured herself a week or so earlier.) She had bigger fish to fry (so to speak) and she did not want to waste time making a couple dimes baking, packaging and selling two loaves of take-out bread.

I really felt sorry for the newly arriving guests. We, like them, were attracted to Buckshot Betty's offering of steaks, pizzas, hamburgers, lasagnas, soups, and "delicious homemade breads and pies" (as quoted from *The Milepost*).

It was still mid-afternoon where the sun sets around midnight. They were excited to be in the Yukon. Likely, they wanted to bike many more miles before setting up camp.

Finally, they got two loaves of bread and walked out.

Of all the places, in all the days of interacting with Canadians, Buckshot Betty gave the poorest welcome. This was likely the European cyclers first stop. Had they not been needing evening bread, it would not have surprised me, after such rudeness, if they had walked out leaving bread on counter and no dough.[51]

It would be a good lesson for those traveling with expectations of conveniences and indulgent service in this sparse land. They will run out of sympathetic settlers and sojourners before they run out of words. Want assurance? Ask Buckshot Betty. The rest of you will thoroughly enjoy the adventure.

---

[51] Dough, as to make daily bread, is a colloquial term for money.

Putting the best construction on a bad incident, I think Betty was exhausted by late afternoon. She worked! Hard and Fast! She was underperforming by her standards. With workers, Buckshot Betty was likely a tough cookie. (Afterall, it was a bakery.) Limited available workers likely found other employment more satisfying than the pace Betty expected.

Hungry customers were waiting to eat after driving many hours. Her facilities were opposite her welcoming. I hope other travelers, including bicyclists try Buckshot Bettys. I am certain, if she is around, it will be a colorful experience.

Tomorrow I expect to leave Canada and head back into the United States. With 309 miles (498 km) remaining, it would be like biking from Boston, Massachusetts to Philadelphia, Pennsylvania, or Indianapolis, Indiana to Windsor, Ontario, Canada.

To be at peace, the mind has to match body. I found it mentally satisfying to equate distances in thirty mile (~50 km) blocks. Multiple blocks clicked off meant arrival and rest.

Consequently, once I arrived at the Alaska border, the distance remaining to North Pole would be like biking about six thirty-mile segments—like from Portland, Oregon 280 kilometers (174 miles) to Seattle, Washington. Mentally, it was easy. Drivers make that in an afternoon.

Chapter 46: 🚲 185 km/115 miles
Day 38, June 28, Beaver Creek, YT to Tok, AK

Depart time: 6:22 a.m.
Arrive time: 7:05 p.m.
Highways: 1, 2
Day—total km/miles: 185/115—4,511/2,803
Day average speed: (kmph/mph): 18.7/11.6
Day—total elevation gain (m/ft): 891/2,921—17,239/56,556
Calories daily/total to date: 4,418/123,376
Daily dangers/excitement: More support.

Begin Blog:

It was twenty miles from the Canadian Customs and Immigration border crossing at Beaver Creek to the Alaska border, then another quarter mile to the U.S. Customs border crossing. Not that it would make any difference; there are no other roads, just the Alaska Highway through the mountain foothills and marshes.

Today's blog photo was not a selfie at the Alaska border. Why?

My back tire went low about three miles before the border, but the tire fluid kept it from going completely flat. I was going to wait at the border for Patricia, since there was no cell phone service. Within a couple minutes a pickup pulled up and offered to take my photo if I would take theirs. We did.

As they were departing, they asked where I was going. I mentioned North Pole, but I had to wait a few minutes for my wife because my bike tire was low. The driver said, "No problem. I have a small air compressor."

233

Gary W. Wietgrefe

As we were pumping up the tire, I asked where they were heading. The driver said, "Kodiak. I'm in the Coast Guard transferring from Florida to Kodiak."

I had biked over 2,700 miles; had two flat tires at that point, and the first vehicle to arrive agreed to help me--they were both U.S. Coastguardsman. With all the Alaska Highway traffic, what are the chances the first vehicle after both flat tires were Coastguardsman?

I needed help, and they were there and willing to help.

The tire went completely flat eight miles later. Unknowingly, Patricia had stopped and took a half hour hike. (Read about her fright as the day is explained in more detail.) I flagged down a vehicle (Europeans on vacation) and they found Patricia returning to her car. She came with our extra replacement tire and tube.

It was a long ride (115 miles) with no town between Beaver Creek and Tok.

My troubles were not over. About 65 miles into my ride, I picked up a small piece of metal that punctured my back tire again. Fortunately, Patricia was close behind, and we repaired the flat quickly with a patch.

Not that it makes any difference, but we asked two people about the Highway between Beaver Creek and Tok. Both reported "It is relatively flat." In reality, there were over 85 miles of mountains and foothills making my total ascent over 4,400 feet. The takeaway: Never trust a driver to give accurate elevation, distance, or road conditions if they had never biked long distances.

Tough day, but we made it to Tok, Alaska. Patricia found a quaint nice bed and breakfast in the woods about three miles from Tok. We had our own log cabin. Very nice way to end a long day.

-----End Blog-----

Between my comments of the last couple days and today's blog, have you notice the paradoxical phenomenon?

It is subtle but real.

To be brief, compare the two groups:

Group one: Six bikers at Thachal Dhal Visitor Centre griped about wind. Camper and RV drivers ruthlessly passed me too closely in muddy construction. The scolding pilot vehicle gal, the carping pilot vehicle guy, the closed Pine Valley Bakery, the manager at Discovery Yukon Lodging, and Buckshot Betty, and her lack of employees were long-day realities.

Group two: Compare demeaner of group one with new arrivals like the two European bikers looking for bread, both Coastguardsmen's help, the foreign vehicle driver I flagged after getting a flat tire today, and Patricia on a relaxing hike rather than fearing remoteness. My satisfaction may be confirmed by my complete mood reversion to peacefulness.

What happened?

Why?

Many times I stated and implied the vastness of the Yukon Territory. It has an effect on people. Some negative, some positive.

Remoteness has its mental satisfaction and frustration.

My quick summary--when forced to live, work, or travel in the nearly empty, vast Yukon, frustration develops. It was magnified by a lack of sleep in summer—especially a week after summer solstice when I biked through.

Approaching the Arctic Circle, it was twilight all night. Dark and cooped up all winter bears hibernate, likewise people up here revive in spring as days lengthen.

We had visited Alaska several times before, summer and winter, visiting our daughter and grandchildren. Vivaciousness was evident between nearly all dark winter days and sunny summer nights.

People are outside as much as possible in the summer. We had seen families going out fishing at 9:00 p.m. and we cleaned fish after midnight taking photos of our stringer casting shadows on our daughter's house.

When the sun stays up too long, people get tired. Irritation develops. It is a type of conflict. Recall bikers at Thachal Dhal, construction pilots, and Buckshot Betty?

Before window blackout blinds became available, Alaskans' covered their bedroom windows with aluminum foil so they could get to sleep during short summer nights.

Those of us still pumped with wonderment, continued to pedal through mud, eat a smell-less protein bar near a bakery exit, wait for Buckshot Betty, smile, and bike on.

For analogy compare people. It would be like opening a new bottle or tube. It is liberally used upon opening—more than needed. Towards the bottom, as it ran low, use would often become conservative—ensuring every drop was used sparingly. Some people have kept stocked shelves and died before all was used.

Commonly, as people age, money, energy and sleep are rationed. When younger our body (bottle) was jam-packed and wallet nearly empty. We partied into the night, hustled about when we could have relaxed, and spent earnings on trivial things.

Senior citizens, like myself, have alternatives. This trip was an eye-opener.

Old bodies can travel while minds marvel with regained muscle, vitality, and serenity. Alternatively, we could sit in a sloppy chair watching television, bitch at the news, our losing team and declining stock market.

Avail oneself of a bit left over (inheritance) for a bicycle, possibly a trip or both, will give life, no matter the age, a new perspective.

Unfortunately, many drivers passing me were impatient. They could not wait to get to the next ALCAN stop, then the next, and next, bouncing through permafrost, splashing through construction mud with flailing arms. Others seem to have had all the time in the world at no expense to enjoy rest areas, overlooks and unending scenery.

Some people do not have enough time in the day to get to all the things they want to do in this beautiful land and others hurry to get through it oblivious.

Why do you think that is?

Look around.

Today, leaving Beaver Creek, was cold. June 28. I was bundled with jacket and gloves.

It was about a two-hour ride to the Alaska border. Though I did not know the temperature, I stopped several times to photograph ice sculptures on marsh ponds after exiting Canadian Customs and the twenty miles (32 km) of muskeg wilderness before entering the Alaska Customs station.

This was beautiful. Cold for summer, but stunning. Quiet. Serene.

At 6:30 a.m. nobody was around. I had the world and nature to myself. Time to watch the low sun casting long shadows trying to wake ice crystals hidden in the shade on roadside ponds was enchanting.

I was at peace.

Why was this area so unusual?

This border buffer was originally established in an agreement in 1825 between Russia (who owned Alaska) and England (who owned Canada). It was virgin--unoccupied as if the cold war never began, never left, and was never settled, but always cold.

It could be a buffer for many. Go at dawn…there will be no one to bother you.

Entering Alaska brought satisfaction. I at least made it this far.

My blog explained the two flat tires. It happens. Far more were expected during this trip.

To me it was more than extreme coincidence that I was helped with my first flat tire, day 26, by the first vehicle, a Coastguardsman and his family on their move to Alaska. Today, day 38, I had the second flat tire and again the first vehicle to arrive were two U.S. Coastguardsmen moving to Alaska. That's Providence.

My flat was worse than expected and deflated before my wife arrived. After inverting my bike on its seat and handlebars (the universal symbol for bike trouble), I removed the tire, found the damage, and repaired the tube. Despite the constant threat of a bear attack, with the used tire questionable and only a small hand air pump, I decided to wait for Patricia.

(Like most blogs, I summarized and often downplayed the dangers to Patricia and me.)

After waiting more than a half-hour, I decided to flag down the next motorist and have them notify Patricia who, I assumed, had stopped at the Tetlin National Wildlife Refuge Visitor Center. The few other places to stop were likely too risky for her.

Like most of the Yukon, there was no cell phone coverage. Several vehicles had passed beforehand and asked if I needed help. I briefly explained I was fine and that my wife would be arriving shortly. They drove on.

Now anxious in mid-morning, the day advanced. I had eighty miles (133 km) yet to bike to Tok.

The next vehicle coming up the hill apparently saw me and slowed as it approached. I waved for them to stop. Inside was a family who had rented an RV in Anchorage and were heading into the Yukon with their family. They were European, perhaps Dutch. I asked if they would be so gracious to stop at the Tetlin Visitor Center and see if my wife was there.

I described Patricia and our silver SUV with a rear bike rack and likely a blue bike on it.

True to Alaskans, Canadians, and even Europeans traveling this remote area, they offered help. Not only did they find our vehicle, they did not leave the Visitor Center until they had found Patricia, who had taken a guided hike on the grounds of the expansive Center. At the time, I had no idea of the bear risks on the groomed trails. Staff at the Visitor Center would not let anyone hike the trails without a prepared and experienced guide while they identified ruins of past settlements.

As Patricia returned from the hike, the European couple approached her in the parking lot. They asked, "Was your husband biking ahead of you?"

Patricia, hyped from the hike, on constant alert for bears, nearly panicked at their question. Quickly recalling a similar situation when our son was in a scary car accident, she knew something was wrong.

Before cell phones were common, one morning Patricia was shopping. Meanwhile, I was working in my home office when our daughter called reporting our son's accident. In a hunt for Patricia, I quickly called a couple coffee shops with no luck. Then, I remembered my brother, Neal, asked Patricia about something the night before. My niece wanted guitar strings so I started calling music stores. Luck would have it that the owner of the first store I called said a lady of similar description was there. (For decades, our personal joke was that I could never find Patricia while shopping in the same store.) Imagine her shock when the music store owner asked if her name was Patricia. She later told me, "My heart jumped as soon as the Europeans said '…Your husband….'" She quickly scurried to find me.

Nearly two hours had elapsed between blowing the tire, Patricia's arrival, and replacing the tire before I biked toward Tok.

Those eighty miles were not flat as was promised by two different drivers. Very poor landscape and road descriptions given by drivers was another indication they were not paying attention to their surroundings.

Around 5:00 p.m. with about twenty miles (32 km) to go, Patricia stopped to offer my last snack for the day. She then drove into Tok and found a secluded bed and breakfast cabin about three miles past Tok.

A bike trail paralleled the highway on both sides of Tok. To my surprise, Patricia not only found a room, took our bags into the cabin, but rode her bike several miles east of Tok and met me.

It has always been pleasurable biking with Patricia. We have biked hundreds of miles together in several (U.S.) states. We mountain biked in southern Mexico. On New Zealand's north island we did a bicycle tour through wineries and stayed at a bed and breakfast. A couple years later, we arrived by train in Christchurch (east side of New Zealand's south island) and bicycled through the city, then fields, pastures, and vineyards to a remote eco-lodge.

Today, after a hundred miles of foothills, I had slowed to a pace we could visit, and transitioned to Tok bike path paralleling the Highway.

Once she had confirmed the cabin, Patricia had planned to cook a scrumptious meal from our plenteous supplies. Unfortunately, the cabin was not equipped to cook, and our camp stove was packed in a compartment below our supplies. Rain clouds appeared.

Our bed and breakfast hosts, Shawne and Tony, suggested a tasty Thai take-out café in Tok. They had no indoor seating, but several picnic tables outside.

Biking side-by-side without a breeze, given time before it rained, we talked about dining on Thai as soon as we arrived. Only once, in Dawson City, had we had an Oriental meal. After 185-kilometers (115 miles), my third farthest day, I was ready for more.

The rain was moving in too quickly.

As we entered Tok, Patricia suggested that she stop for Thai takeout, while I headed straight to Cleft of the Rock Bed and Breakfast. Although it was about another three miles west of Tok and a half mile into the woods, I found the B&B, showered while washing my biking uniform for the 38th time. I had just put on clean (street) clothes as Patricia arrived in the rain.

Our cabin deck would have been a perfect dinner setting among the woods, but rain kept us inside.

How could I be so lucky?

Even rain waited my arrival. As Patricia biked in with volumes of aromatic Thai food, we moved inside as it started to pour.

We ate together and toasted with a glass of wine.

Chapter 47: 172 km/107 miles
Day 39, June 29, Tok to Delta Junction, AK

Depart time: 9:22 a.m.
Arrive time: 8:00 p.m.
Highways: 2
Day—total km/miles: 172/107—4,683/2,910
Day average speed: (kmph/mph): 20/12.4
Day—total elevation gain (m/ft): 462/1,515—17,701/58,071
Calories daily/total to date: 5,083/128,459
Daily dangers/excitement: Animal attacks and looking back.

Begin Blog:

What was likely my second to last day of this trip, I slept in until 7:10 in order to enjoy a huge breakfast at the Cleft of the Rock B&B just outside of Tok.

We were advised the stretch of Alaska Highway from Tok to Delta Junction was mostly flat. It was with only 1,515 elevation gain in the 107 miles.

Today's major event was an animal attack. Actually, two of them. In Alaska most likely I would expect bear or moose. Instead, two fat dogs attacked from a rural cabin. I hollered at them as I picked up speed. At that point, I hoped the owner would appear to defend me.

Dogs like to chase bikes. In all the years of biking, I have always been able to out-bike them. Only four dogs attacked me on this trip with the last being in Alberta at about 1,100 miles.

Good and bad news:

Good: The dogs backed off right away.

Bad: Unfortunately, they were likely overfed house dogs who would be a bear meal or two before the summer was over.

Bad # 2: I broke my new replacement chain as I slammed on the pedals to escape. It was not too serious as Patricia was close behind and saw the attack. We quickly put on the old original worn chain (I replaced at 1,699 miles) and I was biking again within the half hour.

Today's blog photo was my mirror looking back at a different view than I had seen as I passed looking ahead.

Looking back, I am glad I saved my old chain. Secondly, as I neared the end of this trip, I often looked back to see what I may have missed.

Many times over the past month I would stop and look back and really see what my mirror summarized. Too many times we pass what we should have taken more time to observe and understand.

-----End Blog-----

Interactions with people made this trip even more enjoyable. Personal connections were made.

Visiting with Tony while Shawne was setting our breakfast table, I learned he was the full-time maintenance manager a Tok school.

"Really?" I asked.

"Yes, I have been doing it for several years and it supplements our bed and breakfast income."

"Do you have a guy working for you from North Dakota?" I asked.

"Well, actually, he did up until a couple weeks ago." Tony replied.

I went on to explain that young guy was the son of a couple that renovated and managed the Bowbells, North Dakota hotel/bed and breakfast where we stayed. It was my hardest biking day against heavy winds. They not only prepared dinner for me, they waited dinner until I arrived. Patricia also stayed there two weeks later.

Tony brought me up to date. With school out, his young employee, took a summer break. Tony had trained him to operate the school heating system. He became a master boiler operator among other skills.

Tok, a town of 1,200 people, was struggling to keep their school viable. Three staff had been laid off. One of their major expenses was the 65,000 gallons of diesel fuel used to heat the school. Meanwhile, area wood had been rotting nearby unused.

What are everyday issues in rural Alaska? They are educating youth, keeping warm in winter, and getting fresh produce.

Tok school solved those problems. Isn't that the purpose of schools? To educate for public benefit.

What did they do?

In 2013 Tok school installed a biomass boiler system to heat the school. Using excess heat, a greenhouse was built and connected to the school. Tomatoes, cucumbers, other vegetables, even strawberries are now produced for school lunches. It was impossible to get such fresh produce before the school replaced their diesel heating system with biomass from the surrounding area.[52]

There are so few residents approaching the Arctic Circle that personal connections can be made with nearly everyone. The Yukon Territory in total has about 35,000 people. A resident could likely start a conversation with family or friend and talk about everyone through acquaintances.

As I biked today, I reminisced how communication, transportation and circumstances bring people together. Had Patricia not found the Cleft of the Rock Bed and Breakfast in Tok, we would not have been able to tie trip-day six with day thirty-nine.

We should always keep our eyes and ears open to what was around us.

Constantly, for thousands of miles I pedaled looking around always with an eye on the highway shoulder immediately ahead of my tire. With shoes locked into pedals, a bolt, bone, hook, glass, chain link, or walnut sized rock could have caused me to crash and flip.

---

[52] EERE Success Story—Alaska Gateway School District Adopts Combined Heat and Power, May 2013, U.S. Department of Energy, https://www.energy.gov/eere/success-stories/articles/eere-success-story-alaska-gateway-school-district-adopts-combined-heat, (Sourced November 25, 2019).

It was unbelievable what I saw laying on the highway shoulder. Tires are amazingly resilient hitting unknown objects with jabs and jolts. Daily survival--just luck?

Several times I considered inserting a photo of one rabbit foot laying on the highway shoulder. Every instance, for thirty-nine days was I lucky to escape?

The rabbit was not. It was likely hit by a vehicle, then eaten as roadkill. Was it lucky only a foot remained?

Situations simply come down to the way one looks at it.

Have you studied my blog photos?

"A picture is worth a thousand words" was the old, some say, ancient Chinese cliché.

Get real!

We were up north—common sense was a must! Ancient Chinese did not take pictures.

Logic should tell us the phrase came after cameras. Actually, the original modified phrase came from a 1921 streetcar ad by Frank Barnard, "One look is worth a thousand words."

Looking back, in many ways, this trip was scary. Now, I look ahead joyous. It boils down to the way one looks at it.

Isn't perception tense?

What happens when past, present, and future arrive up north?

The past leaves nostalgia. The present questions sensibility with a zestful future.

Not if, but when, you take the opportunity to make your journey, it will be worth a thousand pages. Fortunately, I did not visualize and write everything looking back—too much weight to carry.

How did I remember so many details?

My memory was jogged by daily blogs, daily journal entries, maps, the pre-trip travel guide I prepared, *The Milepost* and our side notes, and thanks to smartphones, my photos are imbedded with time and dates.

I could have written a thousand more occurrences. It is your try next!

Chapter 48: 140 km/87 miles
Day 40, June 30, Delta Junction to North Pole, AK

Depart time: 6:00 a.m.
Arrive time: 2:20 p.m.
Highways: 2, Badger Road
Day—total km/miles: 140/87—4,823/2,997
Day average speed: (kmph/mph): 18.5/11.5
Day—total elevation gain (m/ft): 344/1,129—18,045/59,200
Calories daily/total to date: 4,010/132,469
Daily dangers/excitement: Wolfdog attack, arriving!

Begin Blog:

Made it! Pierre, South Dakota to North Pole, Alaska in 40 days—two days break. Preliminary mileage indicates 2,998 miles. (*Actual biked miles was 2,997.*)

As the North Pole city limit sign came into view, I felt my whole body cave with emotion—a feeling I have never experienced. As I biked off the 4-lane highway exit, I could see a group of people and bicycles waiting with a red Finish Line. I was completely astonished. My nieces, nephew, and three grandnieces were cheering. What an unexpected welcome! See today's blog photo.

It was the support I received that made this trip a reality.

First, my wife, Patricia, has heard my dream—too many times. For decades we have supported each other.

Secondly, our son, Wyatt, an emergency doctor and acupuncturist, was the ONLY reason I could physically bike 3,000 miles. After suffering plantar fasciitis last year for eight months, he gave me two acupuncture treatments on my leg and put me on a

245

muscle stretching regiment. Within two weeks, I was back to my usual ten to fifteen-mile weekly hikes. He allowed me to bike with absolutely no symptoms.

Thirdly, our two daughters have physically and mentally reset their lives. For their children and us, they have set examples to follow.

The fourth support list was long. I cannot begin to list and thank everyone from family and friends to a following of many in many countries.

It was all of you that motivated me. I hope in some small way, I have encouraged you to exercise or take on a challenge too long delayed.

Seven years ago I applied for leave without pay which combined with accrued personal time, I was going to bike from South Dakota to Alaska. The application was denied. Now retired for six years, objective accomplished at age 65. Age was not the limiting factor, it was personal willingness to take on and accomplish something delayed far too long.

Now it is your turn.

-----End Blog-----

To clarify, the actual route since Delta Junction was on the Richardson Highway—not Alaska Highway which began in Dawson Creek, BC and ended in Delta Junction, AK.

Normally, a few details of the day's events were included in my evening blog. Although I did not today, I must relate the scariest incident of this whole trip.

While passing, Patricia pointed. I should stop ahead. As I approached the small village of Salcha, it was evident they were holding a Saturday open-air market along the Highway in the parking lot of the general store. Intuition told me that was where she would be.

Sure enough, Patricia had already ordered fresh caramel rolls for my morning break. Afterwards, I continued toward North Pole, while Patricia checked out the few booths in the morning chill.

246

As I pedaled on, there were a few rural residents scattered with some cabins along the highway, others disguised by woods. Most, maybe all, were guarded by dogs. Every time I heard a dog barking, I picked up speed. Then when well beyond attack, my pace returned to normal.

A few miles west of Salcha, I heard a deep *"woof, woof"* through the woods. Instantaneously, I picked up speed and shifted to a higher gear to quickly outrun what was obviously a huge dog. Unfortunately for me, it was not. In mere moments, I could hear its deep bark as it crossed the ditch onto the Highway.

I had to be approaching twenty miles-per-hour (32 kmph) as the road inclined.

The vicious bark was getting closer. Most dogs do not like bicycles. This one obviously thought I had threatened its territory. My racing away provided a challenge he was not about to lose.

I hoped my old chain would not brake as the new one had during the last dog attack.

Assuming Patricia had caught up with me, I began hollering. Louder and louder.

My pace quickened as I struggled uphill. The barks were getting closer.

Perhaps Patricia could not hear me. In a desperate attempt of escape, I moved left from the shoulder across the west-bound lane to the middle of the on-coming lane. With hope, Patricia could hit the big black beast on my right as it continued to close the gap.

I glanced back. No Patricia.

Worse, the beast was within a car-length.

If a vehicle did not suddenly appear over the hill, I was a goner.

With feet solidly clipped into pedals, I was not afraid my shoes would slip from the pedals, but there was no way I could escape if the beast's huge mouth grabbed my leg or foot.

My feeble plan, if I can call it that, was to be left far enough that an on-coming vehicle would swerve into the empty west-bound lane, hit the beasts, as I veered farther left to avoid getting hit.

Nobody came.

Breathing hard, my heart beat out of control, I remembered thinking, "This close. A couple hours left, and my trip would be complete. Now, …if I live, I'll never be able to finish."

Had I got too cocky? Too relaxed? Too unaware of my circumstances?

There was evidence. More rural dwelling. Sometimes, I could spot a vehicle in the yard. Obviously, people that lived out here did not want to live in town. If they worked, rural freedom in Alaska woods was worth the long commute. No doubt it was beautiful with the Tanana River and some lakes nearby.

At many cabins, guns were more likely than visitors.

How could I fight off this growling attacker?

It was big, dark with a wide head.

Once, and only once, I glanced between my right elbow and hip to see a huge black head with mouth snapping at my right foot.

I kept screaming for help with all remaining effort put into escape.

At some point after clearing the top of the hill, the barking stopped. I kept going as fast as I could for another quarter mile.

In the past, after a couple hundred yards, I had out-biked dogs. On other road trips, a dog or two chasing from a farmstead was not unusual. This trip, it happened in North Dakota, Saskatchewan, Alberta and yesterday in Alaska.

Arctic Circle was more than an arbitrary line. It was also a mental state. Special people have the guts to live in the bush up here. Guard dogs are used to protect owners and property against intruders, be it bears, moose, wolves, or criminals.

My assailant was no ordinary dog. It was a wolfdog with far more stamina than any dog I had raced against. It was not the biggest dog I have ever seen, but it matched a farm dog near Hurley, South Dakota in the early years I was an agronomist (mid-1990s).

Our farmer-dealer recruited a good farmer to plant a corn test plot behind his shelterbelt. Before we arrived, I was advised never to get out of a vehicle in their farmyard. Then our dealer explained his customer had a wolf-dog cross—the meanest dog he had ever seen. He went on to complain, that dog was likely going to kill someone.

He had advised the farmer about personal liability if someone was ever hurt or killed in his yard by that dog.

That fall, I went to weigh their corn test plot. Most of the time I stayed in my pickup truck and only slipped back to the weigh scale by climbing over the pickup box just in case the half-wolf snuck up unnoticed.

Without a doubt, angels were protecting me today. The huge mouth had been snapping inches from my rotating foot. Maybe they heard my hollering—nobody else had.

When Patricia arrived, I motioned for her to stop ahead. I was still so scared I could hardly talk as I tried to explain. She had no idea what had happened. Likely, no driver would have seen the beast as the cabin must have been hidden by trees and brush. The part dog, part wolf had attacked the unusual—a bicyclist—me!

Although Patricia had not seen the attack, she easily could have happened upon a mangled mess of bones, blood, and bike.

Still fearing dog threats for the last twenty-five miles or so (~42 km), Patricia followed closely—closer than she had the whole trip. North Pole was ahead. I knew dog attacks were less likely as Richardson Highway turned to four-lanes.

Patricia has been at my side for decades. A couple days earlier, she had looked at the old drydocked Klondike paddlewheel wondering when I was going to hang up my bike.

Would it be at North Pole?

North Pole city entrance sign appeared. Overwhelmed, I pulled in for photos. Strangely, I never visualized my destination. It was just North Pole, although I knew our first stop was at Liesl and Seth's place (my younger brother's son).

Patricia obliged taking photos as I held my bike next to the candy-cane swirled sign of North Pole.

After reentering Richardson Highway, to my left was a huge, fifty foot-tall (15 meters) outdoor Santa Claus, his pen of reindeer, and a huge Santa Claus House.

Just seeing the place was a gift! Christmas, to little children, was different. I had that little kid feeling again.

I imagined Santa looking down, elves excitedly hopping around, and reindeer likely happy they did not have to make the summer trip Pierre-to-the-Pole.

Unbeknownst to me, for the past three hours, Patricia had been on the phone constantly updating our North Pole reception crew.

I had no idea the real reception was only a few minutes away at the next exit.

Coasting paved Badger Road exit into North Pole was a classic homemade reception with a red crepe paper streamer finish line, paper plates the girls had colored, homemade signs, bicycles scattered on the grassy intersection, and screaming girls shooting green confetti party poppers. My bearded nephew, Seth, had been waiting with a huge smile and bearhug.

My oldest niece, Cheryl, had planned her first Alaska vacation months earlier—before she even heard about my Pierre-to-the-Pole plan. She was certain her timing would mean she had to return to Denver before my arrival.

Cheryl and Seth had played together in grade school, but seldom had seen each other for the past few decades. Cheryl had moved to Denver to start her career. Seth, with his new wife Liesl, moved from Tennessee to North Pole in 2006 and produced the most remarkable girls, Adelaide, Gretchen, and Cora.

After months of planning, Cheryl and Seth had cooked up a plan to take a week to deep sea fish for halibut, stream fish for salmon, and sightsee southern Alaska while camping. Seth was an accomplished outdoorsman and Cheryl was as adventurous. As they returned to North Pole on Richardson Highway, they had written on a series of white paper plates and tied them to highway signs encouraging me to bike on. I saw the paper plates but unfortunately I did not read them because similar paper plates were used in the Yukon as highway construction markers.

Completely overwhelmed, after hugs and photos, we remounted bikes on the two-mile ride from Badger Road exit out of North Pole on a paved bike path. The three young girls had never biked that far from home, but easily lead the way.

After about a mile, I heard Seth say, "Low tire."

After pointing to my air pump, I asked, "Which girl?"

Seth said, "It is your back tire."

Green tire sealant was splattering out a hole in my back tire.

"No worries," I said. "It will last until we get to your place."

It did. Barely. My tire may have been deflating, but not my excitement to finally arrive, sit down and visit family. I had not anticipated being so excited.

We parked the six bikes and went into Seth and Liesl's house. What a shock!

Cheryl, my niece, had worked with the younger girls to plaster the windows and walls with banners, welcome signs and more streamers. No doubt they had also anticipated my appetite. Liesl had the table filled with goodies and the evening's dinner, a pile of pink Alaska salmon, was thawing in the kitchen.

Liesl, a professional music instructor, had not only trained their daughters on various instruments, Seth learned the guitar to complement the family of musicians.

Uniquely Alaskan, that evening in their front yard, Seth and Liesl lead their girls in a singalong around a huge campfire.

What a day.

Pierre-to-the-Pole was a success.

There was no way of anticipating the suffering I would endure the next six months.

Chapter 49: Biker Summary

Depart day: May 20
Arrive day: June 30
Total days biked: 40
Total days break: 2
Total km/miles biked: 4,823/2,997
Original total estimate km/miles: 5,000/3,000
Total minutes: 19,316
Average hours/day: 8 hr. 3 min.
Average speed: (kmph/mph): 16.9/10.5
Total elevation gain (m/ft): 18,044/59,200
Calories average per day: 3,312
Total Calories burned: 132,469.

Each day I looked ahead to see what was around the next curve. It was always something different.

Perhaps my biggest physical accomplishment was to not have sore wrists. My **wrist support bar** worked perfectly and I had no other health issues.

Let me get data out of the way. Many cyclists function off data summarized below.

<u>Total distance</u>: Distances were accumulated by day upon arrival at lodging and was not actual distance in each state or province.

<u>Total trip</u>: Exactly 4,828 kilometers (3,000 miles),

<u>Distance biked</u>: 4,823 km, (2,997 miles),

<u>Distance biked by state/province</u>:

    South Dakota: 166 km (103 miles),
    North Dakota: 486 km (302),
    Saskatchewan: 819 km (509),

Alberta: 837 km (520),

British Columbia: 908 km (564),

Yukon Territory: 1,110 km (690),

Alaska: 497 km (309).

<u>Days biked</u>: A sixty day trip was planned. To maximize sun and weather benefits, I departed May 20th and arrived three weeks ahead of schedule, June 30th, which allowed two rain days and forty days of biking. The list below indicates the number of days lodging in each state after bicycling:

South Dakota: 2 bike days,

North Dakota: 4 bike days,

Saskatchewan: 6 bike days plus 1 rain day,

Alberta: 7 bike days +1 rain day,

British Columbia: 9 bike days,

Yukon Territory: 9 bike days,

Alaska: 3 bike days.

<u>Average per day</u>: 75 miles/121 km. Average hours biking (including breaks): 8 hours, three minutes.

<u>Average bike speed</u>: 16.9 kilometers per hour, 10.5 miles per hour.

<u>Total Elevation gain</u>: 18, 044 meters, 59,200 feet.

<u>Elevation by state/province</u>:

South Dakota: 349 m. (1,145 ft),

North Dakota: 1009 m. (3,309 ft),

Saskatchewan: 463 m. (1,520 ft),

Alberta: 2,069 m. (6,788 ft),

British Columbia: 6,527 m. (21,415 ft),

Yukon Territory: 5,931 m. (19,458 ft),

Alaska: 1,696 m. (5,565 ft).

<u>Total calories</u>: Based on (Garmin®) estimated calories burned biking totaled 132,469 with an average of 3,312 per day.

<u>Personal weight change</u>: My beginning weight was 83 kilograms (183 pounds) and I arrived weighing 82.6 kilograms (182 pounds).

<u>Medications</u>: With a change in eating and exercise habits, six months after retirement I stopped taking cholesterol and blood pressure medications. On this trip, in order to anticipate muscle or joint failure I took nothing for pain relief (except one Tylenol one night).

The new **wrist support bar** worked perfectly and proved to be my most practical invention.

Bicycling requires alert eyes and good eye protection. I wore high quality, polarized, light weight Maui Jim sunglasses to eliminate lens glare. Observation areas proved critical.

Bicycling zones of protection were recognized.

- A meter (three feet) before my front tire was the crucial hazard-avoidance zone.

- A meter to each side was my personal travel zone.

- Ten meters (thirty feet) was protective zone (mainly from incoming animals, but also weeds, brush, trees, and flying debris from ditch mowers and vehicles).

- A hundred meters (about a hundred yards) ahead and to the sides were my signage and attack animal notification zone.

- Three to ten kilometers (~two to six miles) ahead were my stopping, bodily disposal, and destination zones. Most satisfying was the constantly undulating distant landscape.

Soft earplugs were worn to hear nature while blocking traveling wind noise. Filming windy outdoor videos with smart phones disturbed the scenery being captured. Why do you think news reporters interview outside with a foam covering over their microphone? It cuts out wind whisking through the microphone pores. Similarly, try soft earplugs while biking. They help expose nature.

For weather, I watched clouds as I had a child and felt wind just as those throughout the centuries.

May 20th I left with the first seven days of lodging reserved in South Dakota, North Dakota and my first three stops in Saskatchewan. Also, July 20th motel reservations were made in Fairbanks, Alaska because I was anticipating arrival in peak tourist season. Before departure, it was beyond imagination I would arrive June 30th--three weeks early.

You have read about where and when I biked, some thoughts, what I had seen, and how dangers were skirted.

The original Google® Maps mileage estimated 3,012 miles (4,847 km) which did not include distance estimated to lodging. Saskatchewan and Alberta offered a few shortcuts. Actual bike mileage turned out to be 2,997 miles (4,823 km) excluding just about three miles (5 km) day 26 and less than a kilometer (<0.5 miles) day 37.

With those 3 miles ridden after a flat tire and one ride in construction, the trip equaled exactly 3,000 miles (4,828 km).

If you enjoyed daily summaries as much as I enjoyed the ride, I hope you do so at ten-miles-per-hour for hundreds of miles. Always realize:

●   Bears are faster than a speeding bike. They feed near roadways which moose use as paths.

●   Moose mothers violently protect their young.

●   Wood buffalo like ditch grass. Not bikes.

●   Birds find gravel on roadsides for their gizzards and fly north to mate.

●   Wolves, fox, skunk, and coyotes smell and forage roadkill.

●   Remote cabins are protected by half-wild dogs and prey for roadkill bicyclists.

●   Porcupines find ??? I have no clue why porcupines are on highways or shoulders. Take the trip and figure it out for yourself.

There are more foolish things than biking 3,000 miles in forty days—like going for 5,000 kilometers.

Bike wherever. Enjoy it.

If you only focus on data, distance, and distractions, you are focusing on the wrong things.

Consider why you bike….

Chapter 50: Why Bike?

Equipment used, distance and numbers only tell a very small part of the story.

Although I wore soft ear plugs to cut down on road and wind noise, with clarity I could hear people talking, vehicles approaching, cows mooing, dogs barking, rustling in the woods, and birds chirping encouragement.

What I saw yesterday was different than what I saw, felt, smelled and heard the next day.

While people are ignored, static distracts and creates stress. A whole world exists without it—naturally. It always has; it still does. We all have a wonderful opportunity to observe it.

No matter our age, we get distracted from our real life with family by work and fiddling with our devices. I was guilty. It started before laptop computers.

One evening, decades ago, I sat reading the daily newspaper in our family room. Our adolescent son was visiting with his young friends. A friend asked him, "What does your dad do?" Our son said, "He leaves early every morning; drives around, talks on the phone all day, and comes home late for supper." Embarrassed, hidden behind the newspaper, I knew I was not the father I wanted to be.

For the last month, I saw others speed through wilderness looking for something down the road. Always looking beyond surroundings is not real.

Reality is not down the road. It has always been around us--every day! Sometimes, all we have to do is unplug to enjoy family and nature.

It reminds me of how nature adjusts to the mysterious Arctic's midnight sun. Days get longer until summer solstice. It stays up longer and longer each night, and like party animals, it takes a long time rising in the morning. Extended shadows are as cobwebs erased by a new day.

Realization often comes from a thing you cannot invent. It is just there…to be seen, observed, and understood. A wise old man, years ago, told me an innovation is someone realizing and explaining what has always been there.

Biking early allowed me to see and experience the nocturnal animals finishing their nightly feed as they transitioned to daily rest. Daylight allowed me to see and hear celebratory birds--the opening chorus of a new day with my wife nearby.

Uncontrolled beauty is not explainable…nor are unbridled sounds and feelings.

Please do not let my explanations keep others from making this trip nor limit desires for adventure. It was not hard. Whatever ride others take can be done at their pace with whomever they wish.

Satisfaction is also outside oneself.

Although I enjoyed this ride beyond expectations, gratification and reward came from knowing Patricia also made a trip of a lifetime. She saw things, heard things, met people and went places by herself she would have never done had not we taken this adventure.

Maybe a decade ago, one weekend Patricia and I packed panniers on our bikes and rode about fifty miles (83 km) to Pipestone, Minnesota. We stayed at an historic hotel a couple nights, enjoyed wine with our dinner, toured a nineteenth century fort, and watched Natives hand-chip pipestone from a small surface mine (actually just small slabs of rocks).

With simple tools we watched as skilled hands transformed rock into pipes of peace. We leisurely pedaled home having experienced something in another state, yet nearby.

A simple piece of rock transformed to peace of mind. Such pipes brought peace between brothers, peace between neighbors and over the centuries throughout the country brought peace to those at odds often over trivial matters.

With peace of mind, I rode. Nobody pressured me to ride on…nor stop.

Spiritual simplicity and nature were what I wanted. Simple. Clear. Ever-present.

The past hundred years brought electronic confusion into all lives. It was overwhelmingly peaceful without it. What more can one ask for than blending old and new realities to close life's chapter?

One always sleeps better satisfied—not worrying about what others think.

Everyone looks at things differently. One never knows how adventures, stories, social media, blogs, or experiences are interpreted by others. How do others tell your story?

My brother-in-law, Rob Boyer, wrote this poem after we arrived at North Pole.

IF YOU BELIEVE, YOU CAN ACHIEVE

The year has arrived that Gary had planned for
His desire to ride from Pierre-to-the-Pole.
His announcement was met with doubt and smiles
That he would be able, to complete 3000 miles.

With each revolution, more miles he would gain
Each night he would rest, and work thru the pain.
With wildlife beside him and drafting behind
Again many thought he's out of his mind.

With mountains to climb, and valleys to coast
He stayed steady at it, with nature his host.
The mishaps were there, they did not deter
For he was determined, after all he's from Pierre.

As a Veteran he's proud to have served this great land
And of the Coast Guardsmen who stopped to lend him a hand.
His sag wagon near with most of his gear
His comfort was knowing, Patricia was near.

He was met at the Pole with a small proud militia
Seth, Liesl, Addie, Gretchen, Cora and Cheryl
And his travel companion, wife Patricia.

As he finished his quest with emotion and pride
He thanked friends and family for support during his ride.

(*Used with permission from Rob Boyer.*)

With electronic static eliminated, my personal satisfaction came through observation of nature, serenity, and support from family, friends, children, grandchildren and especially my wife.

Retirement is a joy when we can do what we want, when we want with whom we want. That was this trip! I biked when I wanted, if I wanted, where I wanted and with whom I wanted--Patricia.

My wife, Patricia, and I want to thank everyone for your encouragement over the six weeks I biked from Pierre-to-the-Pole. Your thoughts, well-wishes, and prayers meant so much (and the latter worked).

By the grace of God, my ride ended successfully. If only I had known what to avoid, I would not have been injured thereafter.

Most books end with the story. This story happily ends with the epilogue…bike on.

Gary W. Wietgrefe

Epilogue: A Tragic Recovery

Life is metered between birth and death with events bolder hashmarks—some *centi*, some *milli*, and some days apart.

By arrival in North Pole, I felt like I was in my twenties again. Physically, I was in the best shape of my life with muscles in different shapes and not necessarily balanced. Before departure, my wrists were my biggest concern. They never ached once during the trip thanks to the **wrist support bar**.

For nearly a week, we enjoyed seeing North Pole area sites, their annual July 4th parade, family stream fishing, short hikes, visiting  Seth's construction sites, and Liesl and the girls' schools. A short drive (by Alaska standards) sixty miles north, we soaked in the Chena hot springs. It was a truly relaxing day.

Thursday night, after Seth returned from work, niece Cheryl, grandniece Adelaide, Seth and I went fishing on a small diversion of the Tanana River.

Lifting the second canoe off his trailer, I felt something pop, snap, or pull in my back. Brush on the sloping ditch-bank only allowed us to carry the canoes with one hand—likewise, when we returned from the River.

Casting for Arctic grayling and paddling in flowing water from a low seated canoe made my back sorer.

The grayling were biting timidly but frisky when caught. After drifting, casting, and paddling for a couple hours we returned the canoes to the roadside trailer.

My back started hurting worse. That did not stop us from a fly-in fishing trip to a remote cabin the next day.[53] There were no other occupied cabins on the lake with snow-covered, 20,310 foot (6,190 meters) Denali[54] evading in and out of clouds. Northern pike were the only fish we caught. They fought! They were so numerous and fought so hard we had to take breaks every four hours or so, go back to the cabin, relax, and eat.

During breaks, Seth and I rebuilt a log path through muskeg to the ridge where the cabin sat. Carrying five-gallon buckets of water from the lake up hill to the cabin did not help my back. I thought it was out of joint and needed stretching.

Sunday, after two days of fishing, I struggled boarding the outbound float plane.

Patricia and I were going to depart Fairbanks Monday, nine days after arriving in North Pole. In order to hike, relax, and take excursions, our plan was to get back to the Yukon.

However, Monday as I was having trouble walking upright, I told Patricia I needed to get a chiropractic adjustment before leaving. Before I returned from Advanced Chiropractic, Dr. Aaron Shoemaker suggested that I return for another treatment before riding in the car for days. We left Tuesday after that second treatment. Patricia drove while I tried to sit comfortably as a passenger.

Before stopping that night at Delta Junction, we pulled into a quaint park where I tried fishing. Going to and from our vehicle, I used a folding chair for support and used it while casting.

---

[53] Photo: Patricia and Gary fly to remote lake reflecting Denali.
[54] Denali is usually hidden by clouds. As the highest mountain in North America, part of the Alaskan Range, it is the third most isolated mountain in the world. Although phonetically referred to historically as Deenaalee in native language, Koyukon Athabaskans, it was renamed Mount McKinley in 1896 after then U.S. President William McKinley. Alaska politicians, under pressure from natives who petitioned the United States Department of Interior, celebrated renaming the mountain Denali in 2015.

Before we got too far into the Yukon, we wanted to stop at Discover Yukon Lodge for a night. (See Day 37.) Our log cabin was quaint and near the main office where we were served dinners and delectable breakfasts—yes, plural. We stayed three nights. I could barely walk to meals, sit comfortably, and even lying in bed was miserable.

In order to sit with slight comfort, I was given a flat (hot) water bottle to place under my right hip. My body was tilting to the left.

Medical help, we were advised, would require returning west to Fairbanks over 300 miles (~500 km) or attempt to get help in Whitehorse about 400 kilometers (240 miles) east.

Although Whitehorse reportedly had excellent healthcare facilities, we were told, as Americans, my initial appearance would cost $650 (Canadian), and likely they would only give me a prescription for pain medications. As mentioned earlier, I tried to avoid all medications. I certainly was not looking forward to taking addictive pain meds.

Our immediate goal was to find the quickest way back to South Dakota, where our son Wyatt, an emergency room doctor, acupuncturist, massage therapist, and yoga instructor, could advise us. The fastest way, with minimal driving, was taking the Alaska Ferry from Haines, Alaska to Bellingham, Washington, then drive halfway across the United States.

Fortunately, we were able to book a cabin and vehicle passage on the Ferry for the four night inland passage. First Patricia had to drive to Haines Junction where I spent a restless night and could not even walk to the dining area for breakfast. With rain pelting us going south through the Yukon, British Columbia and the Alaskan Panhandle mountains, we arrived in Haines a day before the four-day ferry passage.

Without choice, on the ferry we were thankfully assigned a four-person cabin with in-suite facilities including a shower. Both of us were able to use the lower bunks with the upper steel frame used as my stretching and exercise equipment.

Although hall rails allowed me to get to the front lounge and dining area, I spent most of the time watching mountains, fiords, woods and wildlife slowly pass skirting islands within meters with fast, almost rapid, tidal waters. Several times I saw whales breech. Wow! Had I not had so much back and hip pain, it would have been one of our top trips ever.

On Friday morning, three weeks after arriving triumphantly in North Pole, we landed in Bellingham, Washington where I had pre-arranged for a chiropractic treatment with Valley Chiropractic and Wellness in Mt. Vernon, Washington.

I hobbled in with Patricia's support and was directed into a treatment room by Dr. Lisa Pfeffer, professionally trained and proficiency rated using an activator (instead of manual adjustments). Twice she tried lowering the procedure table as my back, hip and legs screamed in pain. I could not lay on my stomach. Dr. Pfeffer's alternative was to do a standing adjustment while I held the vertical table for support.

It worked. In moments, I was nearly pain free. By the time we returned to our vehicle, pain gained intensity.

Unable to get another appointment with Dr. Pfeffer before Monday, Patricia started driving east 1,160 miles (1,868 km) toward South Dakota. With one unrestful night, and hour-upon-hour of driving, we arrived at our daughter Michelle's home near Whitewood, South Dakota. Our son, Wyatt was waiting.

After struggling to get into the house, Dr. Wyatt checked me over and said, "You have a choice, you can go to the emergency room tonight or tomorrow morning."

"Why wait?" I asked.

With Patricia and Michelle following, Wyatt took me to Spearfish Regional Hospital, the nearest 24-hour emergency room. That Sunday night, July 22, I was observed, x-rayed, given some pain medications and after midnight assigned prescription pain meds for my immediate release.

After a heated discussion with emergency staff, my family was ready to walk out abandoning me in the hospital unless I was put under observation to determine my injuries. Reluctantly, I was admitted, given even more nerve, pain, nausea, and intravenous medications and muscle relaxants.

Tuesday, after a morning consultation, I was told there was nothing they could do and that I was to be released. When Patricia asked what she should do with me, the doctor said, "Take him to a nursing home."

Exasperated, Patricia said, "Do you remember what this man just did? He just bicycled 3,000 miles to Alaska and was in the best physical shape of anyone I know. Now you are telling me to take him to a nursing home?"

With intervention by the hospitalist, head nurse, and administrator, I remained in the hospital four more days unable to walk. I was told my muscles were spasming from sciatica (back pinching the sciatic nerve) and piriformis syndrome. An orthopedic surgeon who observed me, my CT scans and my x-rays said I was not a candidate for back surgery.

Fortunately, the hospital occupational therapist using a wheelchair took me to a room to practice climbing steps, getting into and out of the bathtub, and instructing me to dress and to put on socks with a reaching tool.

My hip and right leg muscles were still tight, pulsating, and screaming with pain. Something was structurally wrong with me. Within a couple days I transitioned from immobile, to a wheelchair, to crutches and released with a long list of medications.

For six nights I was hospitalized. What did I learn?

- Medications replace physical movement and can cause memory lapses.

- Do not assume doctors and nurses know how to treat every injury.

- Seek physical and occupational therapy as soon as possible.

- Avoid prescription drugs whenever possible.

- Wean yourself from meds as quickly as possible.

- Do not suck ice chips, besides possible lung issues, they lower desire for water.

- Drink more than normal water to flush drugs from kidneys and liver.

- Assuming plenty of water was consumed, eat salty foods because hospital foods are unsalted and standardized for heart patients.
- Discuss symptoms and solutions with family or friends and figure out what is wrong yourself. Example: My daily lab tests were good except blood sodium levels decreased every day. Finally, I ordered a bag of potato chips with dinner, and the nurse encouraged me to consume more salt to bring up sodium levels.

Over the next month, I was mainly housebound at our daughter, Michelle's place. Our son, Wyatt, using acupuncture relieved my most immediate threat, muscle pain, although I was still heavily medicated. Multiple treatments were needed, but gradually needles and his instructions on moving and stretching provided relief.

Gradually, I weaned from addictive nerve and pain medications and muscle relaxants. Prescription drug labels advise dosages of continual use but are a cumbrous disservice to patients for not instructing on how to get off their drugs.

Excessive and continuous leaning to my left exasperated a bulged disc. Dr. Christopher Dietrich at Black Hills Surgical Hospital relieved some back pain with a cortisone spinal injection.

Regular appointments for the next month with Dr. Cathy Sulentic-Morcom of Black Hills Physical Therapy in Spearfish, and chiropractor treatments by Dr. Gregory Scherr and his staff at Black Hills Wellness Center allowed me to transition from crutches to a walking cane.

Michelle and Patricia assisted me in and out of a vehicle on regular trips to the Sturgis Community Center pool in order to reactivate my legs.

By September 3rd, over two months since arriving in North Pole, I was able to travel across South Dakota, nearly 400 miles (over 600 km) to Sioux Falls to see our family chiropractor, Dr. Mark Hagen, Hagen Chiropractic. His first x-ray indicated after weeks of correction, I was not only still leaning severely left nineteen degrees, my spine was twisted, and my left foot was extended two inches below my right.

For most of the next two months, Patricia helped me in and out of the house and drove me to physical therapy appointments with Dr. Mark Ponstein as he directed activities for my daily workouts at Avera Therapy-Fitness Center.

While Patricia was my constant companion and support, our daughters Michelle, Charmion, and son Wyatt were my mental balance team.

Meanwhile, for all of September and October, I had chiropractic treatments twice daily with Dr. Mark Hagen's activator accuracy. Every weekday morning shortly after he opened and every evening just before he closed, using only an activator and detailed x-rays, he gradually adjusted my spine.[55]

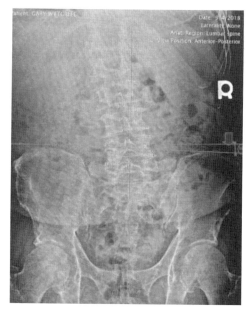

I cannot over-emphasize the benefits from Dr. Hagen's twice daily activator adjustments. By the end of October, his treatments, supplemented with our son's and Dr. Ponstein's directed physical activities allowed me to walk without a cane or other assistance. My wife and daughter, Charmion, massaged essential oils into my lower back and legs to calm irritated muscles and nerves. With patience, I was able to walk slowly to our vehicle and appointments.

---

[55] Gary's back x-rays indicated irregularities two months after treatment by sixteen doctors, six chiropractors, and four physical therapists.

After completing treatment regimes, Patricia and I returned to La Penita de Jaltemba, Mexico hoping the warmer weather would complement my recovery.

By the end of December, six months after arriving in North Pole, I was able to return to regular ten to fifteen mile (16-25 km) hikes.

However, shortly after arrival in Mexico, a Canadian friend mentioned a retired Canadian physical therapist who was spending the winter in the same community. Nana was originally from Denmark and emigrated to Canada to practice her trade. At our second appointment, she brought a huge book with detailed sketches and photos of the body's bones, muscles, and nerves.

Up to that point, after six days in the hospital, three months of medication, four months of physical therapy, five months of daily stretching exercises, advice from sixteen doctors, six chiropractors and four months of treatments from five physical therapists, nobody actually could tell me the cause of my injury.

Although symptoms like sciatica, muscle spasms and piriformis syndrome hip pain were professionally treated, my problem was not identified.

A retired Danish physical therapist, Nana, by way of Canada, observed me over two weeks in Mexico and determined I was highly likely recovering from psoas syndrome.[56]

It was likely while lifting the canoes and supplemental strains, one psoas tore while the other contracted pulling my skeletal structure out of shape causing back, hip, and leg pains from nerve damage. My muscles, especially the heavily used psoas, were conditioned to one position for forty days. Once torn, even slightly, the other psoas wrenched my body to compensate.

Biking forty days, muscles seek efficiency. Psoas muscles lift the legs as required for biking. By being clipped to pedals, forced lifting by one leg improves efficiency as the other leg pushes down on the

---

[56] Psoas syndrome is a rare muscle condition, normally occurring in athletes, where the inside spinal muscle, the psoas, runs inside along the thoracic spine, through the pelvis and attaches to the hip and femur (top leg bone). It is a body muscle used for walking. See https://my.clevelandclinic.org/health/diseases/15721-psoas-syndrome.

opposite pedal when going uphill. Connected to back and hips, psoas flex the hip to walk.

Those forty days my psoas were extremely conditioned for uniform movement. Shoes clipped to pedals provided efficiency but insured uniformity.

My psoas muscle injury likely occurred because they were conditioned for specific use. Psoas injury is hard to detect. Likely, that is why psoas syndrome is confirmed in athletes and usually confused with other muscle tears, sciatica and piriformis pains.

Advice from our son Wyatt, daughter Charmion (a yoga instructor), and physical therapists taught me safe stretching movements. Every morning (likely for the rest of my life) I follow a routine of thirty or so leg, hip, and body movements to strengthen and condition my psoas, hip, stomach and back muscles.

Although I avoid former jolting activities like jogging, horseback riding, 4-wheeling, skiing, boating and bowling, I hike and bike regularly and use massaging oils and bilateral strengthening exercises.

What did I learn during six months of recuperation?

Before and after each day of biking, I should have walked, swam or did other casual activities other than walking to dinner. Although I stretched a bit each morning, I should have done more to loosen my legs, back, neck and psoas muscles. Being laid-up made me more mindful that I want to keep physically and mentally active for my remaining years.

Sitting too long, at least for me, creates aches. Soft cushy chairs that are hard to get out of are worse than cushioned but firm chairs. Poor mattresses, sloped from wear, must be avoided. I must sleep in good beds that are not too hard. When on an extended outing, like *Destination North Pole*, poor mattresses, poor chairs, inconvenient café booths cannot be avoided. More stretching was necessary.

Bicycling, intermixed with other activities, was good--biking forty days without them was not.

How could I have avoided psoas syndrome?

- Do not overcompensate for initial injury symptoms. For example:

- Do not carry canoes on a brush-filled ditch embankment.
- Do not fish-cast and paddle a canoe for hours in a flowing stream.
- Do not manhandle forty-pound (18 kg) packs in and out of a floatplane.
- Do not carry five-gallon (19 L) pails of water from lake to cabin on a hill.
- Do not carry five-foot (1.5 m) logs or rebuild a path through a boggy marsh.
- No matter how much joy gained on a metal boat seat, do not fight northern pike fishing eighteen hours on nightless days.
- Do not sit too long in a doorless toilet overlooking a lake reflecting Denali even if there was a loaded shotgun hanging on the wall. The view—fantastic, but passing delay encourages bears to approach. Assuming survival from attack, firing a shotgun in a seated position could be a messy jolt.

During the trip I learned, and it was certainly confirmed afterwards, that support from family and friends was physically and mentally of infinite value. Patricia made our Pierre-to-the-Pole trip possible. It was not my trip; it was our trip. Our children's visits, support and treatments made recovery possible—compared to the alternative—constant nursing care.

The moral of the recuperation story: No matter what age, life is not what you can do, it is also what you should not do.

Personal advice of what not to do is sit brainless enveloped in a digital maze. Rather embrace nature and the world. Avoid electronic static. Keep moving.

From hospitalized invalid to wheelchair, to walker, to crutches, to walking cane, to cane-free took four months.

Besides hiking Sierra Madre foothills in southern Mexico in the first six months after recovery, the next six months Patricia and I visited civil war/HIV/AIDS orphans in Uganda, Africa. We also explored some of the poorest areas in Europe. Greek islands were beautiful. Moldova allowed us to sip wine in the world's largest winery, Milestii Mici. A training school for servants in a southern Portuguese castle was our host for several days. Their grace and professionalism confirmed servants need good schools and good trainers.

We did not stop.

Guarded by Russian tanks, the Soviet-era flag still flew as we inspected breakaway Transnistria (an autonomous area near the Black Sea in southeast Europe). Also, with the help of a Romanian/Russian speaking driver, I was able to visit the ancestral village where my grandfather and great grandfather were born in South Russia (now called the Ukraine). Since they escaped in 1911, I was the first family member to visit their village.

Buying stuff and surrounded by it could consume our retirement. Instead, we remain societal explorers.

The world is for everyone to experience…sometimes on a bike.

Appendix 1. Bicycle specifications

TYPE BICYCLE: Used 2008 Trek Alfa Aluminum hybrid bicycle ridden about 8,000 miles (~13,000 km).

WEIGHTS:
- 35 ½ lbs. (16.1 kg) bike weight empty (no kickstand with three empty bags under seat and handlebar)
- 41 lbs. (18.6 kg) bike weight with bags full, two odometers, and two water bottles on frame
- 48 lbs.(21.8 kg) panniers loaded
- 183 lbs. (83 kg) my departure weight
- Eight lbs. (3.6 kg) hydration pack (with 100-ounce/3 liter bladder) carried on my back
- Five lbs. (2.3 kg) shoes, socks, jersey, padded pants, jacket, and helmet
- 285 lbs. (129.3 kg) total weight on bike tires at departure
- 240 lbs. (108.9 kg) total weight on bike tires after my wife met me in western Saskatchewan. For the remainder of the trip, with panniers removed, I strapped to the back bike rack an emergency sleeping bivy bag that weighed less than five ounces, plus tire pump, and emergency bottle of water. On warm days, I removed my jacket and leather gloves and strapped them also onto the back rack.

GEARS, TIRES, and PEDALS (in U.S. customary units):
- 24 gears (3 drive; 8 rear)
- Original rims and spokes
- 27 ½ inch tire circumference
    - 1 1/8 inch tread width with ½ inch center traction ridge
    - Loaded about 2 ¼ inches tread on ground
    - Carried one spare (fold-up) tire (three used spare tires carried in my wife's support vehicle)

- o   Four spare inner tubes (Shrader valve stem because they are more universal)
- 68 inches total bike length
- Standard brake pads front and rear
- 40 ½ inches seat height
- Hydraulic seat support (great back shock absorber)
- Two water bottles carried on frame
- Two small bags below seat
- Dual-sided pedal (one side for clip shoes, the other regular pedal surface)
  - o   Used clip-on shoes
  - o   19 inches to top of pedal height, and 4 ½ inches bottom of pedal to ground
  - o   One small handlebar bag (front mounted 3 ½ inches height x 7 ½ inches deep)
- Rear rack support mounted on rear axle
  - o   Expandable horizontal bag on rear rack
  - o   Pannier on each side rear tire carrying approximately 24 lbs. (10.9 kg) each.

HANDLEBAR:
- Straight—like most hybrid bikes
- Ends had wrist support pads
- 24 inches handlebar length
- Eight inches height center of handlebar down to bike frame
- 19 inches center of handlebar to front of seat
- 43 ½ inches handlebar height (top).

WRIST SUPPORT BAR:
- It was quite flexible giving slight shock absorption with hands near center. About 90% of handlebar vibration was eliminated with hands near the far ends. My invention looks like a second inside handlebar parallel to the first straight bar.
- 42 ½ inches height of flexible horizontal bar I named **wrist support bar**
- 29 inches **wrist support bar** length (5 inches longer than handlebar on left to lay down without damaging mirror)
- 4 ½ inch stem (attached to handlebar stem)

- One inch PVC tube with foam pipe insulation wrapped in padded handlebar tape
- End caps not glued (can us for secure money and documents) with red reflection tape
- Extended to protect a 3 inches diameter mirror mounted on left end of handlebar.

ODOMETERS:
- $12.95 Bell Dashboard 150 (purchased from Walmart and mounted the day before trip began) This was the most dependable odometer.
- $99.99 Garmin® Edge 20 cycling GPS (purchased from Amazon and mounted the day before trip began). Note: as advertised, it only has a maximum eight-hour battery life, and it cannot be charged by a lithium charger while using it.

SAFETY:
- Taillight on rear bike frame (uses 2 AAA batteries)—operated flashing red
- Red helmet
- Polarized sunglasses
- Chartreuse bike jersey
- Bright yellow water-resistant jacket
- Mounted light on rear of helmet with zip-tie—operated flashing red
- Lighted arm band on left bicep—operated flashing red
- Padded-palm biking gloves
- 20-ounce (0.6 liter) sealed emergency water bottle.

Appendix 2: Supplies

BIKE CARE:

I always carried two replacement innertubes, a tube patch kit, two extra innertube caps, chain oil (accompanying application rag), toothbrush (for chain dirt removal), tube removal wrench, spoke wrench, three Allen wrenches to fit all connections, Leatherman, and a small tire pump. A fold-up tire was carried until my wife arrived as a sag wagon.

PERSONAL CARE:

Band aids, anti-bacterial ointment, large bottle of 50 SFP sunscreen, large tube and six packets of Chamois Butt'R®, toothbrush/paste, shaving cream, razor, soap, fungal cream, hemorrhoid ointment, dental floss, Ibuprofen, toilet paper, ache roll-on ointment, plantar fasciitis sock, and reading glasses.

CLOTHES:

An extra jersey, long-sleeved biking undershirt, two padded biking shorts, a neck kerchief, three handkerchiefs, removable biking sleeves, a short-sleeved shirt, long-sleeved shirt, long-sleeved insulated undershirt, walking shorts, long pants, three underwear, four pair of socks, a pair of thin-soled walking shoes, baseball cap, and a bright yellow weatherproof jacket. Extra biking jerseys, padded biking pants, street shirts and pants, and a light jacket were carried in our vehicle.

NUTRITION:

On my bike I carried twenty protein bars, two bottles Sports Leg, six energy jell packs, six Sports Bean® Jelly Bean packs, two packs of a dozen peanut butter and cheese crackers, two cans of Spam®, four packs of Spam®, two canned fish, large bag of beef jerky, six nut packs, forty electrolyte water treatments, twenty electrolyte capsules, and a thirty day supply of vitamins (multi-vitamin, magnesium/calcium/zinc, glucosamine/chondroitin, and fish oil). The remainder, about two boxes of non-perishable food items, were loaded in our vehicle before I departed.

275

DAILY USE:

Cell phone, cell phone cable, pocket radio and recharge cord, battery pack and charging cord, Garmin® charging cord, extra flashing armband, headlamp, six AAA batteries, journal, two pens, twenty-five book promotion brochures, a hundred book website business cards, and a bike mileage log.

The sixty-two page 'Pierre-to-the-Pole' booklet I prepared was easily accessible in my rear trunk tote. It contained daily route maps with towns, highway numbers, alternate routes, mileage between turns, lodging suggestions, their addresses and phone numbers. Small and large scale maps were inserted. In case of route changes, I wanted to insure I was daily heading the right direction.

Pages three though six contained an extensive chart with estimated mileage to likely nightly stops. Left blank were actual mileage, elevation, calorie, speed, departure and arrival times, and other tracking data.

HANDLEBAR BAG:

A small day-bag was mounted in front of my handlebars. In it I would usually carry a peanut butter sandwich (or two), an orange, apple, or banana, protein (nutrition) bars, usually some peanut butter or cheese filled crackers, beef jerky, and nuts or trail mix.

BACK DAYPACK:

The small day-pack on my back contained a hundred-ounce (3 liter) water pouch, four nutrition bars, six napkins, tight roll of camping toilet paper, emergency rain poncho, medical kit, billfold, fifteen business cards, driver's license, medical insurance card, credit card, ADM debit card, passport, $300 U.S. cash, $500 Canadian cash, three sets soft earplugs, two tubes 30 SPF lip balm, iodine tablets, snakebite kit, and hand sanitizer towelettes.

In my bike jersey back pockets, I carried my cell phone, handkerchief, and a nutrition bar.

Two 24-ounce (0.71 liter) water bottles were mounted between the triangle frame. One always contained Solstic® Energy (soluble electrolyte mix).

BACKUP SUPPLIES:

Since my wife was to catch up with me in Saskatchewan or Alberta, a large plastic storage tub was packed. It was packed in our vehicle to insure

I could keep the bike running and have overnight supplies in case we had to sleep in the SUV.

The storage keeper contained backup bicycle parts, supplies, and clothes I may need later along the trail. It contained: An extra drive chain, chain lubricating oil, two application rags, three extra tires, three additional innertubes, tire sealant, 8-inch by 10-inch (20.3 cm x 25.4 cm) solar panel (to charge cell phone and Garmin®), small socket set, open-end wrench set, two plyers, two screwdrivers, a crescent wrench, my used bike helmet, a kickstand, assortment of zip ties, tie-down rope, and several stretch-cords of various sizes.

In our SUV's back storage were two compact down sleeping bags, foam futon, portable propane grill, four full propane containers, rain suit, jacket, and small suitcase with long-sleeved shirts, pants and other gear to wear once we arrived in Alaska to fish, hike and explore.

DAILY OUTFIT:

I always wore padded biking gloves, a skull cap under my helmet, chartreuse biking jersey, padded short-leg biking pants, socks, and bike shoes with clips. (Note: My pedals were dual-purpose. One side I could clip my shoes in, the other side was flat for use with normal street shoes.) All but a couple days I wore a white long-sleeved tight-fitting undershirt (for warmth and sunblock).

Most mornings started cooler than I had planned. Long, black, tight-fitting bike pants were worn nearly every day and never removed nor was the long-sleeved undershirt, until I arrived each afternoon or evening.

Once I reached Alberta, my wife bought me leather work gloves which I wore many mornings thereafter as my hands, even with thick gloves, would stiffen to the curvature of the handlebars. By mid-day, I would always remove the heavy gloves and replace them with padded biking gloves.

SAFETY OPERATIONS:

Being seen, is always a concern when biking, especially on highway shoulders. It is the biker's responsibility to ensure they are seen. I was. Each day I wore a flashy chartreuse jersey from Harlan's Bike and Tour (our local bike store). Yes! I wore the same jersey every day (actually 39 of the 40 biking days). I could have gotten by with one jersey, but Patricia insisted that I arrive in a fresh eight-year-old Tour de Kota jersey.

When it was cool (most mornings), a very bright yellow weatherproof jacket was worn.

On my left arm a red-flashing arm band was worn, even over jacket and sleeves. On the back of my red helmet, I zip-tied a small flashing bike headlight. Prominently, behind the rear rack trunk tote, a flashing red bike light was always on. It used two AAA batteries. Panniers were always covered with bright yellow rain covers. As explained earlier, my **wrist support bar** which extended just beyond my left handlebar, had endcaps covered with bright red tape.

If I remembered to shut off my helmet, arm, and rear bike lights, batteries would last a week or longer.

EMERGENCY PROTECION:

Mosquito net (over helmet), thin camping towel, washcloth, thin emergency sleeping bag, a plastic camping fork/spoon combo, plastic knife, three plastic bags (for seat cover when raining), three small resealable plastic bags, emergency rain poncho, a pack of hand sanitizers, head sweatband, 12 ounce (0.4 liter) emergency water bottle, a water purifier, emergency sewing kit, $40 hidden U.S. cash, a dozen zip ties of various sizes, and two bungee cords were carried in my real bike tote.

Bibliography

Boyer, Robbie (Rob), (1958), If You Believe, You Can Achieve (poem), July 2019.

Clemens, Samuel Langhorne, (a.k.a. Mark Twain), November 30, 1835-April 21, 1910, Taming the Bicycle, The Short Story of the Day, May 21, 1919, https://americanliterature.com/author/mark-twain/essay/taming-the-bicycle (Sourced December 1, 2019).

Cleveland Clinic, Psoas syndrome, https://my.clevelandclinic.org/health/diseases/15721-psoas-syndrome (Sourced November 26, 2019).

Fogerty, John, *Who'll Stop the Rain* (song), originally sung by Creedence Clearwater Revival, 1970.

Fournier, Frank, Sustainable Elimination of Iodine Deficiency, progress since the 1990 world summit for children, UNICEF/HQ098-0761/Frank Fournier, https://www.unicef.org/publications/files/Sustainable_Elimination_of_Iodine_Deficiency.pdf (Sourced December 1, 2019).

Google Maps, a mapping service by Google, Alphabet, Inc., https://www.google.com/maps/.

Gullickson, Gill, Is Tillage Steeling Your Soil?, Successful Farming, October 10, 2017, https://www.agriculture.com/machinery/tillage/is-tillage-stealing-your-soil (Sourced November 18, 2019).

Hagen, Mark, x-ray photo, Hagen Chiropractic, Sioux Fall, SD, September 4, 2018.

Horton, John LaGale (1925-1960), *Battle of New Orleans* (song) 1959, written by James C. Morris*; North to Alaska* (song) 1960, written by Mike Phillips released August 22, 1960.

Ideal Software, Restaurant Food Costs: https://idealsoftware.co.za/restaurant-food-cost/ (Sourced December 23, 2019).

Kleinart, Shawn, Quora, https://www.quora.com/When-I-look-out-into-the-ocean-how-far-away-is-the-horizon-How-much-of-the-ocean-can-I-actually-see (Sourced February 2, 2019).

The Milepost 2018, Alaska Highway, (Legendary Alaska Trip Planner), 301 Arctic Slope Avenue, Suite 300, Anchorage, Alaska, 99518, phone (907) 272-6070; https://www.themilepost.com/: 139-229.

Morris, James Corbitt, (a.k.a. Jimmy Driftwood) (1907-1998), *Battle of New Orleans* (song), 1957, sung by Johnny Horton, 1959.

Peace Corp volunteer program, United States Government, Washington, DC https://www.peacecorps.gov/.

Phillips, Mike, *North to Alaska* (song) released August 22, 1960.

Rogers, Jillian, Retreating Yukon glacier makes river disappear, June 22, 2016, https://khns.org/retreating-yukon-glacier-makes-river-disappear (Sourced December 3, 2019).

Scheels® All Sports, Sioux Falls, SD, https://www.scheels.com/ (Sourced December 11, 2019).

Schwartz, Samuel I., *No one at the Wheel: Driverless Cars and the Road of the Future*, PublicAffairs, Hachette Book Group, (November 2018): 212.

SD State Connect, Tour Makes SDSU Stop, Interesting people, good food part of Tour de Kota for SDSU folks, Feature, South Dakota State University, Brookings, South Dakota, June 5, 2011, https://state.sdstateconnect.org/tour-de-kota/ (Sourced January 16, 2019).

Tolle, Eckhart, (1948-), *A New Earth, Awakening to your life's purpose*, Penguin Books, (2005), 227, 271.

U.S. Department of Energy, EERE Success Story—Alaska Gateway School District Adopts Combined Heat and Power, May 2013, https://www.energy.gov/eere/success-stories/articles/eere-success-story-alaska-gateway-school-district-adopts-combined-heat, (Sourced November 25, 2019).

Webster's New World Dictionary, Second College Edition: "mirage," New York: Simon and Schuster (1982): 907.

Wietgrefe, Gary W. (1953), *Culture and the mysterious agent changing it*, *Relating to Ancients* series, GWW Books, Sioux Falls, SD (January 2018): 53, 77.

-----. Daily Journal—Pierre, SD to North Pole, AK, March 2018: 1-62.

-----. *Learning as it influences the 21ˢᵗ century*, *Relating to Ancients* series, GWW Books, Sioux Falls, SD (January 2018): 285, 296.

-----. Pierre-to-the-Pole, https://www.RelatingtoAncients.com/Pierre-to-the-Pole-1.

Acknowledgements

This trip and minute details would not have come together without devoted support of my loving wife Patricia. She found food and lodging each night in the most unusual places. I needed all three more than anyone could realize! My unexpected injury and recovery would not have been possible without her and our three children, Michelle, Charmion, and Wyatt. Prolonged suffering was the alternative when the hospital doctor said, "You need to put him in a nursing home."

People laugh at Cora Wietgrefe's bicycling sketch. My grandniece has a rare talent to express imagination. She captured the raw story—man on bicycle in North Pole white.

Reviews by Doreen Berg and author Charmion O'Day Harris were greatly appreciated. Chad Phillips did an amazing job on the front cover. Likewise, *Google Maps* and *The Milepost* were of extreme value for anyone attempting this ride.

My brothers Mark and Neal, grandson Willie, nephew Andrew, sister-in-law Sharon, cousins Darlene and Bob, and friends (Carol & Joel, Deb & Rob, Adele & Myles, Jan & Joe) and all who met us along the way brought encouragement, humor, and genuineness to life.

My brother-in-law, Rob Boyer, in a few short poetic verses put my journey in perspective and I happily tied it into the story.

An unexpected reception in North Pole organized by my niece Cheryl Williams, nephew Seth Wietgrefe, his wife Liesl, and their three amazing daughters Adelaide, Gretchen, and Cora could not have been more overwhelming. They brought the forty day adventure to an appropriate close. A subsistence grilled pink salmon dinner and front-yard campfire sing-along complimented the warmth of the mid-night sun.

I thank you all dearly….Gary

Gary W. Wietgrefe

Societal Explorer, Author, & South Dakota Native

Wietgrefe's books tie education, school system, parenting, technology, and business with 21st century culture and learning. Pleasurable reading. Intellectually intriguing.

Grady Harp, San Francisco Review of Books Hall of Fame Top 100 Reviewer--Five out of Five Stars

"The aging mind tampers with memory, shrouding elements of yesterday to alter perception, spins moments recalling now outdated themes and traditions and names that once were the commonality of being alive. In this superb book Gary Wietgrefe explores this phenomenon scientifically and philosophically.... In a most intelligent manner, suffused with wry wit... This is one of the most satisfying reading experiences around – take advantage of retrospection to put the world in perspective and become enriched! Very highly recommended."

Dr. Larry P. Arnn, President
Hillsdale College, Hillsdale, MI:

"Your goal to understand modern learning and culture in the context of the ancients is noble indeed. I was especially

pleased to see that you cite Plato's *Republic in Learning.* Perhaps you would be interested in reading his *Meno*, a lesser-known dialogue in which he offers an intriguing theory of learning. Your account and his seem to share many important tenets. Thank you for your diligence. Your books offer a great testament to your love for truth. I wish you every success.

Gary Wietgrefe's books, including e-books can be ordered from Amazon, BCH Fulfillment at 914-835-0015, or anywhere fine books are sold. For more details see
www.RelatingtoAncients.com.

About the Author

Gary Wietgrefe (*pronounced wit' grif*) is an inventor, researcher, military intelligence veteran, economist, agriculturalist, systems developer, societal explorer, cyclist, hiker, outdoorsman, and author. He and his wife Patricia live and travel from South Dakota.

Wietgrefe's **Relating to Ancient** series includes:
Culture and the mysterious agent changing it,
&
Learning as it influences the 21st century.

Wietgrefe's agricultural series includes:
Proso Millet: A Trade Summary,
&
Proso Millet: A Farmer's Guide.

www.RelatingtoAncients.com